The Institute of Chartered Financial Analysts Continuing Education Series

CFA Readings in Real Estate

Edited by
Susan Hudson-Wilson, CFA and Katrina F. Sherrerd

The Institute of Chartered
Financial Analysts

Additional copies of this publication may be ordered from:

The Association for Investment Management and Research
P.O. Box 7947
Charlottesville, Virginia 22906

Phone: 1-804-980-3647
Fax: 1-804-977-0350

Katrina F. Sherrerd, *Managing Editor*
Brett M. Ferguson, *Associate Editor*

Printed in the United States of America

ISBN 0-935015-17-5

Table of Contents

Chapter 5 - Portfolio Management

Acknowledgements

The Institute of Chartered Financial Analysts gratefully acknowledges the following organizations for granting permission to reprint the articles in this publication.

The Actuary
Society of Actuaries
475 North Martingale Road, Suite 800
Schaumburg, Illinois 60173-2226

The Appraisal Journal
430 N. Michigan Ave.
Chicago, Illinois 60611-4088

AREUEA Journal
College of Business
The Ohio State University
1775 College Road
Columbus, Ohio 43210

Industrial Development
Conway Data, Inc.
40 Technology Park-Atlanta
Norcross, Georgia 30092

Institutional Investor
488 Madison Avenue
New York, New York 10022

John Hancock Properties, Inc.
Two Copley Place, Suite 200
Boston, Massachusetts 02117

The Journal of Portfolio Management
488 Madison Avenue
New York, New York 10022

The Journal of Real Estate Research
P.O. Box 6236
Mississippi State, Mississippi 39762-6236

The Real Estate Appraiser and Analyst
225 N. Michigan, Suite 724
Chicago, Illinois 60601-7601

Real Estate Review
New York University
The Real Estate Institute
11 West 42nd Street
New York, New York 10036

Salomon Brothers Inc
Bond Market Research - Real Estate
One New York Plaza
New York, New York 10004

Warren, Gorham & Lamont, Inc.
210 South Street
Boston, Massachusetts 02111

Foreword

CFA Readings in Real Estate covers one of the most important and most rapidly changing areas in the investment industry. New thinking and greater analytic sophistication have occurred at a very quick pace. Unfortunately, information on these recent developments are not readily available to professionals in written form.

This book of readings, edited by Susan Hudson-Wilson, CFA and Katrina F. Sherrerd, has been compiled from the literature in an effort to extend the reader's knowledge and understanding of real estate, with emphasis on portfolio management. It is an extension of the Institute of Chartered Financial Analysts' effort to keep members of the profession on the leading edge of investment literature.

This volume is divided into five sections covering the topics of Valuation, Real Estate Finance, Fundamental Market Analysis, Performance, and Portfolio Management. Both practitioner and scholarly journals, as well as material from corporate research departments, are represented in this collection. This book also contains an introduction and an extensive bibliography. The purpose of the introduction is to summarize the contributions of each article included in the publication and to place it within the context of the body of literature on real estate. The bibliography provides a resource for those interested in reading additional material on the subject. It is not possible to include all the articles that are of interest and importance in one book. Therefore, the reader is encouraged to seek out articles in areas of interest beyond the scope of this book.

The readings included in this book should provide a valuable source of information to the investment professional, particularly those who make or plan to make real estate investments. It is not without gaps, however. As Susan Hudson-Wilson notes in the Introduction, the most glaring gap in the literature concerns international real estate markets. For this reason, as well as the pace of research in this field, this book will need virtually constant updating.

Special thanks are extended James R. Vertin, CFA, Chairman of the Council on Education and Research, who helped make this book a reality. Jim has dedicated many hours to the development of the ICFA's Continuing Education program—of which this book of readings is an integral part. These efforts are evident in the quality, volume, and breadth of material that constitute the publications of the Continuing Education program.

Thomas A. Bowman, CFA
Senior Vice President
Association for Investment
Management and Research

Introduction

Susan Hudson-Wilson, CFA

Real estate's status as an orphan of the institutional investment arena is rapidly ending. The size of the real estate market has encouraged this change. Of the $1.5 trillion worth of U.S. real estate, domestic pension investors own only $113.4 billion. Readers interested in articles that provide an overview of the size and the ownership of the domestic real estate market are encouraged to read Lillard (1988) and Miles (1989).

Right now, the field of real estate research is wide open: Quantitative techniques are just beginning to be applied with some creativity to the analysis of this asset class. As a result, many ideas can be put to productive use immediately. But, as institutional investors' interest in real estate investments grows so will the demand for the same analytic rigor and innovative thinking that is the standard for the traditional asset classes of stocks and bonds. This book of readings in real estate has been assembled as a partial solution to the demand for information on real estate that accompanies the growth in interest in, and the importance of, the asset class..

The analytics in the industry are following a well-trod path forged by the bond and stock industries. Investors are progressing from a focus on individual transactions to a focus on the portfolio of investments, whereby transactions are being analyzed within a portfolio context. Historically, it has been argued that portfolio approaches were not applicable to the real estate asset class because each transaction was unique and real estate markets were inefficient. This opinion is not uniformly held, however. Darrat and Glascock (1989) and Gau (1987) present opposite points of view on this issue. Darrat and Glascock argue against efficiency and provide evidence of lags in the assimilation of market information into prices. Gau argues the other side, claiming that efficiency can be defended if information is capitalized quickly enough, thus models that assume market efficiency are able to be fruitfully applied. Although there will continue to be some "old guard-new guard" debates within the industry, the two focuses are increasingly perceived to be complementary not competing.

The purpose of this introduction is to summarize the articles included in this publication within the context of the body of literature on real estate. This volume is divided into five sections covering the topics of Valuation, Real Estate Finance, Fundamental Market Analysis, Performance, and Portfolio Management. The most glaring gap in the literature concerns international real estate markets. Some productive work is being done on this topic and one can expect to see it represented in future publications. It is not possible to include all the articles that are of interest and importance in one book. Therefore, the reader is encouraged to seek out articles in areas of interest beyond the scope of this book; to that end a bibliography is provided.

VALUATION

The art of property and investment valuation is of particular importance to the real estate asset class because transactions are both more private and less frequent than for other asset classes. As more pension funds invest in the asset, there is increasing pressure to "mark to market" the individual real estate investments. The pressure is an outgrowth of the emergence of the asset as a "traditional" investment. In fact, the completion of the metamorphosis will likely be delayed until the valuation question can be satisfactorily resolved.

A key question in the area of valuation concerns the definition of the appropriate benchmark by which the valuation process may be judged. The "correct" value of a property is hard to define. Is it the appraised value produced through a dispassionate exercise in which the efficient market assumptions about the motivations of buyers and sellers are held to be in effect? Is it the actual sales price—the price at which a property changed hands? Or, as Iain Reid from Richard Ellis, Inc. in London contends, is it the losing bid, the offer that failed?

In the first article in this section, Fisher describes and critiques the three principal methods of valuing real estate: the discounted cash flow method, the market comparables method, and the replacement cost method. The discounted cash flow (DCF) method is analogous to the dividend discount model used in stock equity valuation and requires the use of some fairly complex assumptions. Included in the set of assumptions are an income growth rate, an expense growth rate, a reversion value that entails the use of a "going-out" capitalization rate, and an internal rate of return (IRR).

The market comparables approach requires a depth of knowledge about actual market transactions that few real estate experts have, although many claim to have. Even if a real estate database is seemingly rich with price data, information on the differences between the properties, the buyers, and the sellers typically is not well documented. There is tremendous opportunity for the use of subjective insight in the application of this approach. Whereas the DCF method is largely speculative, the market comparables method is purely historic. For this reason, it can miss market turning points. When a market collapses or becomes very thinly traded, the market comparables method produces less meaningful results. In such an environment, the DCF is superior.

The replacement cost approach, although still presented in appraisal reports, has lost its historic role as a mark of the ceiling value. This approach is considered to be the least reliable because it demands an accounting of depreciation and entrepreneurial profit—two difficult measurement problems.

The paper by Cirz and Sorich (1987) outlines the results of a survey on the inputs used to price real estate using DCF models. According to the authors, investors frequently give responses that could be somewhat inconsistent; for example, high expected growth paired with relatively low discount rates. In today's market, income growth assumptions are in the 3 to 5 percent range, IRRs are in the 9 to 13 percent range, and capitalization rates are in the 6 to 8 percent range. The inflation rate has not changed much during the survey period—the mid-1980s—but investor demand for domestic real estate has. This article provides an interesting extension to Fisher's discussion of the assumptions required to use the DCF method.

The last two papers in this section discuss the reliability of commercial appraisals. In their article, Cole, Guilkey, and Miles (1986) compare actual net sales prices with appraised values, using data on 144 transactions from the Russell-NCREIF database. They discovered that although appraisals exceeded sales prices by 9 percent on average, the differences ranged from a positive 181 percent to a negative 28 percent. After excluding the outliers, the average spread drops to a more comfortable 6 percent. The authors conclude that the most important source of discrepancies is appraisers' missing major changes in real estate markets. Thus, the technique used does not appear to contribute to the generation of errors. In the future, appraisers will probably have to become better skilled at the analysis of the economic fundamentals of real estate markets.

In the last article, Graaskamp (1987) discusses the need for appraisal reform. He points out that the entry of pension funds with fiduciary accountability into the real estate investment arena raises the need for quality control. He is particularly articulate on the subject of the increasing complexities associated with the valuation process and identifies a number of issues that must be addressed, including issues related to the financial structure of individual investments, accounting complexities, engineering obsolescences, environmental concerns, and the legal context. He asks whether the appraiser in today's environment is qualified to operate independently. There is a clear need for an "interface of professions." Due diligence is a multidisciplinary task that may not be adequately addressed now. Graaskamp concludes with the provocative question: Are we paying enough for the type of rigorous appraisal we increasingly require?

REAL ESTATE FINANCE

The broad topic of real estate finance is addressed in the second section. The articles included cover issues ranging from the analysis of favorable or unfavorable leverage, through capital market effects on real estate, to the calculation of duration in real estate. Readers who want a nuts and bolts discussion of this topic are encouraged to read the real estate chapter in Brown and Kritzman (1989).

In the first article in this section, Edwards and Cooley (1984) analyze the effects of leverage on equity returns. The authors contend that leverage is favorable if it contributes to the realization of an enhanced return on equity versus that available without leverage. The analysis appears to be straightforward, but there are two major problems. The authors point out that one must consider the relative risks of the two financial structures and that one must compensate for scale differences that can easily distort the comparisons. Analytic solutions to both problems are provided.

In the next article, "The Triple Revolution in Real Estate Finance," Downs (1983) shares his predictions about real estate markets. This article makes interesting reading because of the author's style and because it was written in 1983, which permits an interesting perspective for readers in the 1990s. The author's revolutions concern the inflation indexation of debt, the end of subsidies to the single family housing sector, and changes in both monetary and fiscal policy and their effects on interest rates and volatility. Downs was right on target with respect to many of his observations. For example, with respect to the indexation of debt, he observed that lenders would have to "smartened up" and shift the inflation risk back to the borrowers. He took this thought to its logical conclusion and stated that because the cost of borrowing had risen, the demand for borrowing—and therefore development—would fall. He did not, however, sufficiently anticipate the effect of the inflow of pension monies to the real estate asset class. Returns to equity have fallen, but demand for the asset has risen. The author's observations on affordability and the housing sector and on the spectre of rising deficits are insightful. All in all, Downs' thinking has proven to be of great interest and, of critical importance to a forecaster, accurate!

In the next article, titled "What Determines Cap Rates on Real Estate?" Froland (1987) asks whether capitalization (cap) rates are a "child of the capital market" or a "unique aberration of an inefficient interplay between real estate buyers and sellers." His paper includes an empirical analysis of the determinants of capitalization rates. The results suggest that real estate is primarily traded on the basis of a current yield that is competitive with risk and maturity-adjusted debt instruments. The yield is discounted to accommodate expected equity returns. The current yield requirement varies with inflationary expectations. The historically very low capitalization rates in today's real estate markets reflect investors' demand for equity real estate and their inflation expectations over the holding period. Incomes and values are clearly expected to grow at a very fast rate.

Duration is a very important concept to the successful integration of real estate as a "traditional" asset class. In the final article in this section, Hartzell, Shulman, Langetieg, and Leibowitz (1988) address this very important subject. Real estate may be viewed as a bond with a fully inflation indexed principal balance. There is some concern, however, that the characterization of the principal portion of the cash flow may be a bit naive. In this article, the authors state that the coupon portion of the duration calculation may be fully indexed, partially indexed, or unindexed. The degree of indexation varies as a function of the relation between supply and demand in the market and of the property's physical viability. The effects of the degree of indexation are examined. The authors conclude that real estate duration may be managed, to a greater or a lesser degree, by the investor, if the investor can control lease structure and term.

In my opinion, the issue of investment maturity has yet to be resolved. The economic benefits of the investment continue beyond a lease term or a particular investor's holding period. Thus, there ought to be a very close relation between time and the asset's duration. The authors are silent on this point

as well as on the problems with the certainty of the cash flow estimates. In the literature on stock equity duration, it is clear that this uncertainty is very troublesome. I am sure we can look forward to a continuation of very good thinking on this important topic.

FUNDAMENTAL MARKET ANALYSIS

The section on fundamental market analysis contains only one paper titled "Review of the Chicago Real Estate Market," by Lauritano and Peterson (1989). The study is representative of the kind of urban and real estate economic analysis that is becoming a staple product of institutional real estate management and investment banker firms. The paper covers the Chicago metropolitan area's economic structure; the political environment; and the office, industrial, apartment, and retail real estate markets.

This type of study is useful for characterizing the environment within which a particular investment will need to perform. The vacancy rates, returns, and rents described by such studies are meant to be suggestive of a "typical" product's performance. Any particular property will, of course, perform either slightly better than or worse than the mean. These market reviews are most often used to enable the careful identification of markets as acquisition targets. There is an increasing interest in using the findings of such studies in a portfolio context. This topic is covered in the section on portfolio management.

PERFORMANCE

The fourth section presents five papers on various issues in real estate performance measurement and expectations. The authors are unanimous in their belief that the industry has a long way to go before the data that are being examined fully reflect the behavior of the real estate asset. The key "problem" with the data used to analyze real estate performance is that it is appraisal, rather than transactions based. It is not clear that the appraisals themselves are the problem. Rather, the problem may be that real estate is not valued frequently enough. If real estate values were marked to market each month—reasonably accurately—changes in discount rates caused by intermittent periods of greater or lesser uncertainty about the property and the capital markets would be reflected in values. This type of value reassessment would be relatively simple and inexpensive to execute and would certainly help to put real estate and stocks and bonds on a more level playing field.

The first paper in this section, Sirmans and Sirmans (1987), consists of a thorough literature search on the topics of real estate returns, returns relative to other asset classes, risk in real estate and other assets, and the utility of real estate as an inflation hedge. Unfortunately, however, the measurement problems in real estate relative to other asset classes are such that it is difficult to have much faith in anyone's conclusions.

The inflation hedge topic is covered well by Hartzell, Hekman, and Miles (1987). In this paper, the authors report the results of their research on the ability of real estate to hedge expected or unexpected inflation. This analysis was conducted within the real estate asset class. The time period covers the very high inflation period of the early 1980s, but does not cover the very soft markets of more recent years in which tenants have become very sophisticated negotiators who are sensitive to the potential effects of inflation on leasing costs. Thus, although the authors conclude that real estate returns compensate for both expected and unexpected inflation, these results might be different if the analysis were updated.

In the third paper, Hartzell and Webb (1988) present the results of a survey they conducted in the fall of 1987. They report that the October, 1987 stock market crash made very little difference in the expectations of the survey participants. They found that real estate experts regard a three-year horizon as short term and that ten years constitutes the long run. The survey respondents believe that inflation will be modest but rising, returns will reflect the increased inflation, property values will rise at a faster rate than net income, real estate volatility is one-half that of stock volatility, and real estate will continue to perform an important role as a portfolio diversifier when combined with stocks and bonds. This survey is now conducted annually and will be monitored for predictive value.

The fourth article in this section, authored by the accounting committee of the National Council of Real Estate Investment Fiduciaries (NCREIF), demonstrates that possible appraisal inaccuracies are far from the only source of complexity in the analysis of the performance of real estate! A survey of NCREIF members was conducted to ascertain the reporting treatment of expenditures on tenant improvements, tenant allowances, leasing commissions, building improvements, and free rent. The discussion revolves around questions of expensing versus capitalizing, the billable basis versus the earned income method, the amortization and depreciation of expense versus no amortization, the merging of the accounting practice used to calculate net operating income, and the appraisal practice used to calculate property values. Although variations in the practices may not affect holding period returns very much, they certainly affect period-to-period comparisons among properties and real estate funds. Investors must make themselves aware of the effects of these practices.

In the final piece in this section, Giliberto (1989) addresses the issue of the usefulness of international diversification of real estate portfolios. It appears that although correlations between real estate returns in the United States and the United Kingdom were high historically, they have recently fallen considerably. As the conditions in the two markets have increasingly diverged—the U.S. market is soft and the U.K. market has experienced rising returns—the correlation has fallen. Thus, there may be increased merit in the idea of achieving diversification benefits by combining these assets in a portfolio.

Giliberto raises a very arresting and thought-provoking possibility in this paper that may render other reseach—even some in this book—moot. He states that the generation of a favorable relation between real estate returns and inflation is generated exclusively by the inclusion of data from the years 1980 through 1982: When this period is excluded, there is no relation between the FRC index and inflation. The United Kingdom's experience is similar. The author speculates that real estate may hedge only high inflation, not all inflation. I would anticipate that considerably more research will be forthcoming on this critical subject.

PORTFOLIO MANAGEMENT

The six articles in this section present the literature on the infant industry of real estate portfolio management. There is considerable controversy, yet a certain inevitability, about the usefulness and appropriateness of modern portfolio theory (MPT) applied to the real estate asset. The bottom line is that the pension fund managers, well schooled in modern portfolio theory applied to stocks, bonds, and asset allocation, are insisting on its use in making allocation decisions among real estate investments. Further, the logic of a risk management concept applied to the highly diverse U.S. real estate markets is compelling. The tools are well-developed, the data is improving rapidly, and the train has left the station.

In 1988, Zisler asserted that real estate portfolio management discipline was either weak or nonexistent. In this article, he describes the uniqueness of real estate and its place in an investment portfolio. This article establishes a foundation for thinking about real estate portfolio management.

In the second article, Conroy, Miles, and Wurtzebach (1986a) present, in very clear language, the logic of the application of portfolio theory and the basic facts about MPT, the capital asset pricing model (CAPM), arbitrage pricing theory (APT), and options pricing. The authors conclude that although the CAPM and APT have practical problems that impair their application, MPT is holding up very well.

The basic principle of MPT is that when two assets that are less than perfectly correlated are combined into a portfolio the following two outcomes occur: (1) the portfolio's return is equal to the weighted sum of the two assets' returns, and (2) the portfolio's standard deviation (the measurement of risk) is less than the weighted sum of the two assets' standard deviations. The reason diversification works is simple: There is no smoke, no mirrors—just math.

The authors go on to describe the whole efficient frontier concept and its usefulness as a way to think about individual assets in a portfolio context. They conclude that as the use of MPT in the real estate investment market widens, the concept of risk will broaden to include, not only the risk of the performance of a particular property, but also the contribution of that property to a portfolio. Ultimately, property values will need to reflect this dimension.

In "Real Estate: The Whole Story," Firstenberg, Ross, and Zisler (1988) examine the principles of diversification. They regard the use of MPT as inevitable and a complement to the more traditional transactions orientation of real estate analysis. They present some very basic analyses of the diversification benefits available to real estate investors, but admit that a four-region model is crude. They believe that a more specific articulation of the dimensions of diversification can and will be done.

Wurtzebach (1989b) addresses the question of the further refinement of the dimensions of diversification. He contrasts the concepts of geographic and economic regions and suggests that the analysis should seek to combine places with common economic structures into regions. Wurtzebach created five economic dimensions based on the growth patterns of places and five based on the structure of various economies. The area mentioned, but unexplored, is that of property type diversification.

Implicit is the notion that locational allocations can be conducted as a separate exercise from property allocations. This implies that a uniform property type allocation would be appropriate for each of the economic regions.

The simultaneity of property and locational allocation decisions is addressed in Hudson-Wilson (1989b). The author believes that each property type in each metropolitan area must be thought of as a potentially unique asset. A cluster technique may then be applied to the investor's investment universe to determine statistically the similarities and the differences among the many investment options. Assets that cluster together are substitutes for one another; assets that appear in separate clusters may be combined in a portfolio to manage portfolio risk. It is clear from this work that it is not appropriate to apply a uniform property type allocation to each of several regions, however defined.

Finally, the last paper presents the beginning of thinking on a product that everyone wishes were available in the real estate investment universe—an indexed portfolio. Hopkins and Shulman (1989) describe a possible structure for an indexed portfolio. They suggest that perhaps the F.W. Dodge construction contract awards, available for over 20 years, might be used to describe the size and the composition of the market of investment real estate. This work decomposes that data by property type, but does not broach the issue of quality differences among all of the included projects. The authors compare the property distribution as captured by the F.W. Dodge data with that found in the Russell-NCREIF data base. It can be concluded, if the analysis using the Dodge data is thought to be credible, that institutional investors are grossly under-invested in apartments and are over-invested in offices. Interestingly, this is consistent with the current thinking of many pension fund investors!

The discussion of the size and composition of the real estate market is key to the continued process of "mainstreaming" the real estate asset class. Much productive work is likely to continue to emerge on this basic topic.

Real Estate Appraisal

Jeffrey D. Fisher*

INTRODUCTION

Real estate appraisal is usually undertaken for the purpose of estimating the "market value" of a property. The appraiser uses information obtained from analysis of the real estate market to develop an opinion about the value of the property being appraised. This paper is directed to the user of appraisals on real estate income property. The primary purpose of this paper is to review and critique the approaches taken by appraisers to estimate market value. The focus is on understanding the key assumptions that the appraiser is making when a particular approach is taken to estimate value. An understanding of the assumptions will contribute to the user's ability to interpret and apply the information in an appraisal.

MARKET VALUE

Market value is defined as "the most probable price which a property would bring in a competitive and open market under all conditions requisite to a fair sale, the buyer and seller each acting prudently, knowledgeably and assuming the price is not affected by undue stimulus."[1] Market value can also be thought of as the price that would result from sale to a typical buyer, that is, the type of buyer most likely to purchase the property. This price may differ from that which was just paid by a particular buyer

*Jeffrey D. Fisher, Ph.D. is Director of the Center for Real Estate Studies and Associate Professor of Finance and Real Estate at the Indiana University School of Business. Dr. Fisher is the 1990 President of the American Real Estate and Urban Economics Association (AREUEA) and served as the 1986-87 Chairman of the Real Estate Center Directors and Chairholders Association. He is a Trustee and Officer of The Appraisal Foundation and is a member of the Advisory Board of the National Council for Real Estate Investment Fiduciaries (NCREIF) Research Institute

[1]This definition was first introduced by the Federal Home Loan Bank Board in Proposed Rules 12 CFR Parts 563 and 571, (Appraisal Policies and Practiices of Insured Institutions and Service Corporations) published in the *Federal Register*, Vol. 52, No. 94, May 15, 1987.

who may not represent the buyer who is most likely to purchase the property as of the date indicated in the appraisal report.

An appraisal deals with measuring value. This is not necessarily the same as analyzing the underlying determinants of that value. That is, appraisal is concerned more with what the property is likely to sell for rather than why it will sell at a particular price. When estimating market value, the appraiser is not judging whether he or she thinks investors are over- or undervaluing the real estate. If the market value is estimated properly, then by definition that is the value to the most likely entity to purchase the property. The appraiser does not necessarily need to understand the particular investment calculus used by the most likely investor. Rather, what is necessary is sufficient evidence that the price being estimated is what that particular class of investors would be willing to pay as of the date of the appraisal. Whether that class of investors appears rational is not relevant, as long as there are a sufficient number of investors to make a market.

The fact that appraisers use some approaches to estimate market value that do not explicitly consider the investor's motivations for purchasing the property does not mean that they do not attempt to analyze buyer motivations. This point will be amplified in the discussion of the "three approaches" to estimating value.

IMPORTANCE OF DEFINING THE RIGHTS BEING APPRAISED

When real estate is purchased, the physical real estate is not being purchased. Rather, an ownership claim—backed in some way by the physical real estate—is being purchased. The ownership rights are effected by leases, mortgages, zoning, deed restrictions, and other legal factors. The more complex the ownership rights, the more abstract the nature of the income to be received by a particular ownership claim. For example, consider the income received by an investor who owns an office building that is subject to a mortgage and has been leased to a variety of tenants. The leases may contain numerous clauses, such as expense stops, inflation adjustments, and renewal options, that affect the projected income. Further, the mortgage may have provisions for participation in the income and resale proceeds and, perhaps, even an option to purchase some of the equity. All of these factors affect the nature and value of the investor's ownership rights.

THE EFFECT OF LEASES ON OWNERSHIP RIGHTS

Appraisal of buildings that are typically leased for several years, for example, office buildings and shopping centers, requires consideration of how the existing lease structure affects the value. The existence of leases creates three "estates" that have different ownership rights and different values.

Fee Simple Value

When a property is appraised as if it is unencumbered by leases at the time of the appraisal, the resulting value is often referred to as the fee simple value.[2] There are several reasons the fee simple value might be determined, even if a property is currently leased. First, the fee simple value serves as a benchmark. The value subject to existing leases should be compared with this value to determine the effect that the leases have on the value of the property.

Second, many states require that property taxes be based on the fee simple value. This is based on the theory that the taxing jurisdiction is not concerned with how leases may have resulted in an allocation of the fee simple value among the lessee and lessor.

When estimating the value of a fee simple estate, the appraiser assumes that the property can be leased at the time of the appraisal at the market rate. It is assumed that there will be a typical lease on the property at current rental rates. This is important because market rents are based on the assumption of a lease for a specified term; the term of the lease is reflected in that rental rate. Valuation of the fee simple estate must also consider expected vacancy during the term of the lease, typical tenant concessions, such as free rent for part of the lease term, and any tenant improvements that would be paid for by the lessor.

Leased Fee Value

The leased fee value is the value subject to any existing leases. Thus, the valuation must consider how the lease terms effect the income expected by the owner of the leased fee estate.

Several issues must be considered in determining the leased fee value. First, an assumption must be made as to what rental rate will apply at the renewal of expired leases. This will require an estimate of the market rental rate at the time of renewal.

Second, the appraiser must consider the risk of the leased fee estate. This risk may be less than for a fee simple estate if the lessees have a good credit rating. Further, if the leases are below market, there is less chance that the lessee will default on the lease. If the risk is determined to be less, a lower discount rate should be used when applying an income approach to valuation (discussed later).

Third, the appraiser must consider how the leases might effect the value of the property at the end of the holding period (reversion). This value will depend on whether any below-market leases that were in effect at the time of the appraisal have expired and been renewed at the market rate. To the extent that there are still below-market leases, the reversion will be lower than market-rate leases. Considerable care must be taken in estimating the value of the reversion for a leased fee estate. The appraiser cannot use the same assumptions about property growth rates that would be used for fee simple estates. The growth rate for leased fee estates could be higher or lower than for fee simple estates, depending on the behavior of the leases over the lease term. For example, there could be several below-market leases at the time the property is purchased that will expire within one or two years and be renewed at a higher market rate. This results in a greater increase in income than the increase in property value because the income from expected lease renewals will already be discounted into the estimated property value.

Leasehold Value

When a property is leased, a leasehold and leased fee estate are created. As has been discussed, below-market leases can lower the value of a leased fee estate relative to that of a fee simple estate. Further, below-market leases can create positive value for the leasehold estate. Because the two values are created by the same divergence between contract and market rates, there is a temptation to consider the value effects as being symmetric. That is, one might assume that the value of the leased fee estate plus the value of the leasehold estate must add to that of a fee

---

[2]This comes from the fact that a fee simple estate is an estate with maximum ownership rights. A fee simple estate is one that can be leased or sold by the owner. The fee simple value would be the value of a fee simple estate.

simple estate. Although this might be implied by some notion of value additivity in a perfect market, in the less-than-perfect real estate market there are reasons why such value additivity may not occur.[3] In reality, purchasers of leased fee estates are investors who want to own—but not use—real estate. Thus, they purchase property that is leased. Typically, purchasers of leasehold estates are lessees who are willing to buy the remaining term on an existing lease because they want to use the space.

OTHER TYPES OF VALUE

The preceding section emphasized the nature of market value estimates. It should be pointed out that there are other types of value that the appraiser may be asked to estimate that are not "market value." The most common are as follows:

Investment Value. Market value is defined in terms of a *typical* investor. In contrast, investment value is based on the investment criteria for a particular investor—either an individual or an institutional investor. Investment value involves a judgement as to whether a property is overvalued or undervalued from a particular investor's perspective. It considers factors such as the tax status of the investor, the investor's particular investment goals, the investor's risk aversion, the investor's existing portfolio, and needs for diversification.

Investment value may be more or less than market value. If it is less than market value, the investor should not pay more than the investment value for the property. If the investment value exceeds market value, the investor can justify paying up to the investment value for the property.

Assessed Value. Assessed value is the value for calculation of property taxes. This value is often affected by state laws and legal decisions that are inconsistent with valuation theory. For example, a state might require that only the cost approach discussed later be used to estimate assessed value. Thus, assessed value may differ from market value.

Value In Use. This is the value to a user of the property. This value may differ from what the typical investor would pay for the space, especially if the property is being used for a special purpose. For example, an industrial plant may have a relatively high value to the user, but have much less value to a typical investor who might have a problem finding other tenants to lease the space.

Value of Proposed Project. Proposed projects require special consideration by appraisers. Because the value is being estimated for some *future* time period, careful consideration must be given to how market conditions might change over the development period.[4] The value upon completion two years from now may be quite different from the value as if it were completed today because of anticipated and unanticipated changes in supply and demand. For proposed projects, appraisers are often required by lenders to estimate three different values as follows: value as is, value upon completion before rentup, and value after rent is stabilized.

Value "As Is". This is the value based on the property as it is currently improved; it may be vacant land. The value considers the contemplated development, assuming that development is the "highest and best use" of the site.[5]

Value Upon Completion Before Rentup. This is the value at the date the project is completed, but before the space is leased and occupied. Obviously, this is somewhat oversimplified in that there may have been preleasing and some tenants may move in prior to completion of the entire project. It is useful, however, to know how much value will be in place at a point when the project is complete and available for rental of unleased space. This provides a benchmark upon which the loan can be based. Most construction lenders will not loan more than a specified percentage of this value.

When estimating the value upon completion, appraisers must be careful to consider changes in market conditions during the construction period. There is a tendency to appraise the project as if it were complete today. Or the appraiser might fail to consider the effect of the new project on market rents, occupancy rates, and so forth. Also, sufficient consideration is often not given to the length of time that will be required to absorb the new space.

---

[3]In a perfect market, the possiblity of arbitrage would make the values additive. For example, if the leased fee and leasehold estates summed to a value greater than a fee simple estate, one would be able to buy an interest in the fee simple estate and at the same time sell short interests in the leased fee estate and leasehold estate creating arbitrage profits if the estates were not additive.

[4]The term "prospective value" is often used for the value of the project upon completion of construction. See William L. Pittenger, "Time/Value Relationships in Development Projects," *The Real Estate Appraiser and Analyst*, Winter, 1986, pages 33-41 for further discussion.

[5]Highest and best use is the use that results in the highest value to the land.

Value after Rent is Stabilized. The value after rent is stabilized definition differs from the value upon completion before rentup definition in the amount of space leased assumption. The value after rent is stabilized assumes that the space has been leased to the extent where a normal vacancy level has been reached. This value will normally exceed the value upon completion but before rentup for several reasons. First, marketing costs and leasing commissions have likely been incurred that add value to the project. Second, the appraiser may feel that the developer has not fully earned a "developer profit" unless the property has been leased. Thus, the value upon completion, but before rentup, is discounted by the amount of unearned developer profit. Third, there may be less risk associated with the project after it is leased up, resulting in a higher value. Furthermore, even if the income upon completion of the project were known with certainty, the mere fact that the income will not flow until the project is completed results in a lower value because of the time value of money.

The three value estimates described above provide guidelines as to how much should be loaned during various stages of project development. Value should increase over the development period from the "value as is" to the "value upon completion before rentup." Then, as the project is leased, value increases to the "stabilized value." Each of these values should consider the risks associated with the investment at each stage of development. A developer has a lot of options as to what to do with the site before construction begins. These options decrease as the project is developed according to a specific plan. Risk is likely to be highest at the time the project is complete but unrented; it declines as the project is successfully leased.

Going-Concern Value. Going concern value is the value increment associated with having an operating business included with the real estate in properties like hotels, motels, regional shopping malls, and congregate care facilities. The rental income for properties where there is an operating business may be very dependent on the success of the business that operates at the property. This is especially true where the underlying business is quite successful. For example, with a successful regional shopping mall, local tenants will pay a premium in their rent to be associated with the mall. This premium is paid not for the space, but for the right to be associated with the business enterprise at the mall. This premium results in an intangible going concern value that goes beyond that of the real estate (land

and building). Depending on the purpose of the appraisal, it may be appropriate to separate the intangible going concern value (sometimes referred to as business value) from the value of the real estate.[6]

CHARACTERISTICS OF REAL ESTATE MARKETS

Real estate appraisal differs in many ways from valuation techniques applied to other investments such as stocks and bonds. In part, this is a result of the characteristics of real estate markets versus other capital markets. An overview of some of the unique characteristics of real estate markets is as follows:

Each Parcel is Unique. Obviously, no two real estate investments are exactly alike. At a minimum, any two properties will be at slightly different locations. Whether this difference has a significant impact on value is a different question. Because each parcel is unique, the price of one property may or may not be a good indication of the value of a different parcel.

Few Buyers and Sellers at One Time. Compared with many other markets, there are usually relatively few buyers and sellers in the market for a particular property at a particular point in time. This can result in transactions prices that differ from market value.

Some Buyers May Influence the Price. In a market characterized by perfect competition, buyers are "price takers." That is, individual buyers do not influence the price. This does not appear to be the case for real estate markets: Prices are often influenced by a particular buyer who is willing to bid much more than the second bidder. This causes some analysts to question whether market value is being paid—especially when it is the "optimist" that ends up with the property! Furthermore, real estate lacks a market mechanism that would permit the pessimists to short sell.

Relatively Large Economic Units. Real estate investments are not easily divisible into smaller economic units (as shares of stock), although this is changing with attempts to secure real estate equity investments. Most real estate must still be purchased as one unit, for example, the entire office building.

[6]For a further discussion of this value concept and the importance of separating this value from that of the real estate for property tax assessment, see Jeffrey D. Fisher and William N. Kinnard, "The Business Enterprise Value Component of Operating Properties: The Example of Shopping Malls," *Proceedings of the International Conference on Assessment Administration*, September 24-27, 1989, Ft. Worth, Texas.

Many Government Controls. Real estate markets are subject to numerous federal, state, and local government controls such as tax laws (federal and property), zoning, building codes, and environmental regulations. This complicates the development of real estate and the transfer of interests in real estate. Further, the possibility of changes in government regulations that adversely affect an ownership position is an additional risk of owning real estate that may be systematic to some degree for all real estate investments.

Supply Adjusts Slowly. It takes time for the supply of real estate to change through development of new properties or even conversion of a property from one use to another use. As a result, supply and demand are not always in balance. This adds an additional complication in attempting to measure real estate values. For example, in "equilibrium," value might equal cost (if accurately and appropriately measured). In the short run, however, value may differ considerably from cost.

No Organized Market. There is no centralized market where interests in real estate are traded. This makes it difficult to know the price of real estate at a particular time. Shares in real estate investment trusts (REITs) do trade, but these shares tend to take on pricing characteristics more like stocks than real estate.

Poor Information about Product and Market Prices. In part, because of the lack of organized markets and of divisible shares of real estate trading on a regular basis, there is very poor information available about real estate transactions. Buyers and sellers are extremely reluctant to have competitors know the price paid for a property. Further, information about the lease structure of the property is difficult to obtain. Asking prices for vacant space in a building may be very difficult from what is actually paid when a lease is signed.

Infrequent Trades of Property. The above-listed problems are not continuous transactions for real estate investments. This makes it difficult to know how prices are behaving over time, which is essential to a meaningful comparison of the risk and return characteristics of real estate versus other investments. For example, lack of transactions makes it difficult to compute holding period returns for real estate. Indexes of real estate returns such as the NCREIF/Russell Property Index[7] must rely largely on appraised values of the property to determine the appreciation in value from period to period.

CONCLUSIONS ABOUT EFFICIENCY OF REAL ESTATE MARKETS

Several conclusions follow from the discussion of the characteristics of real estate markets. First, because information is difficult to obtain, a relatively high price must be paid to obtain relevant information. That is, buyers, sellers, lenders, and others are willing to pay appraisers to provide information about market transactions.

Second, knowledgeable buyers who have better information may be able to profit on their information. In more efficient markets like the stock market, average returns to fundamental analysis may be high (salaries of all the securities analysts), but marginal returns may be low to zero. That is, no additional returns can be earned by doing more than reading existing reports from all the other analysts. In contrast, marginal returns to fundamental analysis in real estate may be high because of a historical lack of a large number of sophisticated analysts in real estate. Because of the opportunities to profit from the relative lack of efficiency in the real estate market, more sophisticated investors—including many institutional investors—have been entering the real estate market.

Third, as appraisers and others take advantage of the lack of efficiency in the real estate market by selling information, and as developers and financial intermediaries take advantage of the lack of efficiency by creating more efficient ways of making real estate investments available, for example, through securitization, the market naturally becomes more efficient.

APPRAISAL VALUATION APPROACHES

Because of the inefficiencies in the real estate market and the difficulty in easily obtaining information that indicates market value, appraisers generally use several approaches to estimate market value. They are the cost approach, the sales comparison approach, and the income approach. The assumptions and limitations of each are discussed below.

Cost Approach

The cost approach is based on the premise that the value of the property is equal to the sum of the land value (estimated by one of the other two approaches)

---

[7]Published quarterly by Frank Russell Company, Tacoma, Washington in conjunction with the National Council of Real Estate Investment Fiduciaries (NCREIF).

plus the replacement cost of the building. The value is also lowered if there is any physical deterioration in the building (e.g., repairs that need to be done), functional obsolescence in the building (e.g., inadequate or outdated design), and external obsolescence (factors external to the property that effect its value).

The economic rational for the cost approach is that a rational investor would not pay more than the cost of replacing the building with one that is equally productive on a comparable site.

For the cost approach to be valid the building must either be the highest and best use of the site or the value must be reduced to reflect the loss in value that results from the building not being the one that maximizes value.

When the existing building is not the highest and best use, appraisal theory suggests that the loss in value be attributed to the building. Stated differently, land is always valued as if it could be used under its highest and best use. Therefore, if an existing use is not the highest and best use, the building's value is assumed to be diminished.

There are many factors that make it difficult to apply the cost approach. First, adjustments for physical depreciation and functional and external obsolescence are hard to measure. Second, consideration must be given to the fact that a developer would not build a building unless an entrepreneurial profit could be earned. This profit must be included in the value of a property for the cost approach to make sense. At the same time, the entrepreneurial profit should only reflect what is earned by a typical real estate developer. It should not include any intangible business value that exists in a successfully operating enterprise associated with the real estate (recall earlier discussion about value in use).

The cost approach also assumes that the property is held as a fee simple estate. That is, it does not make an allowance for less-than-full property rights. Adjustments must be made for valuation of a leased fee estate or other partial interest.

For the reasons outlined above, the cost approach is generally considered the least reliable of the three approaches as an indication of market value.

Sales Comparison Approach

The sales comparison approach assumes that value is based on what everyone else is paying. That is, sales of other properties, adjusted for differences between the properties, are used as a basis for valuing a subject property. Obviously, this means that the appraiser requires information about the sales of comparable properties as well as sufficient information about each of the properties to be able to adjust for differences between the properties. Examples of

factors that ideally should be the same for the comparables and the property being appraised (subject property) are as follows:

- **Same location and type of property**
- **Same income potential**
- **Same lease structure**
- **Same expenses**
- **Same tax benefits to the typical investor**
- **Same risk**
- **Same ability to finance**
- **Similar property rights**
- **Sold under the same market conditions**

It is hard to find properties that can be used to estimate the value of a subject property without some adjustments. The term adjustment means that the price at which the comparable property was sold must be adjusted to reflect what it would have sold for if it were the same as the subject property. For example, if the comparable property had greater future income potential than the subject property, it probably sold for a higher price than could be expected for the subject property. Thus, the price of the comparable property would have to be adjusted downward to provide an indication of the price that might be expected for the subject property.

Another problem with the market approach is that the sale price of comparables often includes more than real estate. For example, the sale price might include a premium paid for favorable financing, that is, assumption of the seller's below-market interest rate loan. The price might also include personal property such as furniture, fixtures, and equipment. Or, the price might include an intangible going-concern value as discussed earlier.

When appraisers use the sales comparison approach they usually take a relatively small sample of the market. That is, they tend to use three to five comparables, which are adjusted to arrive at the estimated value of the subject property. This is in contrast to using a large sample and statistical techniques such as multiple regression analysis to estimate value. Rather, small samples and judgement are used to estimate value.

This approach ignores changes in the market. When using the market approach, there is a tendency to use older sales in the valuation process. That is, the comparable may have sold many months before (sometimes even a year or more where there is a thin market). Therefore, the appraiser must be very careful in adjusting for changes in market conditions.

Income Approach

The income approach is based on the income potential of the property. The idea is to determine what the typical investor would be willing to pay for the stream of income that is expected from the property. Historically, appraisers have analyzed the income on a before-tax basis. Of course, the before-tax discount rate used to value the income implicitly reflects any expected tax benefits. That is, if one knows that there will be tax benefits, a higher price can be paid for the property, resulting in a lower before-tax yield.

The income approach still relies on "market information." For example, the appraiser must estimate income by knowing the market rent for comparable space. The appraiser must also determine what the typical expenses should be for the given type of property. There are many ways of applying the income approach. The most common are discussed below.

Market Derived Overall Rates

One way of applying the income approach to appraise a property is to use overall capitalization rates from comparable sales. That is, one would first examine comparable sales and compute:

Cap Rate = NOI / Sale Price

where cap rate is the capitalization rate and NOI is the net operating income.

Assuming that the sale price is indicative of what the buyer thought the value of the property was, the capitalization rate can be derived from the comparable sales. This rate would then be used to appraise the subject property as follows:

Value = NOI / Cap Rate

Used in the manner described above, valuation with overall capitalization rates can really be viewed as a market approach. The current year NOI is used and would be known to the market if it were revealed by the property owner or manager.

The advantage of this approach is that it is relatively simple to apply. No forecasting of future income is necessary. One of the disadvantages is that there is a lot of misunderstanding as to what a capitalization rate really is. In fact, many people confuse capitalization rates with discount rates. Capitalization rates are analogous to the reciprocal of price-earnings (P/E) ratios for stocks; they relate the value of the investment to current income. Capitalization rates will differ for investments if the expectations for future earnings differ, even though current earnings may be the same for the two investments. Just as growth stocks have higher P/E ratios, real estate with expectations of higher future income

and increasing property values will have lower capitalization rates.

Because capitalization rates rely on a single (usually first) year NOI, it is important that this rate be consistent with first year NOIs for the comparable properties from which the overall rate was derived. It is difficult to compare capitalization rates for investments that will have different future income because of differences in the expected growth in the district or neighborhood where the property is located or because of differences in the leases on the property. Thus, to use a market derived capitalization rate properly, one must select comparable properties that have similar expectations for future NOI. Using capitalization rates to compare properties implicitly assumes the trend in future NOI will be the same for the subject as for the comparable. Also, because capitalization rates are based on the initial NOI, they are easily distorted by any concessions such as free rent that may show up in the NOI during the first year of the lease.

As a final note about market-derived capitalization rates, one must keep in mind that they are based on historical sales. Ideally, those sales were very recent, which by real estate standards might be within a few months. But clearly markets can change dramatically over a few months, if not a few weeks or even a few days. The fact that we do not observe rapid changes in real estate prices because of the lack of transactions for the same property does not mean factors affecting value have not changed.

Capitalization Rate Formulas

Another approach to obtaining capitalization rates is through the use of a formula rather than deriving the capitalization rate from comparable sales. The capitalization rate formula expresses the capitalization rate as a function of the discount rate required by investors and some measure of expected growth in the property's income and resale value. These formulas can be thought of as shortcut formulas for finding the present value of the estimated future cash flows (discounted cash flow analysis).

One common formula states the capitalization rate as follows:

Cap Rate = Discount Rate - Growth Rate

where the discount rate is the rate required by investors over the investment holding period and the growth rate is the expected compound rate of growth for income and property value. The property value would be estimated by dividing the first year NOI by the capitalization rate. Thus, we have the following value formula:

Value = NOI / (Discount Rate - Growth Rate)

This formula is analogous to the dividend growth model that is used for valuing stock. As in the market-derived approach, capitalization rates are applied to the first year NOI and thus suffer from the same problems outlined above. This particular formula only works if income and property value are both assumed to be increasing at the same compound rate each year.

Discounted Cash Flow (DCF)

The availability of personal computers, spreadsheets, and a variety of software for real estate valuation has simplified the process of attempting to capture investor motivations in the valuation process. Appraisers can analyze the cash flows directly, rather than use oversimplified formulas. Discounted cash flow analysis is an approach that involves projecting income and then discounting it to arrive at a value estimate. Actually, shortcut formulas that express capitalization rates in terms of discount rates and income growth rates are also in the family of discounted cash flow analyses, but most appraisers have not thought of it that way. Thus, the perception is that DCF is something new. All that is new, however, is an attempt to capture more carefully the nature of the income and expenses for the property. This is especially important for leased fee valuation because of the great impact that the specific lease provisions can have on the value of the property.

In general, DCF considers the following:

- **Income projected on a lease-by-lease basis**
- **Expenses projected by expense type**
- **Lease renewals at the market rate**
- **Vacancy based on market conditions at time of lease renewal**
- **Tenant improvements**
- **Free rent and other concessions**
- **Financing (if desired)**
- **The impact of taxes (if desired)**

It should be noted that whereas DCF does not solve directly for a capitalization rate, the capitalization rate is implicit in any DCF analysis. That is, once the present value of the cash flows is determined, the resulting value can be divided into the first year NOI to arrive at the implied capitalization rate. This capitalization rate can then be compared with rates obtained from comparable sales (if comparable sales data are available).

The advantage of DCF is that it reflects the way

investors make decisions. The resulting value estimate is a market value estimate as long as the analysis is done from the point of view of the typical investor. If the projections are for a specific noninvestor, then the result is investment value.

DCF requires a projection of the future cash flows. This is both an advantage and a disadvantage of the approach. The point is that because income must be explicitly projected to generate a DCF, it is clear to the reader of the report exactly what income the value is based upon. It is often argued that using market-derived capitalization rates from comparable properties does not require forecasting. But as emphasized earlier, to say that comparables really are comparables, the appraiser must implicitly consider whether the future income will be the same for the comparables as that of the subject property. Otherwise, the capitalization rates must differ.

Use of DCF does requires careful selection of a discount rate. One problem with real estate analysis is that the yield that investors are expecting on real estate investments cannot be observed directly. In the case of bonds, the face value and coupon rate are known; therefore, yields can be determined from observed purchase prices. For real estate, one does not necessarily know what the typical investor has in mind for a resale price. Several approaches may be used to arrive at a reasonable discount rate. First, the discount rate for a free and clear (unlevered) real estate investment should normally be higher than that for the same investment with a mortgage because of the additional business risk. To the extent that the property is levered, equity yield rates would be even higher.

Second, there are numerous surveys that attempt to determine typical yield requirements.[8] This provides an additional way to select a reasonable discount rate.

Third, there are also ways to use comparable sales to select a discount rate that is consistent with what market participants are projecting for increases in income and property values.[9]

VALUATION OF DEBT AND EQUITY INTERESTS

Sometimes it is necessary to estimate a separate value for the debt and equity interests of a property. For example, the investor may want to know the value

---

[8]For example see the "Real Estate Report" published Quarterly by Real Estate Research Corporation, Chicago, Illinois.

[9]See *The Appraisal of Real Estate*, Ninth Edition, American Institute of Real Estate Appraisers (AIREA), Chicago, Illinois 1987, page 534 for further discussion.

of just the equity position. Or, a lender may want to know the value of the mortgage that is backed by the property.

When valuing debt and equity interests it should be realized that the use of debt does not change the value of the underlying real estate. This does not mean that the cost of debt (interest rates) does not affect the value of real estate investments. Rather, the point is that the value of the real estate does not depend on how a particular investor finances the property.

If below-market financing is available from the seller, the equity investor may pay a premium over the value of the real estate to have the favorable loan. But this does not change the value of the real estate. Looked at another way, any premium associated with below-market debt is exactly offset by the discount that would be paid for the below-market debt if it were sold.[10]

Because value is not created by the use of debt, one can start with the free and clear value of the property when estimating the value of the debt and equity components. Next, the value of the debt might be estimated by discounting the payments at a market rate for debt. The resulting debt value can be subtracted from the free and clear value to arrive at a value of the equity component.

Alternatively, one could value the equity position by discounting the estimated cash flows to the equity investor at an appropriate equity yield rate. Subtracting this from the free and clear value of the property results in the value of the debt.

CONCLUSIONS ABOUT THREE APPROACHES TO MEASURING VALUE

In theory, in a perfect market all approaches to estimating value should give the same answer if markets are in equilibrium. In practice, real estate markets are seldom in balance. Even if prices did conform to what would be expected in an efficient market, appraisers (and academics) simply do not have the information necessary to measure (empirically test) that efficiency. Thus, in reality one would be suspicious if an appraiser indicated that all three approaches to estimating value resulted in the exact same answer!

Because all three approaches will not likely give the same answer, it is valuable to use all the ap-

proaches as separate indications of the value of the property. Depending upon the availability of data and the type of property being valued, one approach may be more reliable than another. For example, when appraising apartment buildings in a market where there are a lot of sales of relatively similar apartment buildings, in the same area, of a similar age, and of similar design, the sales comparison approach might provide the best indication of value. Because apartments typically do not have long-term leases, knowing the rent roll for the building is not as critical as for properties like office buildings.

If the property rights to be appraised are a leasehold estate, which depends on the difference between market and contract rents over the lease term, an income approach may be all that can be used. For example, there are not likely to be sales of other leasehold estates that are comparable (same lease provisions, length of leases, etc.), so a sales comparison approach cannot be used. The appraiser might value the leased fee and fee simple estates separately (perhaps using all three approaches) and then back into the value of the leasehold by subtracting the leased fee value from the fee simple value. This can be misleading, however, for the reasons cited earlier under the discussion of leasehold estates.

ISSUES IN REAL ESTATE VALUATION

Real estate markets have changed dramatically in recent years. This has resulted in a host of valuation issues that make it difficult to estimate the value of real estate.

First, the market has become more international with capital from other countries having a tremendous impact on real estate values in the United States. For example, with the Japanese bidding up the price of many "showcase" properties, the question asked is: "Is the price they are paying 'market value?'" Based on the definitions of value, if there are a sufficient number of Japanese investors to constitute a market and if they are the typical investor for a tier of properties, one must conclude that the price they are willing to pay is market value. The fact that their investment incentives—including the yen/dollar relation—may change tomorrow is not relevant. Market values for real estate can change overnight!

Second, institutional investors, especially pension funds, have had an increased interest in investing in real estate for diversification benefits. These investors tend to be very sophisticated in their analysis of real estate markets and the way they structure deals. This has resulted in an attempt to apply more modern portfolio theory to the valuation of real estate, as well as attempts to securitize com-

---

[10]For a further discussion see "Valuation of Equity Interests - Leveraged Properties," September, 1989, a working paper prepared for the National Council of Real Estate Investment Fiduciaries (NCREIF) Valuation Committee, by David H. Trahan and Roger Ollman.

mercial real estate so that it can trade more like stocks and bonds.

The increasing sophistication of the real estate market and the increased involvement from institutional investors raises the issue as to whether real estate should be valued in a portfolio framework like stocks and bonds. If the riskiness of real estate is priced in the market as modern portfolio theory would suggest, then only its systematic risk matters. This is the risk that cannot be eliminated by diversifying the portfolio. This implies that differences in the systematic risk between a comparable and the subject property must be considered. All else being equal, if the subject property has higher systematic risk, then its value should be less. In a discounted cash flow analysis, this means that a higher discount rate would be required for the subject property than would have been required by investors in the comparable property.

More research needs to be done to determine the appropriate measure of risk for real estate. We also need a better understanding of the degree of diversification benefits that can be obtained by investing in properties in different geographic locations, investing in different property types, and investing in properties with different lease structures.

We must be careful not to assume that real estate should be priced like stocks and bonds. The fact that it does not trade like stocks and bonds may mean that its risk is not the same. As we have seen, real estate is unique and its risk may not be viewed by the market in the same way as financial assets.[11]

Third, there has been an increased awareness of the effect that asbestos and other environmental hazards can have on property values.[12] Because so little is known about the health effects of some of these hazards and because federal and state legislation is rapidly expanding in this area, a high risk premium is placed on investing in properties that may have an environmental problem.[13]

Appraisers are being asked to determine the ef-fect of asbestos and other environmental hazards on the market value of real estate. This is difficult because appraisers are not environmental engineers. They cannot be expected to identify different types of environmental hazards and know the cost of eliminating the hazard or know the potential health effects of the hazard. Yet, these environmental hazards affect sale prices. To interpret the market properly (e.g., understand comparable sales) the appraiser must know how different environmental hazards may have affected a sale and the implication of that on the value of a property being appraised. Much research still needs to be done in this evolving area of appraisal practice.

Fourth, there has been a major tax law change (Tax Reform Act of 1986) that significantly altered the tax benefits of real estate investments relative to other investments. Whether the tax law change was good or bad for the economy in general, it clearly changed incentives for real estate investment and, consequently, the type of investor that is now attracted to real estate. For example, this is one reason why pension funds (which are tax exempt) find real estate investments much more attractive now that they do not have to compete with tax-oriented syndications. We must be aware that tax laws may change again, which may result in a change in incentives for investment in one asset class versus another asset class.

CONCLUSION

This paper discussed the nature of the appraisal process with emphasis on how an appraiser attempts to estimate market value. The types of assumptions that must be made to estimate market value properly were reviewed. Because of the nature of real estate markets, this process is necessary. There is not a sufficient amount of public information about property transactions nor a sufficient number of sales of the same or similar properties to judge adequately market values without the use of an appraisal process. Furthermore, the inefficiency of the real estate market requires appraisers to use several approaches to estimate value.

The user of the appraisal must be sure that the appraiser estimates the type of value (e.g., market, investment, going concern, etc.) that the user requires. In most cases, this will be market value even if the client would like it to be investment value!

We have seen that the appraisal process requires many assumptions and is subject to many limitations because of the nature of the real estate market. Fortunately, there are many advances taking place to improve the ability of appraisers and others to estimate market value. First, there is development of

[11]See David J. Hartzell and David G. Shulman, "Real Estate Returns and Risks: A Survey," Real Estate Research Report, Salomon Brothers Inc, February 12, 1988.

[12]For a discussion of the valuation effects of asbestos see Albert R. Wilson, "Probable Financial Effect of Asbestos Removal on Real Estate," The Appraisal Journal, July, 1989. For a general overview of the asbestos problem see "An Asbestos Desk Reference for Corporate Real Estate Professionals,"Industrial Development Research Council, Inc., Norcross, Georgia, February, 1989.

[13]For a comprehensive discussion of the risks associated with environmental hazards see "Coping with Hazardous Waste" by Roger D. Schwenke, working paper presented at the National Council of Real Estate Investment Fiduciaries (NCREIF) meeting October 26, 1989 in New York, New York.

better data bases of real estate transactions and property characteristics are being developed so that more advanced analytic techniques can be used. Second, analytic models (demand, pricing, etc.) that recognize the unique characteristics of real estate are being developed.[14]

Finally, recognizing that a sufficient number of faulty appraisals caused at least some of the problems that the S&L industry has faced, the Financial Institutions Reform, Recovery, and Enforcement Act of 1989 (referred to in the media as the S&L Bailout Bill) included provisions for regulation of appraisers.[15] Among other things, the legislation requires appraisers to become certified if they are to appraise properties that involve federally related transactions. This includes transactions involving any institution that is regulated or insured by the government regulatory agencies as well as transactions involving the Federal Home Loan Mortgage Corporation (Freddie Mac), the Federal National Mortgage Association (Fannie Mae), or the new Resolution Trust Corporation. The legislation gives The Appraisal Foundation[16] the responsibility of developing criteria that the states must follow when certifying appraisers. The Foundation also issues the Uniform Standards of Appraisal Practice that provide guidelines for appraisers to follow in their reports.

Clearly this is a time of change in both real estate markets and the appraisal process. Appraisers must strive to keep abreast of changes in valuation theory and practice if they are going to be able to provide the level of analysis that will be increasingly required by real estate investors and lenders.

---

[14]Organizations such as the Homer Hoyt Institute (HHI) and the National Council of Real Estate Investment Fiduciaries (NCREIF) have made a tremendous effort to bring academics and practitioners together to work jointly on improving the availability of real estate data and enhancing applied real estate research.

[15]Title XI. Real Estate Appraisal Reform Amendments of the Financial Institutions Reform, Recovery, and Enforcement Act of 1989.

[16]The Appraisal Foundation was established by the appraisal industry in 1987 as a source of uniform standards for the appraisal profession.

Developing a Better Cash Flow Projection

by Raymond T. Cirz, MAI, and Michael S. Sorich, MAI

INTRODUCTION

This article will explore the basic elements incorporated in developing a better cash flow projection based primarily on market-derived information.

For the past few years, Krauser, Welsh, Sorich & Cirz has conducted an informal survey of investor acquisition criteria. Through interviews with major financial and real estate-related institutions, acquisition criteria are analyzed to gain a better understanding of investment requirements for institutional-grade real estate on a national level. The survey questions are designed to reflect acquisition/investment situations for a typical property type in a typical market. Although it is increasingly difficult to define the "typical" property in a "typical" market, it is possible to correlate the survey's results within a narrow and consistent range. Monitoring these acquisition criteria to better understand investor motivation is crucial to discounted cash flow analysis.

Figure 1 shows a recent investor survey which sets forth various investor criteria. To understand investor motivation more fully, one cannot simply verify that "we currently purchase on a 13% *IRR.*" Other facets of investment criteria must be explored to ascertain the basis for this internal rate of

Raymond T. Cirz, MAI is a partner in Krauser, Welsh, Sorich & Cirz, a nationally oriented real estate advisory corporation. He received a bachelor's degree in business administration from Fairleigh Dickinson University and is a past contributor to *The Appraisal Journal.*

Michael S. Sorich, MAI, is a partner in Krauser, Welsh, Sorich & Cirz. He has a bachelor's degree in business administration from Arizona State University and has extensive experience in appraising large commercial real estate developments for institutions and investors.

return. The four key elements to be discussed here are growth rates, the overall rate of return, the holding period, and reversion assumptions.

FIGURE 1.

Institutional Investors Criteria For Investment

Summer 1986

	Project Types in Preference Order	Growth Rate Assumptions		Holding Period (Years)	Existing Properties	
		Percent Income	Percent Expense		IRR (Percent)	Overall Rate (Percent)
Citicorp	Office Shopping Hotels Shopping Centers Industrials	5%	5%	10	12.5—13.5%	8—10%
Aetna Life Insurance Co.	Office Shopping Centers Industrials	6	6	10	12.5	8.5—9.5
Metropolitan Life Insurance Co.	Office Shopping Centers Industrials Hotels	4—5	6	N/A	12.0	9—9.5
Equitable Life Assurance Co.	Office Shopping Centers Industrials Apartments w/ Condo Potential	5—7	6—8	10—35	12.5—14	8—10
Lomas & Nettleton, Dallas	Office Shopping Centers Industrials	5—7	5—8	15	13—14	8—11
Prudential Insurance Co.	Major Investment R.E.	5—6	5—6	10—15	12—14	8—10
Travelers Insurance Co.	A Mix of Commercial Properties	4—5	4—5	10	12.5—13.5	8.5—10
New York Life Insurance Co.	Office Industrials Shopping Centers	5	6	10	13—13.5	8.5—11
RREEF	Office Shopping Centers Industrials	5—7	5—7	10	12—13	8.5—9.5
Chase Investors Management	Major Office CBD Quality Suburban Office Parks Regional Malls	5—6.5	5—7	10—15	12.5—14	9—9.5

GROWTH RATE

Growth rate assumptions have a direct impact on the investors' internal rate of return requirements. Certainly, a cash flow projection that assumes a 6% increase in market rent is more aggressive than one based on 4% growth. This additional risk is usually reflected in the *IRR*. In current markets there can be a noticeable difference between quoted (face) rental rates and effective rental rents due to rent concessions. In fact, rent concessions can reduce quoted rental rates by 30% or more in some markets. For example, one investor interviewed applies a 5% market rent growth factor to effective rent rather than the quoted (face) rates. Analyzing the *IRR* requirement of this investor without this knowledge might indicate an aggressive investment posture when, in fact, the investor's expectation could be market-oriented.

Discussions with investors reveal that the specific market and property type may noticeably affect their growth assumptions. In overbuilt markets investors are moderating their income growth assumptions, at least for the time being. In markets where the supply imbalance is not as noticeable, investor expectations are usually more aggressive.

Growth rates for income and expense items may not always correlate. Slow growth in rent levels due to an oversupply does not necessarily mean expenses will follow a similar pattern. Local market conditions have a direct impact on items such as real estate taxes, utilities, payroll expenses, and cleaning charges. In California, Proposition 13 limits real estate tax increases to 2% per year. However, at the end of the assumed holding period a reassessment can be expected, and this could have a negative impact on the resale price. Obviously, growth rate assumptions that are unrealistic and inconsistent with market expectations can result in erroneous value conclusions.

OVERALL RATE OF RETURN

The internal rate of return is also affected by the going-in, or overall, rate of return. Several survey respondents indicated that although cash flow projections must be considered, they prefer a solid, market-oriented overall rate to an above-average forecasted internal rate of return. Investors perceive less inherent risk when cash flow is at an acceptable level rather than predicated on future expectations. If initial leasing is underway, a lower overall rate may warrant a higher *IRR* to reflect the risk of lease-up during the projected absorption period. This is especially true in markets where absorption is difficult to predict.

HOLDING PERIOD

For analyzing major real estate investments, the most widely accepted holding period is 10 years. Interestingly this time period does not necessarily coincide with the investor's planned ownership period. Major investors typically sell an investment in less than 10 years, but proposed tax law changes may alter this tenet in the future.

Some investors use a 15-year holding period, while one investor quoted 35 years. Certain foreign investors are basing their investment decisions on much longer holding periods, and their influence on future market perceptions should be closely watched. Obviously, there is a correlation, and usually an inverse relationship, between the length of the holding period and the associated risk. Projected dollars become more speculative as time increases because their return becomes less certain. Therefore, if the investor's holding period assumption is not known, other factors may appear inconsistent.

In many cases the length of the holding period corresponds with long-term lease encumbrances at nonmarket terms. Here, cash flow analysis is needed to analyze the overall desirability of the investment. However, it may not be necessary to make a projection for a period of more than 10 years if the existing lease structure is typical of the market or if the investment is susceptible to unpredictable, long-term changes such as is the case with hotels and motels.

It is prudent to test the overall yield with varying holding periods, but assume the 10-year investment period unless circumstances dictate otherwise. Capitalizing an eleventh year net income may be illogical if a significant increase or decrease in cash flow can be expected in the twelfth year. In general it is important to estimate a reasonable income flow and resale value.

REVERSION ASSUMPTION

The reversion assumption is the assumed resale price of the property or where financing is considered, the equity position at the end of the projection period. This topic warrants an article of its own. Fortunately, this element has less impact on the overall return and property or equity value due to the effect of discounting over time.

The survey uncovered several methods of calculating an investment's resale (reversion) price. By far the most popular method is to capitalize the projected net income for the year immediately following the assumed holding period. The reversion (resale) capitalization rate typically ranges from 9% to 10%, although one major investor indicated that the reversion capitalization rate could be as low as 8.5%. Reversion rates for specialized properties such as lodging facilities can be significantly higher; the overall rates and *IRRs* of these properties may be higher as well.

Some acquisition specialists prefer to use a reversion capitalization method, adding from 50 to 150 basis points to the property's going-in rate. However, this practice can be arbitrary and not give full consideration of the other elements used in developing the cash flow projection. Certainly, the property's expected leasing position at the time of resale is a consideration. If a reversion capitalization method had been applied to the analysis conducted in purchasing the Pan Am Building several years ago and an overall rate of 4% had been used, an inappropriate value conclusion could have been reached.

Another method of calculating reversion is to apply an overall rate to the projected net income based solely on current market rent levels. This assumes that all leases will be at market levels when applying the reversion capitalization rate. If actual, below-market leases are in place at the end of the projection period when this rate is applied, the reversionary value conclusion could be erroneous. Based on the survey, this method has not gained wide acceptance in the industry. Reversion can also be estimated by calculating current construction costs and the property's land value at assumed inflation rates and then deducting an amount for depreciation. Any or all of these methods may be acceptable if they are based on sound conclusions and consider the other elements included in the cash flow analysis.

We prefer to let investors identify an acceptable reversion capitalization rate range for the type of investment under analysis and then subjectively select a rate giving consideration to the assumptions in the cash flow analysis. Critics may claim that this subjective selection is unreliable, but it parallels the traditional method of capitalizing a stabilized net income. The reversion assumption can be tested by calculating the implied average annual property appreciation rate. We find that the annual appreciation rate is near our assumed inflation rate unless there are unusual circumstances.

The income stream to which the reversion capitalization rate is applied must also be considered. Usually an overall capitalization rate is applied to the forecasted *NOI*, to produce a property value reversion estimate. If assumable, low-interest financing encumbers the property, however, it may be prudent to capitalize the cash flow after debt service. This results in an equity reversion value estimate to which the current mortgage balance is added to produce an overall reversion property value estimate. The debt service constant and the remaining term of the existing loan should be considered in the analysis to determine if refinancing would be more advantageous.

Typically, an allowance is deducted for resale costs such as commissions and closing costs, but this adjustment, usually has little effect on the overall value due to the effects of discounting.

CONCLUSION

Cash flow analysis has a definite place in the valuation process, particularly when valuing institutional-grade investment properties. It is certainly not the only valuation method available to the appraiser, and its importance varies depending on the investor's preference. Valuation theory is a compilation of techniques and analyses used to interpret the motivation of sales activity. A key element in the successful use of cash flow analysis is understanding investor motivation. Investigating investor requirements and understanding the basis for these requirements allow appraisers to consider empirical evidence and not rely solely on subjective intuition in making projections. Cash flow projections are based on a variety of empirical and subjective factors, but real estate appraisers and consultants must also seek empirical evidence. Our profession requires this type of investigation and today's real estate market demands it.

Toward An Assessment of the Reliability of Commercial Appraisals

by Rebel Cole, David Guilkey, and Mike Miles

INTRODUCTION

The appraisal of a major commercial property is a complex and challenging task. Typically, the client requests an opinion of market value, often with his or her own unique definition of value. Although definitions vary and "a current definition of market value" cited in the Appraisal Institute's principal text[1] is quite distinguishable from a most probable selling price,"[2] most practitioners are comforted when arms-length transactions between astute buyers and sellers take place at prices close to appraised market value.

---

1. American Institute of Real Estate Appraisers, *The Appraisal of Real Estate,* 8th ed. (Chicago: The Appraisal Institute, 1983), 33.
2. Developed by Richard U. Ratcliff and popularized by James A. Graskamp, University of Wisconsin, and Halbert C. Smith, University of Florida.

Rebel Cole is a Ph.D. candidate in real estate economics at The University of North Carolina.
David Guilkey is professor of economics at The University of North Carolina and an econometrician who has contributed to both theoretical and applied literature.
Mike Miles is Foundation Professor of Urban Development at The University of North Carolina, where he specializes in real estate investment. He is a regular contributor to the *The Appraisal Journal.*

The authors appreciate the help of Kim Smith of the Frank Russell Company in preparing this article and also gratefully acknowledge the financial support of the National Council of Real Estate Investment Fiduciaries. NCREIF neither endorses nor rejects the results of this study and any errors in it are the authors' responsibility.

This article examines a series of sales of commercial properties that had been recently appraised in an effort to assess the reliability of commercial appraisals. While there can probably be no perfect test of an opinion, we believe the data are informative. On average, the absolute difference in sales price and most recent independent appraisal was almost 9%.

THE DATA

The National Council of Real Estate Investment Fiduciaries (NCREIF), who, together with the Frank Russell Company, publish *The FRC Report*, has a membership that includes most of the major real estate investment managers. There have been 147 sales from their data base, which now includes the operating history of nearly $9 billion of commercial real estate. A comparison of the sales prices to preceding appraised values provides a test of the reliability of the commercial product.

Table 1 provides a breakdown of the data base which includes *all* FRC property sales occurring between January 1978 and June 1984. The sold property data base (like the complete *FRC* data base from which it comes) is generally well diversified by region, property type, and size.[3] An independent fee appraiser appraised

TABLE I

Characteristics of the Data Base
(Number of Properties in Each Category)

Region	East	19
	Midwest	33
	South	49
	West	43
	Total	144*
Type	Apartments	4
	Hotels	3
	Industrial	68
	Office	36
	Retail	33
	Total	144
Size	<$2,000,000	60
	$2–10,000,000	70
	>$10,000,000	14
	Total	144

*See text for an explanation of why three sales were deleted from the data base.

---

3. The one major exception to this statement is the lack of any large retail properties.

108 of the sold properties within the 18 months preceding sale. The remaining 36 were appraised in-house by a staff that included several MAIs and numerous MBAs. In total, the group of appraisers who produced these opinions of value includes the nation's largest and most respected appraisal firms.[4]

The direct appraisal client (the real estate investment manager) sets the unit value of its portfolio based on these appraised values. In the open-end funds (which constitute well over 50% of the properties in the data base), pension funds may buy into or sell out of the manager's funds at these unit values. Clearly, there is a strong incentive to have appraised values reflect investment values to the pension fund.

REASONS WHY SALES PRICES MIGHT NOT EQUAL THE APPRAISED VALUES

In this section several reasons why sales prices might deviate from appraised values are considered. Some result in adjustments that are reflected in the analysis presented in the following section. Others are necessary qualifiers to conclusions drawn from that analysis.

Terms of Sale

Fortunately, the vast majority of these sales were cash sales with no guarantees beyond typical general warranty deed covenants. In the four cases involving seller debt financing, the contractual payments were discounted to present value at one point above the then current yield on similar maturity treasury obligations. The differences from face values were small, and none of the sales involved high degrees of leverage which would have required additional adjustments for risk.[5]

In cases in which the seller owned less than 100% of the fee, the sales price was "grossed up" to match the appraised value, which was of the property in single ownership. (For example, if the seller had owned a 75% interest, the sales proceeds were multiplied by 100% ÷ 75% before comparison with the appraised value.) In three cases there were complex seller guarantees of future income which would possibly result in material deviation of actual seller cash proceeds from reported sales price. These three sales were dropped from the sample.[6] For the remaining 144 properties, the sales price was definitionally comparable to the interest being appraised by the appraiser, i.e., the definition of value was consistent with the terms of the sale except for the adjustment described above.

---

4. One of the larger NCREIF members, Prudential Insurance, now spends nearly $2 million annually on outside fee appraisals.

5. The fact that few of these sales involved unusual financing does not mean that the appraisers could ignore adjustments for atypical financing or trends in what the market considered typical financing. Their opinions of value were extracted from the market. Many market transactions involved significant financing and, thus, necessitated adjustments before they could be used as comparables in the subject property valuation.

6. Two of these sales also involved seller debt financing, so that of the 144 remaining sales, only two involve seller debt financing.

Thin Markets and Buyer Motivation

For very large transactions there may be but a few large buyers actively bidding. In such cases the prices obtained may not reflect a true market consensus.[7] Additionally, for a few industrial properties, the buyer was the existing tenant. When the buyer has additional investments in unique tenant improvements, surrounding investments that are used in conjunction with the subject property, or other extra incentives to purchase, the market conditions surrounding the sale may have been less than perfect. Since there is no way to adjust for such effects, it is necessary to condition conclusions drawn from the subsequent analysis accordingly.

Logistics and Seller Motivations

There are two general types of seller motivation in this data base. As in many investment property sales, the seller often had a less optimistic forecast of the property's future than the buyer. This motivation involves the quality of the individual manager's market research and presents no problems concerning our reliability assessment. A second seller motivation, which is more unusual to this data base, deals with management efficiency. Given operational logistics and the compensation structure of the investment manager, some managers may have tended to sell smaller properties that were not located near their other investments. Since there was usually a large number of potential buyers, even this seller motivation should not substantially affect the appraisal versus sales price comparison.[8]

Capital Improvements between Date of Appraisal and Sales Date

If the real estate investment manager increased investment in the property between the appraisal date and the sales date, the sales price should exceed the appraised value. Assuming a reliable appraisal and only justified and timely capital improvements by the manager, the value difference should be approximately the inflation-adjusted cost of the capital improvements.[9] In this data base all appraised values were adjusted upward by the amount of any capital improvements (not maintenance or normal operating expenses) occurring between the appraisal date and the sales date.[10]

---

7. Of the 108 sold properties for which outside appraisals were available, only 14 sold for more than $10 million, one for more than $50 million, and none for more than $100 million. Thus, thin markets should not be a major problem in this sample.

8. There are two other possible seller motivations. If the managers sold only their losers, there might have been a downward bias in the sales prices since the dates of outside appraisals preceded sales dates by as much as 12 months. This would also be true (with a reverse bias) if the managers sold only winners in an effort to impress their pension funds. There is no evidence of either of these motivations.

9. There is some possible slippage between appraised values (forward looking) and accounting entries (historic) for capital improvements. After checking all material capital improvements, the authors believe that the capital improvements added were all physically made after the appraiser's last visual inspection of the property so that no double counting occurred.

10. These adjustments assume that a capital improvement occurs at the midpoint of the quarter in which it is reported.

Changes in the Discount or Capitalization Rate[11]

It is possible that the discount or capitalization rate could change during the interval between the dates of sale and appraisal. This is especially likely both when the preceding appraisal occurred more than one quarter prior to sale and also during periods of interest rate volatility. If the discount or capitalization rate does change during this interval, the sales price would be expected to diverge from the appraised value.

Closing Costs

Since the appraiser's value is not typically adjusted for closing costs (i.e., the opinion of value is more comparable to gross than net selling price), net proceeds received by the sellers might be less than appraised value by the amount of the closing costs. In the sample, closing costs varied substantially but averaged slightly over 2%.[12] Due to the variation in closing costs, net proceeds were used in calculating the difference between sales price and last appraised value. However, since the appraiser would typically not consider closing costs, the average 2% should be considered in interpreting the results of the analysis which follows.

Date of the Last Appraisal

This is the most complicated issue involved in using this data base as a test of appraisal reliability. There is an appraisal every quarter for each property. However, in most cases there is only an outside fee appraisal once a year. The timing and the frequency of outside appraisals varied over the period (1978-1985) so that seasonality effects were both unpredictable and nonstationary. Still, for the majority of the properties (those held in open-ended funds), the managers should have been conscientious about inside appraisals (their staffs are equally well trained),[13] since pension funds could buy in and sell out at the fund's unit value which was based directly on the quarterly appraisals. In the tests that follow we report both the differences from the last appraisal and the last outside appraisal.

Another potential bias in the data results from the length of time needed to close a large commercial transaction. It is possible that at the end of the quarter preceding the sale the property was already under contract, and that the appraiser properly adjusted the opinion of value to reflect this information. Since some closings

---

11. While many money managers generally argue that all appraisals should contain discounted cash flow analysis, some appraisers still rely upon the capitalized value of stabilized net operating income.

12. This is the actual average cost of sale, i.e., the difference between gross and net proceeds reported by the investment managers.

13. While levels of experience may vary, the staffs included both MAIs and MBAs and, thus, had similar training to the fee appraisers.

may have been even more than one quarter after the contract signing, we report differences from the last six quarters' appraised values.[14]

Given the length of time between the appraisals and the sales date (now up to six quarters), appraisals are adjusted for inflation during the intervening period. This adjustment assumes mid-quarter sales and appraisals and uses the Consumer Price Index (CPI) as a measure of inflation. Clearly, this CPI adjustment is imperfect since prices move for a series of reasons other than inflation and at different rates in different markets. Still, inflation is a major factor and additional adjustments would be rather small, given the relatively short period of time involved.[15]

TABLE 2

Comparison of Net Sales Prices to Appraised Values
Mean Absolute Difference (in percentages), CPI Adjusted

	N	Last	2nd qtr.	3rd qtr.	4th qtr.	5th qtr.	6th qtr.	Outside
Total	144	7.57	9.34	10.02	10.85	10.86	12.55	9.58
By region								
East	19	5.26	7.28	7.43	8.78	9.14	9.29	6.49
Midwest	33	5.95	9.30	10.44	12.64	11.83	12.11	9.01
South	49	9.60	10.20	11.18	10.97	11.89	13.85	11.52
West	43	7.52	9.31	9.53	10.30	9.61	12.86	9.05
By type								
Apartments	4	22.61	23.06	26.50	25.65	19.32	20.26	23.90
Hotels	3	1.40	6.19	7.12	11.10	11.75	12.87	5.50
Industrial	68	9.91	11.65	11.88	13.23	13.22	14.48	11.73
Office	36	4.11	5.96	7.85	8.33	9.11	10.92	6.14
Retail	33	5.27	6.73	6.76	6.86	7.05	9.46	7.30
By size								
< $2,000,000	60	8.86	10.97	11.05	12.05	12.15	13.83	11.33
$2–10,000,000	70	7.15	8.53	9.02	9.94	9.47	11.29	7.80
> $10,000,000	14	4.15	6.19	10.70	10.35	12.25	13.10	10.60

---

14. Last appraised value equaled the sales price for three properties. In three cases, the appraised value also equaled sales price two quarters prior to sale.

15. Without the adjustments for inflation, we find that the mean absolute differences are larger in magnitude and increase with every interval between date of sale and appraisal. For example, the mean absolute one quarter and one year differences of the total sample were 7.6% and 10.8% when data was inflated to constant dollars, but were 7.9% and 12.1% when no adjustments for inflation were made.

Table 2 presents the mean absolute percentage differences[16] in the sales price and the appraised values for appraisals one through six quarters preceding the quarter in which the property was sold, as well as for the last outside appraisal. Absolute differences are examined because the use of signed differences would result in an averaging inappropriate in a reliability test.[17] These differences are also broken down by property type, region, and size. In all categories presented in Table 2, the differences are not significantly different from zero at the 5% level when the nonparametric Wilcoxon signed rank test[18] is used to test for differences.

The results are very interesting. For the entire sample, the last appraised value was, on average, over 7.5% (inflation adjusted) different from the sales price, while the last outside appraisal was over 9.5% (inflation adjusted) different. While these differences may be slightly greater than most appraisers would have guessed, the range is even more instructive. The greatest positive and negative differences for the last outside appraisal were +181% and −28% respectively. In fact, 11 sales had an absolute difference of more than 20% from the last outside appraisal. Eliminating these sales, the mean absolute difference from the last outside appraisal drops to around 6%.

It appears that the largest differences were in southern properties, industrial properties (the apartment and hotel samples are too small to be meaningful), and very small properties. However, after removing the major outliers noted in the preceding paragraph, none of the differences within categories remain statistically significant. Thus, it appears that a few appraisals were the major causes of the significant differences within categories and for the whole sample.

This is the expected result, given the extreme outliers noted above. Unfortunately, this means that the confidence interval around any one opinion of value is very large. Since the absolute percentage difference distribution is highly skewed and definitionally nonnormal (lower bound of zero and a mean relatively close to zero), it is not possible to construct standard formal confidence intervals. Still, the ranges and the frequencies reported in Table 3 clearly indicate that any confidence interval would be quite large. Even more disturbing is the failure of the standard deviations to shrink materially as we move from six quarters prior to sale to one quarter prior to sale. The most current appraisals exhibit nearly as great a standard deviation as the more distant appraisals. Additionally, since the

---

16. The mean absolute percentage difference is average of the absolute values of the differences in sales price and preceding appraised value.

17. If one were concerned with the level of confidence a pension fund might place in the unit value of a portfolio of real estate, then actual or signed differences would be more appropriate.

18. The Wilcoxon signed rank test is a significance test that requires the analyst to make no assumptions about the distribution of the variable in question, such as the assumption of a normal distribution. This test is used because of the observed nonnormality of the distribution of absolute differences.

TABLE 3

Frequency Distribution: Mean Absolute Differences

Difference	Mean	SD	Range		Frequency Distribution			
			Min.	Max.	0–10%	10–20%	20–30%	>30%
1st qtr.	7.50	17.48	0.11	192.22	81.9%	13.2%	2.1%	2.8%
2nd qtr.	9.34	17.35	0.04	184.68	73.2%	17.6%	4.9%	4.2%
3rd qtr.	10.02	17.34	0.02	183.07	70.0%	17.1%	7.9%	5.0%
4th qtr.	10.85	17.39	0.08	180.85	66.4%	21.9%	5.8%	5.8%
5th qtr.	10.86	17.09	0.01	178.27	65.2%	22.7%	8.3%	3.8%
6th qtr.	12.55	18.45	0.31	171.91	59.2%	23.8%	11.5%	5.4%
Outside	9.58	18.60	0.08	180.85	73.1%	16.7%	6.5%	3.7%

magnitude of the mean differences increases for more distant appraisals, it is clear that other forces besides inflation (for which we have adjusted) are causing these differences.

In an effort to determine statistically if nonzero absolute differences were systematically related to the sample breakdowns listed above (i.e., type, region, size), ordinary least squares regressions were run of the form:

$$Y = XB + E$$

where Y is the mean absolute difference, B is a vector of parameter estimates of the vector X of independent variables, and E is a disturbance term. The results of these regressions, presented in Table 4, indicate that not the size or type of the property, region of the country, or year of sale were significant explanatory variables. Interestingly, the dummy variable indicating whether a property was sold in the third quarter was highly significant in explaining the nonzero means in the first regression. This result clearly indicates that the majority of the 11 largest outliers (mean absolute difference greater than 20%) occurred in the third quarter. An examination of the 11 major outliers confirmed this, since 6 of these 11 properties were sold in the third quarter.[19]

---

19. This concentration in quarter 3 appears to result from chance alone.

TABLE 4

OLS Regression Results*

Dependent variable: mean absolute difference in sales price and last appraisal

Variable	Parameter Estimate	Standard Error	T for HO: Parameter = 0	Prob. > |T|
INTERCEP	4.202885	4.797367	0.876	0.3826
YR78	7.596765	8.877448	0.856	0.3937
YR80	4.143596	9.964811	0.416	0.6782
YR81	− 4.186445	9.343266	− 0.448	0.6549
YR82	10.971887	6.849403	1.602	0.1116
YR83	1.356125	6.088714	0.223	0.8241
YR84	1.997131	5.838109	0.342	0.7328
HOTEL	− 5.334000	10.649212	− 0.501	0.6173
APT	16.653312	9.280603	1.794	0.0751
RETAIL	− 5.979722	3.715027	− 1.610	0.1099
OFFICE	− 3.820697	3.777605	− 1.011	0.3137
Q2	− 1.286401	4.989359	− 0.258	0.7969
Q3**	12.264460	4.986533	2.460	0.0152**
Q4	1.368898	4.633668	0.292	0.7681
SALEPR	− 1.24342E-07	1.50000E-07	− 0.829	0.4087

Dependent variable: mean absolute difference in sales price and last outside appraisal

Variable	Parameter Estimate	Standard Error	T for HO: Parameter = 0	Prob. > |T|
INTERCEP	6.918931	5.516594	1.254	0.2129
YR80	4.484858	14.854448	0.302	0.7634
YR81	− 3.051471	11.404971	− 0.268	0.7896
YR82	11.035803	8.251043	1.338	0.1843
YR83	0.619687	7.295982	0.085	0.9325
YR84	1.811404	6.667415	0.272	0.7865
HOTEL	− 12.194120	19.013798	− 0.641	0.5229
APT	18.109900	11.464537	1.580	0.1175
RETAIL	− 5.828061	4.511809	− 1.292	0.1996
OFFICE	− 3.758697	5.063195	− 0.742	0.4597
Q2	− 3.003571	6.315530	− 0.476	0.6355
Q3	12.148697	6.315412	1.924	0.0574
Q4	0.456769	6.005649	0.076	0.9395
SALEPR	− 1.28587E-07	1.89262E-07	− 0.679	0.4985

*Individual and small group regressions show similar results.
**Statistically significant at the 5% level.

SUMMARY AND CONCLUSIONS

Without the outliers, the mean absolute difference from the last outside appraisal was a respectable 5.9%. Unfortunately, the outliers do exist and the overall results (over 9.5% average absolute difference) do not indicate a high degree of reliability in the individual commercial appraisal product. (Still, as indicated by the REIT and stock index figures provided in the Appendix, 9% may not be bad in an investment world that exhibits considerable variation over time.)

The outliers are not confined to one property type, location, or size. Since all of these appraisals were reviewed by the investment managers, it is not likely that a methodological error caused the outliers. Thus, it appears that the major appraisal errors concern real estate, not financial or technical aspects. In the outliers, the appraiser appears to have missed major market changes and, at times, even the highest and best use. Certainly, improvements in technique are possible, but an understanding of the underlying land economies appears to be more important.

APPENDIX

The REIT Experience
NAREIT Share Price Index
(January 1972 = 100)

	Index (December)	Price Charge (%)	Dividend Yield (%)	Total Yield (%)	Index of Total Yield
Dec. 1972	103.54	3.54			
Dec. 1973	69.46	−32.91			
Dec. 1974	35.05	−49.54			
Dec. 1975	42.85	22.25			
Dec. 1976	58.46	36.43			58.46
Dec. 1977	64.35	10.08	8.01	18.09	69.03264
Dec. 1978	58.86	−8.53	8.43	−0.10	64.28470
Dec. 1979	69.44	17.97	10.67	28.64	75.72306
Dec. 1980	76.70	10.46	9.68	20.14	83.42179
Dec. 1981	76.53	−0.22	9.48	9.26	83.80116
Dec. 1982	88.88	16.14	9.97	26.11	96.51004
Dec. 1983	102.96	15.84	9.62	25.46	111.5102
Dec. 1984	106.97	3.89	9.20	13.09	116.4423
Mean	73.38846	3.491926	9.3825	17.58573	84.35369
Variance	470.8631	488.2441	0.622693	83.25665	366.5139
SD	21.699938	22.09624	0.789109	9.124508	19.14455

The figures are taken from data compiled by the National Association of REITs. As the dates indicate, these figures primarily describe the 1970s-style REITs (equity, mortgage, and combined), not the 1980s REITs which have investment strategies designed to fit pension fund investors better.

One-year differences in other indexes are reported to provide some insight into long-term market stability. While the comparison is anything but perfect, the change in major stock market indexes from year to year is interesting.

Statistics of Selected Stock Return Indexes 1978-1984

	SP 500	% Return	NYSE	% Return	NASDAQ	% Return
Dec. 1977	98.20	−2.22	53.69	0.02	105.50	11.83
Dec. 1978	96.02	7.28	53.70	8.60	117.98	28.11
Dec. 1979	103.01	15.31	58.32	16.77	151.14	33.88
Dec. 1980	118.78	7.80	68.10	8.69	202.34	−3.21
Dec. 1981	128.04	−6.51	74.02	−6.88	195.84	18.67
Dec. 1982	119.71	34.00	68.93	34.38	232.41	19.87
Dec. 1983	160.41	0.03	92.63	−0.18	278.60	−11.22
Dec. 1984	160.46	—	92.46	—	247.35	—
Mean		7.9555		8.7724		13.990
SD		12.582		12.658		15.058

Appraisal Reform and Commercial Real Estate Investment for Pension Funds

by
James A. Graaskamp

Summary and Conclusions

The integrity of the appraisal process has always been critical to social equity in terms of eminent domain, real estate taxation, legal disputes, and contract administration. However, the credibility of appraisal for income properties has been undermined over the past 25 years by an implicit conspiracy between financial institutions and the real estate development fraternity for appraisal *form*, rather than substance. Traditional appraisal formats might have upset a profitable deal at a time when Regulation Q guaranteed infinite spread, and lending officers were driven by fees, arbitrage and fear of inflation. Credit and interest risk smothered concern for property risk.

● The impact of faulty appraisal on fiduciary institutions has been examined in a recent congressional study that blames the attitudes and policies of the Federal Deposit Insurance Corporation (FDIC), the Office of the Comptroller of the Currency (OCC), the Federal Savings and Loan Deposit Insurance Corporation (FSLIC), and other regulators. The study proposes legislation (HR 4956) that would place direct Federal sanctions on appraisers, investment officers and others, as well as tight procurement controls intended to protect appraisal independence.

● The FSLIC was recognized for efforts to define appraisal procurement through Memorandum R 41 (b) and the newly defined R 41 (c). These standards are enforced by an engagement letter with the appraiser and the placement of fiduciary liability for obtaining the required appraisal on the lending officer. This precedent will shape legislation and dramatically modify the power of the appraiser to protect his professional independence.

● Pension fund real estate investors need reliable real estate values to bring unit values of commingled funds and owned real estate to market value at least quarterly, to measure asset performance in terms of cash income and realizable appreciation, and to evaluate the relative performance of the asset manager. This creates an urgency for greater quality control in the procurement of appraisal services. Those responsible for guarantees under the Employee Retirement Insurance Society Act (ERISA) might find it useful to be included in HR 4956.

● The appraisal process is a key part of the larger business of providing objective financial information, and, like the accounting profession, needs to enhance the appearance (and the reality) of its own independence in the execution of the appraisal function, either through outside appraisers or inside fund management committees.

Intensive research of appraisal procurement procedures for pension real estate investments has identified joint but divided responsibility for improved appraisal practice.[1] Pension fund trustees must have an explicit statement of appraisal policy that will produce timely market prices, standard price communications formats, and preservation of appraisal independence. Pension sponsor rules on in-house quarterly appraisals must be contained in its contract with the asset manager, while its goals for the outside appraisal must be spelled out in a letter of engagement between the asset manager and independent appraiser — and reflected in more realistic compensation. However, the independent appraiser must protect his independence through his professional society, which will determine the protocols of independent information processing. Thus, appraisal

---

[1] *Implementation of Minimum Appraisal Standards for Valuation of Pension Fund Real Estate Unit Values*, Professors Robert Gibson and James A. Graaskamp, Research Committee of the Pension Real Estate Association, unpublished, October 1986. The report is available from PREA.

reform depends on greater sophistication and effort by the pension trustee, the asset manager, the appraiser, and the professional appraisal societies, which are the arbiters of ethics and practice.

The board of directors or trustees of pension real estate assets should require certain standardized output from the appraisal report, including probable price of the property sold as encumbered for cash, premiums or discounts to price for assumable financing or other entitlements not in the real estate fee, and probable value of leasehold interests.

• Appraisers should also take total probable price and, in some basic way, allocate total price among present value of cash flow under contract, additional cash flow assumed to be contracted for, present value of debt reduction during ownership, present value of reversion of original equity and additional equity investments recovered from resale, and present value in any growth in equity assumed to be realized upon resale. Unbundling the sources of return will pinpoint the forecasting risks in total value and also provide a benchmark for measuring asset enhancement over time.[2]

• The appraiser should test his probable price conclusion for reasonableness with a pattern of financial ratios, yields, and tests of investment returns to the next buyer based on assumed resale price.

• To avoid the risk of sophistry, the appraisal profession has defined market value as cash to the seller for real estate interests. The appraiser must report separately value premiums or discounts for financing, entitlements, or other business benefits included in the sale.

• Probable value of leaseholds is the best indicator of the upside potential value that can be recovered by aggressive property management, compared with value increases that depend on general market conditions beyond the control of the asset manager.

The appraiser should be the economic interpreter of the relevant facts about the property and its economic context. However, the impact of accounting procedures, engineering obsolescences, potential liability for environmental impact and toxic material, and anticipated revenues and outlays are part of an information explosion and exchange that modify the traditional independence of the appraiser and his use of declarations of nonresponsibility.

• Explicit professional protocols are needed to define when the appraiser can accept at face value data processing media on future leases and operating expenses, engineering reports, or property management programs. Replication and auditing by the appraiser might be expected, but cost-effective reports will lead the appraiser to rethink his relationships with other designated professionals and to take advantage of their expertise.

• Must the appraiser concur, validate, or simply assume that other designated professionals are providing independent information? Restrictions on the use of limiting conditions and assumptions should also be spelled out, lest appraisers abuse the credibility by indiscriminate hold-harmless declarations.

• Should the pension sponsor or asset manager provide express permission to use or to omit certain data sources without independent due diligence by the appraiser? The protocols of information sources and completeness require a policy statement by professional appraisal societies.

---

2 "Component Capitalization," Gene Dilmore, *Real Estate Issues*, Volume 10, Number 1, American Society of Real Estate Counselors, Chicago, Spring/Summer 1985. For ease in accounting, certain components can be simplified to serve as a proxy; for example, cash flow under contract could be the first year's cash flow to avoid accounting allocation of current and future expenses.

The general objectives of value, benchmarks for measurement of performance, and communication of critical risk factors in the appraisal forecast assumptions desired by the investment trustees should be implemented by means of a standard letter of engagement between the asset manager and his independent appraiser; by contract between the trustees and the asset manager; and by an occasional spot-check of appraisals on file with asset managers by independent valuation consultants hired by the investment trustees.

Clearly, a better product from both in-house appraisal committees and independent appraisers will cost more money — at least three times as much as is currently spent.

● However, most of the unsystematic risk in real estate investment stems from the poor quality of information with which decisions are made, or the skepticism with which investors discount performance records based heavily on the appraisal process.

● Sincere efforts to establish the appearance (and reality) of reliable appraisal estimates of probable price must presume that the additional expense will be offset by lower risk premiums within expected investment yields, as well as by increased investment in real estate and in asset managers' fee income.

Responsibility of Pension Fund Sponsors and Asset Managers

A survey of pension fund sponsors and asset managers found that trustees and directors provided detailed policy statements on the procurement of insurance or the selection of asset managers, but had little to say in terms of written policy controlling the procurement of appraisals or, in the case of asset managers, the reporting of appraised values. For open funds, an independent appraisal is generally required once a year, but quarterly adjustments of value are provided by the in-house committee. Most committees could roll values forward on their own judgment, so there is little "independence" left in reported values other than the threat of a rollback of an in-house value by the next independent appraisal. However, most in-house committees were not required to abide by the independent appraisal. Asset managers would argue that appraisals tended to be more volatile than the market, and were often so far from the mark that they injected an element of unfairness in setting unit prices.[3] On the other hand, smoothing of erratic appraisal results may tend to suggest that the real estate market is less volatile than the stock market, leading to over-investment in real estate as a way of stabilizing portfolio values.[4]

One apparent reason for the cautious acceptance of independent appraisers seems to be the budget or average price per appraisal of a major income property. The average price (including both original and updated appraisal) was $3,000-$4,000, when well-trained commercial appraisers should bill out at $750-$1,000 per day. Even allowing for efficiencies of scale for an appraiser frequently operating in the same market, a $25-million building or shopping center cannot be fully inspected, comprehended, researched, and written up in three or four days without the risk of a significant oversight and misvaluation. An appraiser under these time constraints must take information provided by others at face value, and not exercise the due diligence required of an independent observer. In addition, such a budget does not allow any time to present value conclusions in several formats, which convert the data into appropriate measurements, information about the asset opportunity, comparative performance, or risk implicit in the appraiser's assumptions.

---

[3] See *Toward an Assessment of the Reliability of Commercial Appraisal*, Rebel Cole, David Guilkey, and Mike Miles, Appraisal Journal, vol. LIV#3, July 1986.

[4] See *The Relative Risk of Equity Real Estate and Common Stock: A New View*, David Shulman, Salomon Brothers Inc, June 30, 1986.

The small number of funds eager to maintain the dominance of the independent appraisal were also concerned about maintaining the economic independence of the outside appraiser and occasionally controlling systematic bias as a check and balance on innocent or malicious bias in the appraisal process. These funds limited the number of annual reviews of a specific property by a given appraisal company, as well as the dollar volume of business done with a specific appraisal company. Appraisal has much to learn from the accounting profession in terms of protecting its members against unacceptable pressures from clients. At the same time, the appraiser and the accountant must work together to define the accounting rules for measuring income defined on an accrual accounting basis.

These concerns have led to a proposed statement of appraisal procurement policies, which can be used by pension sponsors and their real estate asset managers (see Appendix 1).

Protocols Controlling Data Sources and Proper Appraisal Assumptions

Need for Data Protocols

The explosion of data, the recognition of the investment risk inherent in the quality of data provided, and the discipline and cost of electronic data processing have outstripped the working ethics and rules provided by professional appraisal societies. Many appraisers use outside market and engineering studies as a starting point for their work, using limiting conditions to provide a hold-harmless assumption on the reliability of the outside data. At the same time, the professional societies argue that use of an outside data source requires concurrence by the appraiser, implying that the appraiser has exercised due diligence regarding its quality. Some recent prospectuses have contained appraisal value conclusions wherein leases were read by one professional group of investment bankers who forecast revenue, while an accounting firm studied expenses and forecast outlay with or without engineering assistance — requiring the appraiser to place a value on a net income figure estimated by others.

These practices conflict with the concept of an independent valuation, at a time when the professional appraisal societies and accounting groups want to strengthen the appearance of independence. However, the cost of assembling detailed financial information suggests the practicality of allowing the appraiser to accept abstracts of leases, legal descriptions, accounting data, and engineering data prepared by others. Extensive hold-harmless clauses undermine the usefulness of an estimated sales price that does not consider legal, engineering, or environmental pitfalls. The appraiser has become the economic interpreter who must synthesize the significance of information from multiple professional sources into an estimate of the price at which a property would likely sell if buyer and seller were *fully* informed about all available facts. Such data must be available to the appraiser and assumed acceptable if received from a professionally designated accountant (C.P.A.), certified property manager (C.P.M.), professional engineer (P.E.), attorney (J.D.), or registered architect (A.I.A.).

Alternatively, the client or investment banker could provide necessary data with a guarantee of reliability and financial guarantee of damages for misrepresentation. Indeed, in the future, appraisers may have these other professionals in their office as part of a natural clinic of professional real estate services. The professional societies must issue a statement on data protocols, and major data incompatibility issues must be addressed regarding the appraisal and accounting interface, legal concepts of real property, pitfalls inherent in land use control, legal liability for environmental degradation, and the risk of future subtle distortions based on the future by extrapolation of the past.

Major Data Gaps for Appraisal/Accounting Protocols

The valuation of income real estate properties now relies more on discounted cash flow simulation of property performance or a single price/earnings ratio method called direct capitalization with a single overall rate. Discounted cash flow presumes the real estate is simulated on a strict cash accounting basis, while the Financial Accounting Standards Board (FASB) advocates accrual accounting for real estate including adjustment of nominal debt to economic equivalents. This will become extremely confusing for both appraiser and those who will rely on appraisal reports. The asset management association can have an impact in this regard by setting a standard to which all members must subscribe. Ironically, the direct capitalization rate method is often based on an economic accrual method with reserves for replacement of short-lived items — a method of smoothing net income that would be unfathomable to FASB and its goals of measuring economic productivity. Our review of many appraisals revealed unwarranted manipulation of direct capitalization. Rates derived from market transactions relied on engineered prices and estimated incomes, while those that came from a loading of points to some base rate — such as a tax-exempt bond or middle-rated industrial bonds — were never supported by evidence from interviews with institutional buyers. The method of building a capitalization rate conceals implicit assumptions about a trendline of future property income.

The major accounting/appraisal conflicts regard the amortization of deferred expenditures or tenant improvements, leasing commissions, points paid for long-term financing, and deferred maintenance combined with capital improvements.

Another major area of concern is the need to allocate or attribute income to land, building, tangible personal property, intangible personal property, and working capital. When should the appraiser delineate revenues from the real estate enterprise, and when should he value the whole as a going concern? This also provides the asset management association the opportunity to set standards for the accountants (see Appendix 1, Section G and H).

Major Issues for Appraisal/Engineering Protocols

Traditionally, the appraiser side-stepped encroachment on the other professions by denying responsibility for legal or engineering issues, unless physical structural failures were clearly apparent. However, appraisal evaluations that ignore basic obsolescence in terms of energy consumption, maintenance cost, or environmental risks for such things as asbestos and toxic waste can be construed as misleading, and a major concern of appraisal reform is to avoid the sin of omission — which is implicitly misleading. Therefore, the logical sequence of appraisal would be to incorporate engineering surveys of the structure, its equipment, and its site done before the appraisal.

The Appraiser and Building Management

The appraiser relying on discounted cash flow is forecasting future productivity, but many dollars depend on execution of the property's management plan, which will alter size, tenant mix and operating characteristics. Should the appraiser accept the management plan of current ownership in forecasting, or review several alternative scenarios for the future of the property? One view would be that pension sponsors have a right to know that an independent appraiser has reviewed the asset manager's plans. The other view is to assume the professional property manager will enhance the asset, and subsequent updates of the appraisal will recognize failure. A third perspective would be to value the property exactly as it exists on the day of valuation, extrapolated into the future as though the property were not to be enhanced. To avoid a systematic upward bias of value that hinges on the successful completion of grand plans, we believe that the latter method should be used.

Professional Society Standards and Interface of Professions

The appraiser's expertise is the collection and analysis of market data and off-site transactions, while the accountant and designated property manager are responsible for on-site data collection and control. Traditional appraisers were expected to reconstruct lease roles, profit and loss statements, property management strategy, and a buyer's probable financial structure, rather than simply accept data from others. Given the costs of microdata review, should the appraiser be expected to audit data generated internally? The appraisal societies and asset managers must define the following:

1. Responsibility of the appraiser to flag legal, engineering, traffic, or structural issues requiring professional review;

2. Legitimacy of the appraiser's accepting audits of leases, operating budgets, and revenue collections provided by other professionals;

3. Legitimacy of the appraiser's accepting data on such electronic media as floppy disks for use in cash flow or data management models provided by the asset manager client, the accountant for the client, independent purveyors of software and operating data, and investment broker/ marketing.

4. Legitimacy of the appraiser's accepting a property management program implemented by the asset manager as a point of departure for future revenues, expenses, and project characteristics of extrapolating the status quo.

The complexity of the appraisal question in terms of income properties is illustrated in Figure 2. In the past, the appraiser was superficially conversant in property management, finance, marketing, and basic engineering — and this general level of expertise presumably protected his independence. Now, a pool of intensely technical data from numerous sources is used, and the appraiser must rethink the protocols of using other sources of data for efficiency and reality while maintaining neutrality and independence.

Institutional Forces Accelerating Appraisal Relevance and Reliability

The appraisal process was not prepared to provide a large volume of valuation services with tight quality control once pension institutions recognized the validity and necessity of real estate equity investment, as such a commitment had to be supported by a constant feedback of performance, safety, yield, and liquidating value information.

Concurrently, traditional intermediaries of mortgage debt euphorically shifted surplus capacity toward construction financing of the real estate product, presumably to exploit the new equity markets. Coincidentally, foreign investors were also willing to expand their participation in U.S. real estate capital markets. These major players, their regulators, and their beneficiaries perceived the need for reducing the information risks in real estate investments and for adapting real estate data formats to be compatible with other portfolio financial reporting standards.

The ultimate control of the appraisal product will be a letter of engagement, with certain requirements sanctioned by such trade groups with a common interest as pensions, investors in Federally insured projects, or group equity pools. This letter will be subdivided into four sections: specifications of the assignments, appraisal protocols, appraisal methodology, and appraisal business arrangements.

Each section will incorporate the current standards and practices for appraisal and accounting relative to investment properties that have been promulgated by the following groups.

Federal Regulators for Financial Institutions

Congress has been investigating the impact of inadequate appraisals for commercial real estate lending, as well as failures of residential lending appraisal and its adverse impact on mortgage insurance and secondary market investors (see Appendix 1).

Congressional investigators lament the relatively limited opportunities that professional societies have for policing appraisal quality, but are harsh critics of the Federal agencies regulating the fiduciaries that failed to act when audit procedures revealed widespread weakness and fraud in the appraisal control of the investment process.

Congress points out that the FDIC, the OCC, or the National Credit Association (NCA) do not require appraisals for all real estate loans, and suggest that these agencies' attitude toward appraisal is naive at best and irresponsible at worst. Its report suggests that commercial real estate borrowers are shifting their loan applications to banks and insurance companies and away from thrifts because Memorandum R 41(b) is being enforced.

Congress can be expected to force corporate fiduciaries to modify and improve appraisal procedures greatly or to face personal liability for dereliction of duty, as is true under R 41(b).[5]

The Federal Savings and Loan Deposit Insurance Corporation has issued the most comprehensive appraisal procurement standards in the United States. This is currently referred to as Memorandum R 41(b), but will soon be corrected for certain ambiguities as R 41(c). This document is appropriate for income properties under development, and it also imposes a breach of fiduciary trust on the asset manager who does *not* insist on receiving an appraisal according to R 41(b) standards.

The Federal National Mortgage Association and Federal Home Loan Bank Mortgage Corporation have redefined market value, best use, and the relevance of sales to control the underwriting of apartment projects and condominiums. These controls emphasize cash equivalency of investment value.

Professional Appraisal Societies

The American Institute of Real Estate Appraisers and the International Society of Real Estate Appraisers have reaffirmed their codes of professional conduct and removed possible ambiguities from their terminologies.

Market value has been clearly defined as the most probable price at which a property would sell for cash to the seller, assuming knowledgeable buyers and sellers under no special duress and including time on the market. This benchmark value must then be adjusted for financing, other entitlements, or encumbrances that would modify the cash value (see Appendix 2).

The appraiser is expected to exercise due diligence in the selection and utilization of all relative data, and concur in the data used. The basic standard is that the appraiser must report all data and procedures used so that his work can be replicated and validated to avoid miscommunication, disinformation or sophistry.

---

[5] For recommendations and provisions of HR 4956, see Section IV in "Impact of Appraisal Problems on Real Estate Lending, Mortgage Insurance, and Investment in the Secondary Market," Housing Report 99-891, by the Committee on Government Operations, September 25, 1986, based on a study made by the Commerce, Consumer and Monetary Affairs Subcommittee.

As the groups receive legislative help in protecting the appraiser against economic intimidation from the client, they will take advantage of the wave of reform to establish significant controls on their membership and methods.

Credibility will mean higher fees, longer apprenticeships, and more reliance on college training — specifically in land economics and land valuation. These professional characteristics are already found in Europe and in the British tradition of value surveyors.

The FASB has published a report about the appropriate use of cash or accrual accounting that will conflict with traditional appraisal and pension fund practices.

Several of the Big Eight accounting firms have set up special appraisal review departments, since accounting practice no longer permits the auditor to sign off on appraised asset values without judging the adequacy of the appraisals.

The European Common Markets Accounting Fraternity, aided and abetted by the Royal Institute of Charted Surveyors, has implemented a 250-page set of standards for the appraisal of fixed assets (including real estate) for various financial reporting services; a special section is devoted to pension fund real estate. These standards are incorporated by reference into appraisal letters of engagement. There is continuing review and improvement by the International Assets Valuation Standards Committee.[6]

Other Institutional Changes

The quickest way to introduce better appraising methods is for a particular user group to define appropriate methods and inappropriate logic in the procurement of appraisal through a standard letter of engagement. Both the Pension Real Estate Association (PREA) and the National Council of Real Estate Investment Fiduciaries (NCREIF) are about to endorse such a letter for their members. These define property interests and definitions, appraisal methods, reporting requirements, and the business relationship between appraiser and asset manager, including the following:

(1) Full disclosure of comparable-market sales data.

(2) Reliance on discounted pretax cash flows, with emphasis on consistency of financial ratios.

(3) Full disclosure must incorporate engineering and other professional studies, rather than ignore them by means of hold-harmless clauses.

The universities have developed several appraisal systems that can drive off computer data banks to automate market comparison valuations of industrial land, farm land, wilderness, and swamp land, as well as match attributes of major commercial properties.

Conclusion

Recognition of the pivotal social and financial responsibilities of appraisal by sophisticated investors and public regulators will cause the appraisal profession to leap into the 20th century of financial information. The carrot will be the opportunity to be paid well for providing the best valuation material technically possible because of the value-added from reduced information risk. The leap will be assisted by sharp prods from the Securities and Exchange Commission (SEC), bank regulators and appraisal professional societies who will otherwise be replaced by the accountants.

---

[6] For additional information, write the Secretary, TIAVSC, 103 Mount St., London, W17 6AS, United Kingdom.

* * *

Appendix 1. Pension Fund Managers' Appraisal Policy Statement to Inform Investors of Real Estate Appraisal Policy

A. Definition of real estate investment categories and appraisal value relevant to the following:

Investment-grade properties (operational and 80% occupied)

1) Market value of leased fee;

2) Leasehold value to be recaptured by property management; and

3) Financial or contract agreements to be transferred with sale that add or detract from market value of leased fee (such as discount for high-interest mortgage without right of prepayment, or additional value of transferable development rights or surplus land).

Development Properties[a] (Vacant, Transition, or Less Than 80% Leased and Occupied)

1) Cost outlays or market value, whichever is lower in value; and

2) Future value discounted by cost to complete, and value created by development process, as in R 41(b) prototype.

Financial Participation Contracts[b]

Investment value as discounted cash flow less reserve for resale cost (custom-crafted, hybrid equity contract unlikely to meet presumptions of fair market value).

B. Specific questions to be addressed by independent appraisal value determination:

Market value of a specific interest in a specific property, given income and resale prospects for the underlying collateral as of a specific date.

Appraiser shall provide selected tests of appraisal conclusion that may indicate reliability, including illustrative tests that will vary according to the nature of the property and critical assumptions and are intended to reveal error or suggest reliability:

1) Indicated compound growth rates for effective gross rent, operating expenses, and net operating income, compared to assumed market rental growth rates or expected rates of inflation.

2) Financial risk ratios such as debt-coverage ratio, cash break-even ratio, or range of tenant turnover cost to projected revenue, compared to average vacancy loss in the local market.

3) Ratio of projected potential rent rate to current market rental rate projected at standard growth rate.

4) Sensitivity analysis should be applied to critical assumptions.

5) Whatever formula is used to hypothesize resale price at the end of the investment, the appraisal should compare the resulting resale cap rate with the inferred "going in" cap rate, computed by defining net operating income for year one by appraised value conclusion.

Where appropriate, the appraiser should unbundle the value conclusion as to the proportion of total value contributed by certain categories in order to facilitate understanding of the relative significance of existing contracts, operating assumptions, and future contingencies.

---

[a] Not subject of current study; recommend R 41(b) model.
[b] Valuation process subject to PREA research under the direction of Professor William Brueggeman of Southern Methodist University.

C. Definition of frequency of appraisal by independent appraisers:

Annual appraisals for open-ended fund.

Three-year appraisals for closed fund.

Whenever value changed by in-house managers exceeds 5% of previous independent appraisal or 1% of total portfolio value.

Change of more than 10% in capital investment through partial sale or expansion and refurbishment.

Independent appraisals scheduled to reappraise approximately 25% of portfolio value each quarter.

D. Protection of appraiser independence and control of accidental or systematic bias in the independent appraisal process:

Requirement that appraiser be controlled by a specific professional code of ethics and standards of practice and definition of terms, regardless of whether he's a member of that professional organization.

A specific individual with experience in property type must sign the appraisal and be accountable for it (compared with the accounting practice, for example, where a firm name can be used).

Sponsor should provide guidelines limiting the percentage of portfolio value assignments to be given to the same appraisal firm and percentage of appraisal firm gross income comprising fees generated by one asset management firm. Fees to be due and payable upon receipt of report, rather than upon review or acceptance.

Appraiser should be guaranteed at least one update before reassignment to reduce intimidation.

Appraisal assignment should be reassigned to an alternative appraisal firm after a specified number of updates, such as three consecutive annual valuations.

E. Supply appraisers with engineering report, investigation allowance or waiver of responsibility, for the influence of the following:

Engineering reports on structural matters, expansion capacity or programmed improvement budgets.

Analysis of HVAC system in terms of BTU and kilowatt-hour deficiencies, or the cost to cure known trouble spots.

Toxic wastes in the ground or spilled on the site.

Asbestos removal or other building code internal hazards.

Survey, deed restraints or development code restrictions whose impact could hurt building value in the marketplace.

Existing studies of programmed renovation budgets or cost-to-cure studies of parking, life safety, vertical circulation, or other systems critical to long-term value trend.

F. Pension sponsor should set guidelines that permit the appraiser to accept the abstracts of leases, engineering studies, electronic accounting data, and other information from others subject to some guarantee about the authenticity of the data and the appraiser's degree of accountability for spotting errors or due diligence review of the data. Pension sponsor may ask the appraiser to indicate the alternative cost of using proffered material or independent study by the appraiser and his subcontractors.

G. Definition of in-house appraisal procedures to protect reliance of investor on independent value estimates:

All valuations are ultimately the responsibility of an in-house valuation, since the in-house procedure will set the value during at least three quarters each year and may override the conclusions of the independent appraiser. The independent appraiser is essentially auditing the objectivity of the in-house group, by referring to external market facts, local conditions, and freedom from collective optimism of the ownership. The in-house committee must avoid the subjectivity of a single individual, must establish a consistent procedure, and must record critical factors in their valuation process to be addressed explicitly in the next independent appraisal. Fund management must limit the deviation of annual independent values from in-house values to not more than 5% from the lower value, before calling for an independent update.

The in-house review committee will consist of no less than three persons, one of whom must have appraisal background; the third may be the property manager responsible for the asset. Acquisition agents, general management personnel or institutional officers involved in fund marketing cannot be official members of the in-house review committee.

In-house appraisals of individual properties shall be provided as necessary to set portfolio values for official purposes, and a summary of appraisal considerations must be put in writing in the property file each time the appraisal is reviewed or adjusted, indicating the reasons for the action taken. Key assumptions of the in-house committee must be analyzed explicitly by an outside independent appraiser at the time of the next independent appraisal.

Period values should be reported in a format to indicate value reported by the last independent outside appraisal, value added by additional capital investment from that date, value lost from partial sale, equity withdrawal, or other financial adjustments, and value lost or gained due to in-house adjustments and the net value at the close of the subject period. Finally, the report should indicate the total change in value since the previous period of valuation.

Fund managers must define accounting rules for operating income distinct from capital investment outlays for amortized leasing commissions, tenant improvements, lease repurchase, and for renovations. Added investment between independent appraisals will be superceded by the next independent appraisal with an appropriate adjustment to additional capital investment.

H. Optional policies of pension fund sponsor or fund management:

Explicit rules for spot-checking appraisals on a random-audit basis by contracting with a real estate counseling, appraisal, or qualified pension fund consulting firm for an appraisal review (not unlike similar review of property-specific insurance).

Specific rules for property inspections by an independent engineer/architect observer to spot-check properties owned and managed by a commingled fund in which the pension sponsor has invested.

Specification of accounting format for real estate assets by class of asset or enterprise unit, with possible asset allocation among land, building, tangible personal property, or intangible going-concern values.

Special studies where fund sponsors or asset managers perceive a risk concentration by property type within a specific market area. (It may be desirable to contract for specific research on supply and demand trends related to economic base and demographics, fiscal trends in the community that will affect the real estate tax and resulting cost of occupancy, and other land use trends or plans that may have a foreseeable effect on investment concentration or changing institutional ownership patterns in the market.)

Appendix 2. Appraisal Protocols Regarding Data Sources and Assumptions

Appraisal protocols are concerned with responsibility for supplying data and critical appraisal assumptions and the degree to which the appraiser must concur, be held harmless, or empirically validate through independent research the data in question. The issues raised by protocol grow out of the availability of electronic data files, the increasing conflicts in accounting and valuation procedures, the growing legal and engineering pitfalls of land use control, liability for environmental degradation, and a trend toward computerized modeling of future property market and financial performance.

	Appraiser Supplies	Appraiser Reviews	Appraisal Society Standards	Appraiser's Engineer	Owner's Legal Services	Owner's Policy Statement	Property Manager	Owner's C.P.A.	Owner's Architect	Asset Management Standards
Legal Description of Property Interest					X					
Deed Restrictions and Covenants					X					
Five-Year Chronology of Ownership and Transactions Involving Transfer of Fee		X			X					
Lease Abstracts		X					X			
Engineering Assumptions					X		X		X	
Strategic Management Plan		X					X		X	
Definition of Values to be Reported			X			X				
Application of Market Comparison Method and Unit of Comparison	X		X							
Application of Cost to Replace Method and Accepted Cost Service	X				X	X	X		X	
Application of Normalized Income Capitalization	X		X							
• Adjustment of Accounting History to Establish Normalized Statement	X						X	X		
• Treatment of Existing Financing	X		X		X	X				
• Logic for Income Capitalization Rate								X		X
Cash Flow Format		X								X
Cash Flow Forecast	X									X
• Revenue Under Contract							X			
• New Contract Revenue		X					X			X
• Lease Turnover Costs		X					X	X		X
• Rental Concessions		X					X			
• Market Conditions, Leasing Strategy, and Net Capture	X									
• Gross and Net Operating Expenses		X					X	X		
• Gross and Net Real Estate Taxes	X	X						X		
• Third-Party Financing Format for Most Probable Buyer	X									
• Present Value Disaggregated by Source of Financial Interest	X									X
Economic Environment	X		X							

Note: X equals source and/or responsibility.

* * * * *

Three basic changes will alter the benefits of real estate investments.

The Triple Revolution in Real Estate Finance

Anthony Downs

SINCE 1979, a triple revolution has occurred in U.S. real estate finance. Dramatic changes have taken place in the following areas:

- The attitudes of lenders and other capital suppliers toward inflation;
- The formerly favored position of housing in credit markets; and
- The nation's basic monetary and fiscal policies.

These changes will profoundly affect nearly all aspects of real estate for many years. They will make the 1980s a more difficult decade than the 1970s for everyone who borrows money—which includes most people who generate real estate activity. On the other hand, these revolutionary developments will improve the financial rewards of the largest money suppliers, including both individual savers and financial institutions.

Anthony Downs is a senior fellow at the Brookings Institution in Washington, D.C. The views expressed in this article are solely those of the author, and do not necessarily reflect those of the Brookings Institution, its trustees, or any of its other staff members. This article is part of a study funded by the American Counsel of Life Insurance, the Ford Foundation and the FNMA.

THE REVOLUTION IN LENDERS' ATTITUDES TOWARD INFLATION

For thirty years before 1980, most lenders either ignored the rate of inflation or believed that whenever it went up it would soon return to "reasonable" levels. Therefore, suppliers of money were willing to lend it at fixed, relatively low rates. These suppliers included both households that deposited their savings in thrift institutions or bought insurance policies and financial intermediaries that loaned funds to real estate developers and households. These intermediaries made millions of fixed-rate loans for long periods, up to thirty years.

A Decade and a Half of Negative Interest Rates

But inflation accelerated in the 1970s to record levels. The Consumer Price Index (CPI) rose at a compound rate of 7.8 percent, compared to 2.7 percent in the 1960s and 2.1 percent in the 1950s. Moreover, the CPI reached "double-digit" levels three times from 1974-1980, when its compound average annual rise was 9.2 percent.[1] As a result, loan repayments, fixed in nominal terms, fell in real value. The "true cost" of mortgage borrowing declined sharply from about the mid-1960s to about 1978, even though nominal interest rates were rising to record levels. Real rates were even lower for borrowers when the effects of income tax deductions are taken into account. On mortgage loans made in every year after about 1963, borrowers in the 25 percent income tax bracket were actually paying negative real, after-tax interest rates.[2]

This situation was a bonanza for borrowers. The beneficiaries included home buyers, developers, and speculators. By leveraging their small investments with no-cost capital during an inflationary period, they raised their rates of return on equity to unprecedented levels. This profitability motivated millions of other households and thousands of developers and speculators to enter the market, thereby driving up prices of real estate faster than the rate of inflation. Hence, a form of "self-fulfilling prophecy" developed, fueled by money borrowed from the financial intermediaries.

While borrowers were enjoying immense profits, lenders and savers were earning abnormally low real rates of return on their capital because of inflation.

Thus there arose a fundamentally unsustainable imbalance between borrowers and lenders.

Lenders Revise Their Expectations

Consequently, in 1980 the nation's financial community drastically revised its expectations concerning inflation. A second consecutive year in which the CPI increased more than 10 percent apparently convinced lenders that relatively high inflation rates were here to stay, perhaps indefinitely.[3] The shift in expectations caused financial institutions and other major lenders to change their behavior in two ways. First, they demanded higher real yields to "cushion" against both possible future increases in inflation and the greater volatility of interest rates. Second, they changed the forms of their investments to protect themselves against uncertainty about how fast prices will rise in the future.

If future inflation rates could be forecast reliably, lenders could write loan contracts in advance that specified annual interest rates that would exactly offset those future price increases. But no one can forecast future inflation rates reliably. The only way capital suppliers could protect themselves against such uncertainty was to adopt forms of investment that vary nominal payments with inflation as it occurs and, thus, keep real yields approximately constant.

This was done in three ways. They offered loans with interest rates that varied in accordance with some other indicator sensitive to inflation, as in *variable rate mortgages*. They developed loans that required the interest rate to be renegotiated at frequent enough intervals to quickly "catch up" to changing conditions, as in *renegotiable rate* or *rollover* mortgages. They began to take *equity positions* in properties because a property's net income presumably will vary with inflation.

In 1980, most major financial institutions switched from making long-term, fixed-rate mortgage loans to using one or more of these approaches. All three forms shift most of the risks of unanticipated inflation from lenders to borrowers.

Consequences of the Revolution in Lenders' Attitudes

These two changes in lender behavior *will raise the real cost of capital to borrowers in the 1980s, compared to its abnormally low level in the 1970s.* Capital suppliers are demanding much higher real interest rates at the outset. For example, in late 1982, new mortgage loans on single-family residences were being made for about 13.5 percent when the inflation rate (as measured

---

[1] *U.S. Statistical Abstract: 1981*, 467.

[2] See Downs & Giliberto, "How Inflation Erodes the Income of Fixed-Rate Lenders," 11 REAL ESTATE REVIEW 47 (Spring 1981). Computations of real interest rates assume each loan is held for ten years and then fully repaid (except those made after 1970, which are repaid in 1980). All payments, including the final repayment, are converted back into dollars of purchasing power equivalent to those of the year in which the loan was made, and then the real return is computed.

---

[3] The CPI rose 11.3 percent in 1979 and 13.5 percent in 1980. *U.S. Statistical Abstract: 1981*, 467.

by the CPI) was about 5.0 percent. The real interest rate on such loans was therefore around 8.5 percent, compared to real interest rates of 2.5 to 4 percent in the 1950s and 1960s.[4]

Moreover, *real capital costs will remain high no matter what happens to inflation*. If inflation rates soar higher than either lenders or borrowers have anticipated, the forms of investment recently adopted by most lenders will adjust nominal repayments so as to keep real yields roughly constant. Thus any underestimation of actual inflation rates by lenders in the 1980s will not greatly favor borrowers, as happened in the 1970s. In fact, high inflation in the 1980s will produce high real interest rates too—just the opposite of the low rates that such inflation produced in the 1970s.

On the other hand, the reappearance of relatively low inflation rates will not immediately cause sophisticated lenders to abandon these new investment forms. In the first quarter of 1982, the CPI increased at an average annual rate of only 2.3 percent. Yet lenders did not go back to making long-term, fixed-rate mortgages at low rates. Nearly all believed inflation could easily accelerate again to much higher levels. With the experience of the 1970s in mind, most of the financial community is not going to believe high inflation has truly been eliminated until the inflation rate has fallen to very low levels and stayed there for several years in a row. So capital suppliers are likely to continue the two key changes in their behavior described above for many years.

THE REVOLUTION IN HOUSING'S FAVORED CREDIT AND TAX POSITIONS

During the period from World War II until about 1980, housing enjoyed favored credit and tax positions in the nation's financial markets. The beneficiaries of these positions included the home building industry (builders, material suppliers and mortgage lenders), the home sales industry (realtors, title companies and mortgage lenders), and households that purchased new or existing homes.

Housing's favored credit position was brought about by the regulations that governed financial institutions. These made residential mortgage funds available at lower cost than would occur in a "free" money market. The favored tax position created benefits from investing in home ownership rather than stocks, bonds, or small businesses. These advantages caused the flow of

financial capital into housing to be larger than it would otherwise have been, and presumably reduced the flow of such capital into alternative investments. However, recent developments have greatly reduced the effectiveness of both these advantages.

Bank and Thrift Industry Regulations

Before 1980, households and developers could obtain mortgages at rates lower than would have prevailed in the absence of regulations, especially during "tight money" portions of business cycles. This favored position arose from two types of regulations: (1) federal ceilings placed upon the interest rates that thrift institutions and banks could pay savings depositors, and (2) the requirement that thrift institutions invest most of their assets in housing. The rate ceilings allowed thrifts to pay depositors slightly higher interest rates than banks. Hence households were encouraged to save in institutions that were legally bound to invest primarily in housing. This increased the relative supply of residential mortgage money and reduced its relative price.

Furthermore, during portions of the business cycle when short-term interest rates rose above federal deposit rate ceilings, thrift institutions were prevented from paying market rates to savers. So they did not have to charge mortgage borrowers full market rates either. Savers were thus deprived of the higher interest rates that they could have earned in the absence of regulations. In effect, this arrangement forced small-scale savers to subsidize mortgage borrowers. In contrast, large-scale savers could obtain market interest rates on certificates of deposit of $100,000 or more or by directly purchasing Treasury bills and other securities.

As long as average inflation rates remained low, periods when short-term interest rates exceeded deposit ceilings were relatively short, and the "gap" between these rates was small. Hence total subsidies provided by small-scale savers to mortgage borrowers were not large. But when inflation accelerated, short-term interest rates rose well above federal deposit rate ceilings and stayed there for long periods. This increased the size of the rate subsidies paid by small-scale savers and prolonged their duration.

The Money Funds and Their Consequences

This situation created an opportunity quickly seized by Wall Street entrepreneurs. They developed unregulated money market funds that offered interest rates to small-scale savers well above those provided by thrift institutions. The money market funds lent their deposits on the short-term market, mainly by buying com-

---

[4] These real interest rates are computed on a before-the-fact basis by subtracting the current rate of increase in the CPI from the current nominal interest rate. The real interest rates discussed earlier were computed on an after-the-fact basis, but differ only slightly from the ones used here in the text. By definition, it is impossible to compute after-the-fact interest rates for loans of any duration at the time of making those loans.

mercial paper and bank certificates of deposit. The rapid rise of these funds from under $11 billion in 1978 to over $200 billion in 1982 shows how appealing they were. By early 1978, thrift institutions were beginning to lose deposits to these funds. Federal regulators attempted to help thrifts retain funds by creating a new instrument that would let them pay savers closer-to-market rates too. These "money market certificates" required minimum deposits of $10,000 for six months and paid .0025 percent above the Treasury bill rate. They successfully slowed thrifts' deposit losses but raised the average cost that thrifts had to pay for funds. That cost rose steadily from 6.44 percent in 1977 to 11.53 percent in the last half of 1981 as more and more depositors transferred money out of passbook accounts.

Since thrifts could no longer avoid paying their depositors high market interest rates, they had to raise the mortgage interest rates to their borrowers accordingly. The average effective mortgage rate on new loans by savings and loan associations rose from 8.82 percent in 1977 to 14.39 percent in 1981—up 63.2 percent. Moreover, thrifts experienced an increasing financial squeeze as the cost of their deposits rose, while the income from their large portfolio of low-but-fixed-rate long-term loans lagged. Hence they had to cut back on lending. Whereas all savings and loans made $110.3 billion in mortgage loans in 1978, they made only $100.5 billion in 1979, $72.5 billion in 1980, and $53.3 billion in 1981—a drop of 52 percent in three years.

Inflation and the Economics of Thrift Institutions

Inflation had made inoperable the basic concept underlying thrift institutions: borrowing funds for short terms via savings deposits and lending them for long terms via mortgage loans. This concept presupposes that short-term rates will usually remain lower than long-term rates. But high rates of inflation that are *not expected to last* produce short-term interest rates higher than long-term rates. As long as this condition prevails, thrift institutions cannot profitably borrow short and lend long.

Even when long-term rates rise higher than short-term rates, "normal" profitability does not return to thrift institutions as long as short-term rates stay high. Then thrifts still have to pay their depositors higher rates than they earn on their asset portfolios, which contain billions of dollars of old low-rate mortgages. The low yield on those portfolios creates an upper limit on the ability of thrifts to pay interest to hold deposits without suffering capital losses. Recognizing this limit, regulators have kept at least some deposit rate

ceilings in effect for thrifts. Even so, in 1981 and most of 1982, short-term interest rates rose so far above the average yield on thrift assets that thrifts could not match the rates offered by money market funds, which have no portfolios of old mortgages. As a result, savings and loans sustained a $25.4 billion loss of net new savings in 1981 (although their total savings balances *rose* 2.5 percent because of interest payments credited to savings accounts). And the net worth of the industry as a whole was rapidly being eroded. Late in 1982, short-term rates fell well below both long-term rates and the average yield on thrift institutions' portfolios. This will stop their loss of equity capital for as long as short-term rates remain low.

To help thrifts cope with their worsening financial plight, federal regulators carried out a series of "deregulations" from 1979-1982. They authorized several new accounts offering higher rates to small-scale savers, and almost every imaginable type of mortgage instrument. Thrifts began featuring different combinations of variable rates, short terms, increasing principals, and other elements that shift some of the risk of future inflation onto borrowers. Regulators have also expanded the types of assets thrifts can buy, thus permitting them to enter other businesses, such as consumer finance. These changes recognize the realities caused by rising inflation. But they also reduce the favored credit-market position formerly enjoyed by housing.

Some home builders advocate restoring that favored position by restoring low deposit-rate ceilings and imposing both ceilings and reserve requirements on all competitive instruments too (such as money market funds). But that would force savers to accept below-market-rate yields. Congress is not likely to compel small-scale savers to accept abnormally low returns in order to benefit mortgage borrowers, realtors and home builders. The alternative, providing a huge new federal subsidy to housing, seems both unlikely and undesirable in this era of large cutbacks in federal domestic spending.[5] Thus, housing's loss of regulatory shelters in credit markets is almost certain to be permanent.

THE REVOLUTION IN HOUSING'S FAVORED TAX POSITION

The second pillar under housing's favored position consisted of tax advantages for investing in home ownership that were not available to investors in rental housing, stocks, bonds, or small businesses. Many people think housing's biggest tax advantage is the

---

[5] Congress did pass a subsidy to savers in thrifts and banks in the form of the "All Savers" certificate, presumably aimed at aiding both thrifts and housing. It did benefit thrifts somewhat, but not housing.

ability of homeowners to deduct mortgage interest and property taxes from their taxable incomes. But those who make most other investments can also deduct interest and even more expenses from their taxable incomes. However, they must then pay income or capital gains taxes on any remaining profits. Homeowners get these key deductions without paying taxes on the imputed net incomes they earn by renting their homes to themselves.

This freedom from taxes on the net incomes from their investments constitutes the biggest indirect subsidy to homeowners. In addition, profits from the sale of owner-occupied homes are free from all capital gains taxes if equities are rolled over into new units within twenty-four months after sale. Also, $125,000 in capital gains are exempt from any taxation for persons 55 or over.

These positive tax advantages of home ownership were made relatively even more attractive by some tax penalties for investing in corporate and other businesses during inflationary periods. The most important penalty was excessive income taxes from overestimating "true" net income during rapid inflation. Net taxable business income is computed after deductions for depreciation of plant and equipment. But standard accounting practices required those deductions to be based upon the actual original costs of the plant and equipment, not their current replacement costs. During periods of rapid inflation, actual replacement costs soared far above original costs. Hence the depreciation allowed did not cover the true costs of replacing the plant or equipment when it wore out or became obsolete. Because businesses were systematically understating their "true" costs when computing profits, they overstated their "true" profits. Thus, inflation interacted with tax laws to impose excessive income taxes on many businesses.

There are no comprehensive data on the total size of this penalty to business. However, one accounting authority estimated that corporate taxes were increased by as much as 25 percent above what they really should have been.[6] Several econometric studies have asserted that housing received significantly larger financial capital investment during the 1970s than it would have in the absence of its relative tax advantages.[7]

The Economic Recovery Tax Act of 1981 greatly reduced this penalty by changing the methods of computing depreciation allowances. Much shorter depreciation periods were assigned to most assets, and other tax advantages were extended to businesses. These changes greatly reduced the relative tax advantages of investing in home ownership, even though they did not alter homeowners' specific tax benefits. So the second support for housing's favored investment status has also shrunk in size and effectiveness.

THE REVOLUTION IN FEDERAL MONETARY AND FISCAL POLICIES

The third revolution affecting real estate finance in the 1980s consists of radical changes in the nation's monetary and fiscal policies. Until 1979, a key goal for both policies was smoothing out typical short-run business cycles. Monetarily, the Federal Reserve often manipulated the supply of credit to raise or lower interest rates so as to affect the economy's real growth rate. It sought to slow growth during "booms," and to speed growth during recessions, although these attempts did not always succeed.

Fiscally, federal administrations also tried to stimulate the economy during recessions by increasing federal spending. They used both "automatic stabilizers" such as unemployment compensation and discretionary actions such as public works programs. Such spending plus the normal drop in tax receipts often created large budget deficits during recessions, as in 1975. During "booms," the progressive federal tax system had a dampening impact upon growth because rising nominal incomes pushed both households and firms into higher tax brackets.

The New Monetary Policy

In 1979, the Federal Reserve drastically changed its policy. Alarmed by rising inflation, it decided to focus monetary policy almost exclusively upon slowing inflation in the long run by limiting money-supply growth. It chose money-growth "targets" that required gross national product (GNP) in nominal (current-dollar) terms to increase much more slowly than in recent years. At first, much of this slowdown would consist of lower real growth rather than lower price increases. That means more unemployment, excess capacity, and business failures. In theory, once real growth had declined significantly, the rate of general price increase would fall too. Faced by weak demand and intensified competition, business firms could no longer raise prices as rapidly, and would more strongly resist large wage increases. Faced by mounting unemployment and stronger employer resistance, workers could no longer win as large wage increases. Hence the rate of inflation would gradually be forced down by a prolonged recession.

---

6 Kullberg, "Inflation and Its Impact on Financial Executives," undated speech published by Arthur Anderson and Company.

7 See Hendershott, "Real User Costs and the Demand for Single-Family Housing," in *Brookings Papers on Economic Activity, 1980:2,* 401-452, Brainard & Perry (eds.) (Washington D.C.: The Brookings Institution, 1980).

This is not a very attractive prescription for curing inflation. But it is the only medicine that is almost sure to work—if the patient can endure the pains of treatment for a long enough period. When the Federal Reserve abruptly shifted to this new policy in October 1979, it essentially abandoned its previous attempts to counteract the business cycle or moderate interest rates in the short run. Since then, long-term interest rates have exhibited unprecedented volatility, often changing more in one week than they previously changed in several years. This volatility increased the financial community's uncertainty about future interest rate movements.

New Fiscal Policies

Shortly after the Reagan Administration took office in early 1981, it radically changed past fiscal policies too. Abandoning past efforts to ameliorate short-run swings in the business cycle, the Administration instead adopted three basic goals: (1) massively increasing defense spending, (2) severely cutting federal domestic spending, and (3) drastically reducing federal tax rates. However, achieving those goals simultaneously under prevailing economic conditions required huge federal budget deficits, even though President Reagan had decried such deficits in his election campaign, and continued to do so. Hence the Reagan Administration proposed several federal budgets involving record peacetime deficits. Moreover, if Congress fails to cut federal domestic spending in 1983 as much as the Administration requested, then actual budget deficits will be even larger than the Administration initially estimated.

Large federal deficits stimulate rapid growth in nominal GNP; so this fiscal policy is very expansionary. That is quite desirable during recessions, such as the one that gripped the U.S. economy in 1981-1982. But it is not desirable during periods of rapid private-sector growth, such as forecast for 1984-1985 by the Reagan Administration. Then massive federal deficits would have two negative effects. One is intense competition in credit markets between the federal government and the private sector that would drive up interest rates. The second negative effect is creating such strong excess demand that inflation accelerates to undesirable levels, also causing high interest rates. So the Administration's expansionary fiscal policy may raise interest rates quite high around 1984-1985, if the private sector is also prosperous then.

Whither Interest Rates?

As a result, in most of 1982, in spite of recessionary conditions that usually reduce long-term interest rates, the financial community was reluctant to cut those rates. Why should lenders in 1982 commit funds for long periods at rates they believed were lower than those that would prevail two to three years later? It was clearly more prudent to hold funds in short-term instruments and wait for those higher long-term rates to appear, especially when short-term rates were high. This held long-term interest rates quite high (in spite of the recession) until late 1982, when the Federal Reserve at least temporarily eased its tight money policy.

In fact, after 1981, there was a direct conflict between the Federal Reserve's restrictive monetary policies, aimed at slowing inflation, and the Administration's expansionary fiscal policies, aimed at achieving its three goals. This conflict kept both short-term and long-term interest rates very high, on the average. Whenever expansionary forces caused the economy to begin growing in something like a "normal" business-cycle recovery, the demand for money rose rapidly, as usual. This rising demand collided with the Federal Reserve's restrictions on money-supply growth, causing short-term interest rates to increase sharply. That tended to choke off further growth before the expansion could become a "normal" three-to-four-year recovery. Moreover, uncertainties about future interest rates and inflation induced by large proposed federal deficits kept long-term rates from falling even when overall economic growth stopped altogether.

Because most real estate activities depend heavily upon borrowed funds, they are very sensitive to interest rates. So the high-rate climate produced by the revolution in monetary and fiscal policies after 1979 was extremely unfavorable to real estate activities. This climate persisted until late 1982, with a short hiatus when rates fell temporarily in 1980.

IMPACTS OF THE TRIPLE REVOLUTION

This triple revolution in real estate finance is already having, and will continue to have, major impacts upon real estate markets during the 1980s.

Lower Returns to Equity

The first effect is that equity ownership of real estate will be less profitable in the 1980s than in the 1970s. This will be true even if real properties produce operating profits just as high as those in the 1970s. This conclusion applies to all types of real estate, from owner-occupied homes to multiuse commercial projects.

One reason is that the real cost of capital borrowed by equity owners to finance their properties will be much higher in this decade, as explained earlier. Furthermore, except for owner-occupied homes, the meaning of the term "real estate equity" is different from what it was before 1980. The term formerly referred to the small fraction of total project cost that was put up by the developer or purchaser, who borrowed the bulk of the required capital from a long-term lender at a fixed rate of interest. The equity owner was therefore in a highly leveraged position that during periods of inflation produced high yields on the initial equity investment. If the owner of a property has invested only 10 percent of its cost and borrowed the rest, a 10 percent rise in the property's market value represents a 100 percent increase in the initial equity investment.

But today most long-term capital suppliers want to be equity partners with developers or purchasers of most real properties. If they do not share ownership directly, they do so indirectly by sharing in cash flow and sales profits. This relationship drastically reduces the positive impact of leveraging upon equity yields. If the combined equity investors in a property have put up *all* the funds, when the property's market value rises 10 percent, that is only a 10 percent increase in their equity investment. Even if equity ownership does not constitute 100 percent of required capital, its increase from the very "thin" percentages formerly supplied by developers and purchasers will greatly reduce the profitability of equity ownership.

From the perspective of developers and purchasers, this is a highly undesirable change. But from the perspective of capital suppliers, it is quite desirable because their real investment yields may be higher than the depressed real returns they received from fixed-rate mortgage loans made in the 1970s.

Real Property Values Will Appreciate More Slowly

As a result of the lower levels of equity returns, the real values of real estate properties are not likely to appreciate as fast in the next decade as in the last. Lower profits from owning real properties will reduce the demand for such properties by developers and investors. Although the nominal values of properties will rise because of inflation, their real values may or may not rise, depending upon the particular supply and demand situation in each market. Most nonresidential markets have become heavily overbuilt through a record surge of new construction from 1978-1981. Hence real values in those markets will probably not rise much for at least two to three years. However, that is part of the "normal" real estate cycle rather than any permanent negative development.

Also, if the average inflation rate in the 1980s falls below that in the 1970s, the demand for real estate equity as a hedge against inflation will decline too. These findings do not mean that investment in real estate equities will no longer be profitable. But it will definitely be less profitable than in the 1970s.

Changes in Property Usage

The higher real cost of capital will also raise the "true cost" of creating each square foot of space. This higher cost will generate strong pressures to economize on the use of space. Therefore, nearly all types of space use will shift toward smaller areas per user than in the past. The era of "small is beautiful" has finally hit real estate development. As a result, housing units, hotel rooms, retail shops, office space per worker (net of office machines), and industrial space per worker will all become smaller in the near future compared to the past. This trend is already evident in housing, with units as small as 400 square feet now being sold in many regions.

Also, *more users of space will subdivide their activities and move those not absolutely requiring expensive space to less expensive space.* Examples are retailers storing their inventories in warehouses instead of their shopping center outlets, and downtown office firms shifting many lower-level employees to less expensive space outside the downtown core. Space economizing will be greater in newly built structures than older ones, because the latter were built when capital cost less in real terms.

The rising demand for older properties will escalate the cost of space in these properties too, relative to other business operating costs. Thus, space use in older structures will also be economized. But even a small decline of existing office space consumption could free enormous amounts of space, depressing the demand for new space. For example, if the average area per worker occupied by U.S. office workers dropped by just five square feet (about 2.2 percent), that would vacate over 185 million square feet of office space. That probably equals a full year's "normal" absorption for the entire nation.[8]

Renovations Continue Important

Older structures have lower real capital costs built into them than new ones. Hence, the value of older structures will rise relative to that of new ones. It will frequently be more economical to renovate or expand existing properties than to build new ones. Hence redevelopment will rise as a proportion of all real estate activity, especially in built-up areas. This conclusion applies to all types of real estate, including single-family homes, apartment projects, shopping centers, and office buildings. In time, the shift of demand at the margin toward existing properties will raise their prices relative to new ones.

Changes in Housing Patterns

Three other impacts of the triple revolution all concern housing. The real costs of home ownership will remain higher in the 1980s than in the 1970s, even if inflation abates. That will be true because (1) real interest rates on borrowed funds will be higher; (2) lenders will use mortgage instruments that raise nominal payments if inflation escalates; and (3) slower real home-value appreciation will result in smaller resale profits with which to offset occupancy costs. As a result, *a higher fraction of households that seek shelter will rent rather than buy because they cannot afford home ownership. The demand for rental housing will rise compared with that for home purchase.*

Residential rents will escalate faster than the Consumer Price Index as a whole for one of the few times since 1960. (In fact, this relative change has already begun, in spite of the negative impact of the recession on rental demand. From September 1981 to September 1982, the rent component of the CPI rose 7.1 percent, whereas the overall index rose 5.0 percent.[9]) After

rents have risen faster than living costs for a while, in many locations it will become economically feasible to develop new rental housing.

However, new rental housing will also be financed with higher real capital costs than older existing housing. Hence, *all* new housing will consume a greater portion of household incomes than did housing in the 1970s. The real cost of housing is a key factor that influences the rate at which added households are formed. When real housing costs are low, as in the 1970s, many people can afford to separate from others and occupy their own housing units. Any given increase in population generates a rapid increase in housing demand. But when real housing costs are high, fewer people can afford to separate from others; so a much smaller added demand for housing is generated by the same increase in population. Thus, *the rate of added household formation in the 1980s will fall well below its 1970s levels, even though it would be higher than those levels if purely demographic factors prevailed.* Hence, the overall demand for new housing units will be lower in the 1980s than in the 1970s, even if inflation and nominal interest rates fall well below their record levels at the beginning of the decade. How much lower that demand will be depends in part upon whether high or low inflation predominates in the remainder of the decade.

This future change in housing demand is consistent with future changes in financial capital flows. *The declines in housing's relative advantages as an investment described earlier are likely to lower the share of total financial capital flowing into housing in the 1980s, compared to the 1970s.* From 1970 to 1979, mortgages on homes in structures containing one to four units absorbed 24.2 percent of net funds raised in nonfinancial sectors of U.S. capital markets. This was by far the largest single use of such funds. U.S. government borrowing by both the Treasury and other agencies absorbed the second largest fraction (15.4 percent). The 24.2 percent share of total financial capital flowing into home mortgages in the 1970s was lower than that from 1950 to 1965 (28.1 percent), but considerably higher than that from 1966 to 1970 (16 percent). But this share began dropping as the 1980s started, falling to 19.3 percent in 1981.

HOW LONG WILL THE TRIPLE REVOLUTION LAST?

Most sophisticated capital suppliers will not soon become complacent enough about future inflation to make long-term, fixed-rate loans at relatively low rates. True, some thrift institutions are already willing to commit at least some funds for twenty to thirty years at rates as low as 13.5 percent. One reason is their

---

[8] These calculations assume there are 8.5 billion square feet of occupied office space, the average worker occupies 225 square feet, and average annual absorption of office space for the entire nation in recent years has been over 175 million square feet.

[9] Information obtained by telephone on November 1, 1982, from the Bureau of Labor Statistics CPI information desk, (202) 272-5160.

desperate need to acquire assets earning much higher yields than their older mortgages. Their managers are gambling that inflation will not surge into double digits again for at least the next decade, and perhaps longer. Perhaps they are wiser than I am, but I do not believe this is a prudent strategy for any large share of an institution's total assets. Uncertainty about future inflation rates remains too great to expose such institutions to a repetition of the financial squeeze they have experienced in the past two years. I believe most capital suppliers will not make such loans in any great volume until inflation rates have fallen to low levels (below 6 percent) and stayed there for several years in a row.

The second revolution—housing's loss of its former sheltered position in credit markets—is also likely to persist. The main reasons are that no one is willing to bear the subsidy costs of sheltering housing again and Congress is not willing to suffer the political heat of imposing those subsidy costs on anyone. We may hear stirring rhetoric about restoring the nation's "unwritten covenant" to permit middle-class households to own their own homes. But rhetoric does not pay for subsidies. Yet the same high-inflation, high-interest-rate conditions that would stimulate political demands for restoring housing's former advantages would also tremendously increase the subsidy costs of doing so.

POLITICAL FACTORS MAY CHANGE MONETARY AND FISCAL POLICIES

Only the third revolution—the one involving public monetary and fiscal policies—might greatly change in the near future. Some people think the Federal Reserve has already abandoned its commitment to fighting inflation by tightly controlling the money supply. They cite the fact that the Federal Reserve cut the rediscount rate several times late in 1982 and announced it would ignore M1 for a while. Though Federal Reserve Chairman Paul Volcker denied any basic change in policy, these observers contend he will not allow interest rates to rise sharply again for fear of a deepening recession and perhaps an international liquidity crisis.

Without doubt, it would take extraordinary political courage for the Federal Reserve to force interest rates back up in the presidential election year of 1984 if an economic recovery then under way is strong enough to cause renewed inflation. Moreover, Chairman Volcker is up for reappointment in August 1983. If Volcker is reappointed, he might have enough courage to do just that if he thought it necessary to restrain inflation. But if President Reagan appoints someone else, that person is not very likely to cause a renewed recession right during a presidential campaign. Hence there is a good chance within the next year or two that the Federal Reserve might alter its part of the economic policy revolution described earlier.

There is an even bigger chance that the administration will moderate its deficit-generating fiscal policy by 1985. A policy change is certainly likely if a Democrat were to be elected President in 1984. But that could lead to higher rates of inflation resulting from efforts to combat unemployment if there has been no significant recovery by mid-1984.

But, as pointed out earlier, resurgent inflation would *not* produce the same low or negative real interest rates to borrowers that it generated in the 1970s. This time, capital suppliers are warily anticipating future inflation by charging very high real interest rates and adopting instruments that will rapidly adjust nominal payments to keep real interest rates high. Therefore, *the major impacts of the triple revolution described above will all prevail in the remainder of the 1980s regardless of whether monetary or fiscal policies are changed in the near future.*

What determines cap rates on real estate?

"The cap rate is a child of the capital markets, just as it should be."

Charles Froland

Capitalization rates, technically the ratio between net operating income and the market value of a property, have long been an enigma to many real estate investors.

A good deal of hand-waving characterizes the explanation real estate players give when they are asked about the level of cap rates or where they will go. Syndicators and foreign investors are said to drive cap rates down. Tax reform and overbuilding are thought to drive cap rates up.

To be sure, these types of influences are important, but only at the margin. The larger question, however, is what will happen to the overall real estate market, given that real estate is one of many investment opportunities.

CAP RATES AND THE CAPITAL MARKETS

We should approach cap rates in the context of competitive yields provided by the asset trading markets. From this vantage point, cap rates appear as a composite indicator of debt and equity yield expectations for real estate. Cap rates are in part a function of investor requirements for current returns, which means that they must be competitive with risk-adjusted money market returns of similar duration. In addition, cap rates reflect the ownership of a real asset and, by implication, an expectation of equity appreciation upon sale. Returns based on this expectation must also be priced competitively with alternative equity markets.

When we compare real estate cap rates with other capital market yields, the results have proved favorable to real estate from the standpoints of both risk and yield. Yet, an important question remains: Are real estate cap rates tied to the capital markets, or are they a unique aberration of an inefficient interplay between real estate buyers and sellers? Further, if cap rates are both debt and equity driven, how much do opportunities in each of these areas determine the pricing of income streams in real estate? Moreover, what role do tax benefits play in this process?

THE COMPONENTS OF CAP RATES

The results of several different investor requirements are embedded within the behavior of cap rates. Current return requirements should be competitive with debt instruments of comparable risk and duration, most simply, fixed-rate mortgages. Future returns should be priced competitively with alternative risk-adjusted equity returns.

Much of the long-term return to holding real estate seems to parallel trends in inflation, so investor perceptions of equity appreciation may be a function of inflation expectations. In addition, investors should be willing to give up some amount of current return

CHARLES FROLAND is Vice President and Director of Research Services at Grubb Ellis Company in San Francisco (CA 94104).

in comparison to alternative debt-only investments for the possibility of future equity returns. This offsetting relationship between current and future return expectations may dampen the effects of interest rate swings on cap rate variability.

Additional aspects of cap rate behavior concern the expectation of tax benefits accruing to real estate. For many real estate investments, tax benefits can be mathematically determined to be a sizable proportion of total return. On the other hand, the impact of taxes on pricing will depend on how many tax-advantaged investors are trading in the market and the combined valuation of their tax benefits; unless expectations of tax benefits change, cap rate variations due to this source should be minimal. Given a stable tax policy, cap rate adjustments should be constant with only minor variations resulting from changes in the composition of investors entering or exiting the market.

Variations in yields should also occur because of changing perceptions of the riskiness of holding various underlying assets. Nevertheless, we do not know for sure whether changing marketwide real estate risk conditions, such as overbuilding, have greater effects on the overall level of cap rates or more simply on the spread between cap rates for high risk versus premium grade real estate projects. Yields may characteristically discount the possibility of future overbuilding, because the cyclicality of real estate is well known. Unanticipated changes, however, should cause revaluation of risk premiums, because overbuilding may be anticipated, but perceptions may change during parts of the cycle as more information is presented to investors.

Hence, cap rates should have several key properties:

1. Cap rates should provide a current yield that is competitive with debt instruments adjusted for risk and maturity.
2. Cap rates should provide a yield discount reflecting compensation for equity ownership returns; the amount of the discount will be:
   a) competitive with alternative equity investments, and
   b) influenced by inflation expectations.
3. Cap rates should include an expectation for tax shelter returns, and
4. Include risk premiums that may vary with supply and demand cycles in real estate.

Other factors associated with a particular real estate asset will be included in the determination of an asset-specific cap rate. From the viewpoint of real estate as an asset *class*, however, these four major pricing considerations should exert a significant common influence on the behavior of marketwide cap rates.

The following equation is a more formal expression of these relationships:

$$Y_t = c_1 d_t + c_2 i_t + c_3 e_t + c_4 t_t + c_5 r_t + c_6 k_t, \qquad (1)$$

where, in time t:

Y_t = cap rate,

d_t = maturity and risk-adjusted current yield on debt,

i_t = inflation expectations,

e_t = expected equity returns,

t_t = expected tax shelter benefit,

r_t = expected risk premium for cyclicality,

k_t = non-capital market determinants, and

$c_{1,2,3,4,5,6}$ = constants.

CAP RATES IN PRACTICE: THE DATA

To find evidence of the relationships proposed in Equation (1), we used data from the American Council of Life Insurance "Investment Bulletin" to derive quarterly average cap rates for the period 1970:1 to 1986:2; these data are based on transactions completed by major institutional investors. In the first quarter of 1986, these transactions totaled $6 billion. Institutional investments are biased because of requirements for credit quality, but their scope and coverage is significant in geographical range and categories of real estate. Therefore, we were able to collect cap rates specific to apartments and office, retail, and industrial property categories to derive an unweighted composite of cap rates to represent cap rates for the real estate market as a whole.

The next step was to measure broad capital market influences on real estate transactions.

For debt, we used quarterly yields in mortgage securities specific to each property category, based on transactions in the portfolio of institutional investments. Mortgages are the most competitive debt instrument from which to compare current yields to owners of real estate.

We measured inflation expectations by examining the Treasury yield curve, which contains implicit investor forecasts of inflation. The spread between short- and long-maturity interest rates indicates market judgments as to whether inflation may be increasing or decreasing in the future. We chose thirty-day bills to proxy short rates and ten-year bonds to proxy long rates. An eight-quarter rolling average of the spread provided our estimate of inflation expectations.

The S&P Composite price index and the earnings–price ratio level on the S&P were employed to identify competitive equity returns available in the capital market. We measured risks due to cyclicality by national vacancy rates associated with each of the four property types. In addition, we selected changes in real GNP and industrial production operating ratios to reflect cyclicality in the broader economy.

No specific measure of tax shelter premiums was employed in the analysis of cap rates. Tax changes significantly affecting real estate values occurred at only a few points during the period under study, and these were relatively recent. Minor changes involving the lowering of maximum marginal tax brackets occurred in the early 1970s. Tax changes in 1981 significantly added to depreciation benefits, while revisions occurring in 1984 lessened tax benefits. More recent reforms in late 1986 occurred outside of the study period, except insofar as investor expectations may have begun to reflect impending changes by late 1985 or early 1986. The impact of tax changes was assessed from patterns of residual differences between actual and predicted cap rates during periods of changing tax legislation.

The data series from 1970:1 through 1986:2 for average cap rates and mortgage yields appears in Figure 1. Broad trends are similar in direction between the two yield indicators, but mortgage rates are more volatile than real estate cap rates.

Table 1 shows simple correlations over sixty-

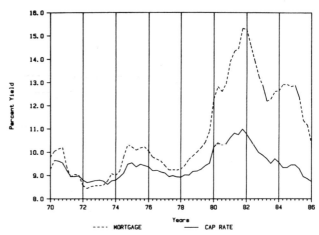

FIGURE 1

AVERAGE CAP RATES VERSUS MORTGAGE YIELDS

six quarterly observations between the property-specific cap rates and measures of debt and equity yields, inflation expectations, and risk. Correlations with the unweighted average of the four cap rates are also shown.

CORRELATION RESULTS

Debt Yields

Correlations with debt yields, particularly mortgages, are high, reflecting the close kinship between cap rates and current yield. Not surprisingly,

TABLE 1

Cap Rate Correlations
(N = 66)

			PROPERTY TYPE		
Debt Yields	Apartments	Retail	Office	Industrial	Composite
Property-Specific Mortgages	0.90**	0.94**	0.93**	0.89**	0.92**
FHA Mortgages	0.84**	0.87**	0.88**	0.79**	0.85**
Treasury Bonds (ten-year)	0.80**	0.83**	0.83**	0.77**	0.81**
Inflation Expectations					
Inflation	0.26	0.09	0.18	0.23	0.19
Bond–Bill Spread	−0.25	−0.10	−0.19	−0.29	−0.22
Bond–Bill Spread 8-Quarter Average	−0.64**	−0.57**	−0.61**	−0.65**	−0.63**
Equity Yields					
S&P 500 Composite	0.11	0.22	0.21	0.14	0.18
% Change S&P	0.05	0.10	0.08	0.05	0.07
Earnings–Price Ratio	0.60**	0.48**	0.51**	0.44**	0.52**
Risk					
National Vacancy Rates	−0.39**	0.51**	−0.30*	0.37**	—
% Change Real GNP	−0.28	−0.33*	−0.27	−0.23	−0.28
Capacity Utilization Ratio	−0.53**	−0.58**	−0.53**	−0.45**	−0.53**

* p < 0.05

** p < 0.01

the closer the debt instrument matches the risk and maturity characteristics of the asset investment, the higher the degree of correlation. An additional 20% of the variation in cap rates can be explained by property-specific mortgages over a ten-year Treasury bond index of debt yields. Overall, approximately 80% to 85% of the total variance can be explained by property-specific mortgage yields, depending on the particular type of property. This suggests that cap rates, and hence real estate prices, trade largely on the basis of current yield.

Inflation Expectations

Inflation expectations also showed significant relationships to cap rates. Although inflation did not prove to be significantly correlated with cap rates on a contemporaneous basis, the eight-quarter average of the bond-bill spread was highly correlated. The negative correlation implies that cap rates rise when the yield curve inverts (i.e., yields on bills rise in relation to bonds). Inverting yield curves reflect periods of high current inflation together with an expectation for inflation to subside, which explains the lower long-bond yield relative to short-term yields. Declining inflation expectations imply a reduction of the appreciation component of future real estate returns and therefore will stimulate a requirement for greater current return by investors. Altogether, the measure of inflation expectations accounts for about 40% of the variance of cap rates.

Equity Returns

Cap rate variations show little correlation with changes in equity prices as measured by the S&P index, but the earnings-price ratio is positively related to cap rate variations. Thus, increase in earnings-price ratios is associated with an increase in cap rates, which is effectively a lowering by investors of the value of operating incomes from real estate properties. As investors pay less for current earnings performance, future earnings potential is being more severely discounted. When investors have lower equity return expectations, they shift their emphasis to current return requirements.

The pattern of correlations reveals that apartments and office building properties correlate most closely with the equity return expectation measure, suggesting that these properties are more sensitive to investor equity considerations. The correlations of retail and industrial properties with equities are only a little lower, but the difference is consistent with the tendency of ownership of those properties to be tied more closely to the operating economies of property users than to purely investment criteria.

Risk

The final category of correlations reveals a complex pattern of response to risk-related indicators. To the extent that vacancy rate variations reflect a threat to property income streams, vacancy rates should be positively related to cap rates, because higher vacancy rates imply greater threat to income, higher risk, and therefore a requirement for greater compensation.

Although this pattern holds for retail and industrial properties, the correlation between vacancy rates and cap rates on office and apartment properties is negative. This result is counter-intuitive. Closer inspection of the cyclicality of vacancy rates for the property types reveals that the correlation is confounded by the characteristics of building cycles for each property type. Vacancy rates for office buildings and apartments exhibit negative correlation to the inflation cycle for the period, with the resulting pattern more influenced by these secondary relationships. Conversely, vacancy rates for retail and industrial exhibit the opposite pattern. The results raise the question of whether vacancy rate cycles per se influence investor perceptions of riskiness or whether broader economic factors are more important.

Results of correlations with indicators of broader economic cycles provide further suggestion that property-specific vacancy trends are not a clear indicator of real estate risk. Capacity utilization rates appear to be a more general indicator of risk by generating consistent negative correlations with property-specific cap rates. This negative correlation means that rising operating ratios — implying increasing economic strength — are related to declining cap rates. Increasing economic strength could influence a change in investors' perceptions of risk, leading to a lowering of required risk premiums. GNP growth also shows a similar pattern of negative correlation, but it was significant only for retail properties. Retail sales performance is a fundamental underpinning of shopping center properties and is also highly dependent on GNP growth. This suggests that investors may perceive that risks are specific to each property type and are influenced by separate sectors of the economy.

ESTIMATING CAP RATES

The analysis of simple correlations in Table 1 confirms a number of the general propositions stated earlier, particularly the trade-off between current yield and future returns. The question that now remains is to determine how important are the combined effects of capital market expectations on cap rates. To address this question, I ran stepwise regression equations against cap rate data and the selected capital market indicators in Table 1: property-specific mortgage rates, the eight-quarter average bond-bill spread, and the S&P earnings–price ratio. The results appear in Table 2.

Except for the category of industrial properties, all the equations were able to explain more than 90% of the variation in cap rates, with the unweighted average cap rate equation reaching 95%. Mortgage rates are the main determinant, although more so for retail properties and less so for apartments. The magnitude of the partial beta coefficients suggests that approximately 65% to 70% of cap rate variation can be explained by this variable. The bond–bill spread was second in importance, explaining about 20% to 25% of the variance. The stock market earnings–price ratio contributed the least to explaining cap rate var-

basis. If we could explain all of the residual by changing investor perceptions of tax benefits, the amount would be relatively minor, amounting to the five to ten basis point discrepancy observed earlier.

This finding is particularly surprising in view of popular judgments of the importance of tax benefits to real estate. To be sure, the finding does not actually contradict the importance of tax benefits, because a certain constant proportion of a cap rate yield may be due to tax considerations. Yet, changes in tax benefits, as occcured in 1981, 1984, and 1986, do not seem to have had a major effect on marginal cap rate variations. Indeed, estimated cap rates were below actual rates during the early 1980s, at a time when tax reform initiatives were under active discussion and significant tax benefits ultimately became a reality — a move

TABLE 2

Beta Coefficients for Cap Rates

| | PROPERTY TYPE | | | | |
	Apartments	Retail	Office	Industrial	Composite
Mortgage Rate	0.59	0.81	− 0.72	0.70	0.70
8 Quarter Bond–Bill Spread	− 0.44	− 0.33	− 0.40	− 0.43	− 0.41
Earnings–Price Ratio	0.27	0.08*	0.12	0.07*	0.13
% Variance Explained (R^2)	0.94	0.92	0.95	0.86	0.95

* Beta coefficient *not* significant; all other coefficients significant $p < 0.01$

iation. In fact, this measure was insignificant in the equations for retail and industrial properties.

THE IMPACT OF TAX CHANGES

How well do cap rates estimated on the basis of capital market factors track actual cap rates? By looking at the residual variation in the regression, we can identify the possible effect of tax changes.

Figure 2 shows the graph of actual and estimated average cap rates based on the regression equation in Table 2. Generally speaking, the estimated cap rates do not stray much more than five to ten basis points from actual rates during the period under study. Extreme variations of between twenty to thirty basis points occur at about three time periods: mid-1970, early 1980, and late 1983 to early 1984. There is no apparent commonality among these three periods as regards tax changes, so either an unspecified influence is at work or the departures are random error.

The residual unexplained variance in this regression amounts to only about 5% to 10% of the total variation in cap rates yields. This close agreement between actual and estimated cap rates makes a significant statement about the degree of influence exerted by changes in tax benefits on a marketwide

FIGURE 2

AVERAGE CAP RATES
1970:1 TO 1986:2

that should have spurred a decline in cap rates relative to the competitive requirements of the capital markets that are embedded in the estimate. Similarly, beginning in 1984 and culminating in 1986, tax changes moved toward significant reductions of tax benefits for real estate, which should imply an increase in cap rates relative to capital market derived estimates. This trend is not evident in Figure 2.

IMPLICATIONS FOR PRICING

As a determinant of the value of an income stream from a property, cap rates are to real estate what price–earnings ratios are to stocks and current yields are to fixed-rate debt instruments. Because of their role in pricing real estate assets, they must reflect investor opportunity costs in the broader capital markets.

The results presented here offer several important conclusions for pricing.

First, current yield requirements are the primary basis upon which real estate is traded. Fully 65% to 70% of cap rate variations were accounted for by measures of current yield. Therefore, the majority of real estate current yield is priced as a bond and will be exposed to the interest rate risks of fixed-income instruments.

Second, real estate is also priced as an equity, with appreciation largely determined by inflation expectations. This component of real estate returns is further conditioned by equity return expectations that are independent of real estate assets. The equity appreciation components account for 25% to 30% of cap rate fluctuations.

Third, with only about 5% to 10% of the variance unexplained, factors such as marketwide changes in perceptions of tax benefits or asset risks assume a relatively minor role in the determination of cap rate behavior. These factors may be important for a specific individual investment, but they do not appear to be influential in the broader market on the basis of the evidence examined here.

In short, this analysis suggests a marketwide hierarchy of pricing considerations. Current yield requirements are about two to two and a half times as important as appreciation expectations in established cap rate yields. Tax and risk considerations do not appear important to marketwide pricing behavior, although they still may be influential at the individual property level. As practitioners often argue for the importance of tax and risk considerations, the implication is that there may be a normal distribution among transactions that effectively reduces the impact of these trends in the aggregate. This has attractive meaning for well-diversified portfolios, for losses from these sources will be muted.

Cap rate behavior is only one part of the pricing equation, with trends in operating incomes and expectations for market rents obviously important to valuation considerations. While stability and growth in income will reflect the fundamental economic value of a real estate asset, the role of a cap rate is to reflect what an asset's earning power will be worth. In this respect, the pricing of real estate will depend upon competitive, alternative returns on other real and financial assets, not just among real estate opportunities. The essential conclusion is that a cap rate yield is a child of the capital market, just as it should be.

REFERENCES

American Council of Life Insurance. Investment Bulletin, 1969 to 1986. Washington, D.C.

Fabozzi, F., and I. Pollack. Handbook of Fixed-Income Securities. Woolford, W. D. "Forecasting Interest Rates," pp. 1001-1049, Homewood, Illinois: Dow Jones-Irwin, 1983.

Gibbons, J. E. "What to Do About Capitalization." Appraisal Journal, October 1986, pp. 618-627.

Robichek, A., R. Cohn, and J. Pringle. "Returns on Alternative Investment Media and Implications for Portfolio Construction." Journal of Business, July 1972, pp. 427-443.

Webb, J. R., and C. F. Sirmans. "Yields and Risk Measures for Real Estate, 1966 to 1977." Journal of Portfolio Management, Fall 1980, pp. 14-19.

Zerbst, R., and B. R. Canbon. "Real Estate: Historical Return and Risks." Journal of Portfolio Management, Spring 1984, pp. 5-20.

Leverage Financing Choices for Real Estate Investments

Charles E. Edwards and Philip E. Cooley*

An article published in 1977 in *The Real Estate Appraiser* (*and Analyst*) by Zerbst, Edwards, and Cooley (ZEC) presents an analysis of debt financing for real estate investments.[1] Their investigation, utilizing an after-tax cash flow model of equity returns, explores the *explicit* cost of debt financing for its effect on the rate of return on equity investment. Favorable leverage exists in their model when the rate of return on equity is increased by the use of debt. Acknowledging the importance of judgment in evaluating the additional risk inherent in debt financing, they suggest further that consideration of the *implicit* cost of debt financing—the tradeoff of risk and return—is essential as a second step toward complete analysis of leverage effects.

In a subsequent paper published in 1979 in the same journal, Mao offers an alternative methodology for evaluating the effects of debt financing.[2] Using an after-tax model of cash flow similar in form to that employed by ZEC, Mao computes the net present value (NPV) of the cash flows to estimate their net effect on the wealth of the equity investor. Relying on Modigliani and Miller's proposition that the required return on equity is a function of financial risk,[3]

Mao's analysis depends on the seemingly simple inclusion of the implicit cost of debt financing by discounting the cash flows at the "market" required return. Mao's analysis offers a one-step procedure for evaluating debt financing as opposed to ZEC's two-step procedure.

As evidenced by extensive discussion of both ZEC's rate-of-return (ROR) and Mao's NPV procedures in a recently published book by Jaffe and Sirmans,[4] interest in the complexities surrounding the evaluation of financial leverage continues apace. Jaffe and Sirmans express concern regarding the accurate measurement of market required returns, partly because financing alternatives are often limited in relatively illiquid financials market for real estate. Sizable transaction costs prevail, and information may be poorly distributed in real estate markets.

Aside from the obvious difficulty inherent in accurately assessing the real estate investor's response to increased risk attending the use of debt financing, an important conceptual problem confronts the real estate analyst. Although an analyst may share Mao's belief in wealth maximization as an appropriate objective of the investor, routine application of the NPV model as illustrated in his 1979 article may actually misrepresent the effects of project financing on the wealth of the real estate investor. Implicit in Mao's illustration of financial leverage is a disregard for possible scale effects of alternative financing arrangements, which leads to important questions for an analyst. For example, should the focus be on the wealth effect of a single project with alternative financing arrangements or should the analyst's focus be on increasing the total wealth of the investor derived from all feasible opportunities? This article explores the significance of the perspective from which wealth effects of leverage are viewed.

*Charles E. Edwards is Professor of Business Administration at the University of South Carolina. He is the author *of Dynamics of the U.S. Automobile Industry* as well as numerous articles in business and financial journals, including the *Real Estate Appraiser and Analyst*. He received his Ph.D. from the University of North Carolina. Philip L. Cooley is Professor of Finance at the University of South Carolina. The holder of a Ph.D. from Ohio State University, he is a frequent contributor of articles to professional journals, including *The Real Estate Appraiser and Analyst*.

[1] R.H.Zerbst, C.E. Edwards and P.L. Cooley, "Evaluation of Financial Leverage for Real Estate Investments," *The Real Estate Appraiser*, July-August 1977, pp. 7-11.

[2] J.C.T. Mao, "Wealth-Maximizing Criterion for Profitable Leverage in Real Estate Investments," *The Real Estate Appraiser and Analyst*, May-June 1979, pp. 51-54.

[3] F. Modigliani and M.H. Miller, "The Cost of Capital, Corporation Finance, and the Theory of Investment," *American Economic Review*, June 1958, pp. 261-297.

[4] A. J. Jaffe and C.F. Sirmans, *Real Estate Investment Decision Making* (Englewood) Cliffs, New Jersey: Prentice-Hall, 1982), especially Chapters 10 and 11.

The Alternative Procedures

The effect of financial leverage can be examined by the following cash-flow model for after-tax return on equity (r_e):

$$P_0 - M_0 = \sum_{j-1}^{n} \frac{(1-t)(NOI_j - D_j - I_j) - F_j + D_j - A_j}{(1+r_e)^j} +$$

$$\frac{P_n - t_c[P_n - (P_0 - \sum_{j-1}^{n} D_j + \sum_{j-1}^{n} F_j)] - (M_0 - \sum_{j-1}^{n} A_j)}{(1+r_e)^n}$$

where:

P_0 = original purchase price of property;

P_n = sale price of property at end of n periods;

M_0 = original amount of mortgage loans;

I_j = interest payment in period j;

A_j = amortization payment in period j;

NOI_j = net operating income in period j;

D_j = accounting depreciation in period j;

F_j = capital expenditure in period j to sustain NOI at desired level;

t = ordinary income tax rate; and

t_c = capital gains tax rate.

In the ROR formulation, the equation is solved for the internal rate of return on equity, r_e, which is the rate that equates to zero the NPV of the cash inflows and outflows.

If a project is financed entirely by equity, the variables related to debt financing, M_0, I_j, and A_j, fall from the equation. In this case, the return on the equity is also the return on assets. In the ROR procedure, favorable leverage occurs when the return on equity is increased as a result of debt financing. A favorable leverage effect must then be examined further in the context of a risk-return tradeoff as a second step toward reaching a final decision on whether to use debt financing.

The NPV procedure employs the same set of cash flows as included in the ROR procedure. The cash flows are evaluated, however, at an estimated market required return on equity, k_e. Whereas r_e appears as the solution value in the ROR formulation, k_e is now substituted as a given value, and the cash flows are evaluated to determine their NPV. By definition, favorable leverage in the NPV procedure occurs when NPV is increased by the use of debt financing.

The Problem

The problem manifests itself in the application of NPV to assess the favorability of financial leverage. The nature of the problem is best understood in the context of an illustration. For this purpose, Mao's original illustration provides a convenient basis for discussion.

The project under consideration is an eight-unit apartment building with a prospective cost of $400,000. If financed with 100 percent equity investment, the project is expected to generate after-tax cash inflows of $100,000 per year for four years, at the end of which it is believed that the property can be sold for an after-tax price of $200,000. Alternatively, the project can be financed with $200,000 of equity and $200,000 of debt at a ten percent interest rate, with the loan to be repaid in four equal installments. If the developer's tax rate is thirty percent on ordinary income, the interest rate has an effective after-tax cost of seven percent.

Under the hypothetical conditions, the anticipated cash flows of the equity investor are as follows:

Year End	All Equity	Debt + Equity
0	($400,000)	($200,000)
1	100,000	42,906
2	100,000	41,613
3	100,000	40,191
4	300,000	238,626

Year-end 0 amounts are the outflows of the equity investor under the two alternatives. The inflows for year-end one through three are net after-tax operating cash flows, after allowance in the debt + equity combination for interest and loan amortization effects.[5] Year-end four net cash flows include the net after-tax operating cash flow and expected after-

---

[5] A $200,00 loan at ten percent per year for four years is fully amortized by an annual payment of $63,094, of which $20,000 represents interest expense for the first year. To illustrate the cash flow computations, consider the cash inflows for year-end one:

	All Equity	Debt + Equity
Operating Revenue	$150,000	$150,000
Cash Operating Expenses	20,000	20,000
Depreciation	30,000	30,000
Interest Expense	-----	20,000
Net Income Before Taxes	$100,000	$80,000
Income Taxes (30%)	30,000	24,000
Net Income After Taxes	$70,000	$56,000
Plus Depreciation	30,000	30,000
Minus Principal Repayment	-----	43,094
Cash Inflow	$100,000	$42,906

tax sale proceeds, again after allowance in the debt + equity combination for interest and loan amortization effects. Evaluation of the net cash flows under the alternative financing arrangements reveals the essence of the analytical problem.

Using the cash flows shown, Mao calculates the rate of return on equity for each of the financing alternatives. The rate r_e is 20.6 percent using debt financing, compared to r_e at 15.0 percent for the all-equity investment. This is indicative of favorable leverage under the first step of ZEC's ROR procedure.

Using the NPV procedure, Mao finds the NPV of the all-equity investment to be $30,839, assuming a 12 percent required rate of return. He next presumes that the real estate investor requires a higher return on the leveraged project because of the financial risk attending the use of debt. Assuming that the required return on equity now rises to 15.5 percent—reflecting the implicit cost of debt—he computes the NPV of the $200,000 equity investment to be $28,513. By comparing the $28,513 NPV for the leveraged alternative to the $30,839 for the unleveraged case, he concludes that the leverage is unfavorable. Hence, the ROR and NPV procedures can produce conflicting signals on the favorability of financial leverage.

Analysis of the Problem

Figure 1 contains the NPV profiles of the two financing alternatives, with NPV and the discount rate represented by the vertical and horizontal axes, respectively. Evaluation of all-equity financing at the presumed 12 percent required return yields the indicated NPV of $30,839. Evaluation of the leveraged case at the 15.5 percent required return yields a slightly lower NPV, $28,513. Since $28,513 < $30,839, the NPV criterion indicates that financial leverage is unfavorable. The internal rate of return on equity for the leveraged case is shown graphically at 20.6 percent, which exceeds the 15.0 percent for the all-equity case. Under the ROR procedure, therefore, the financial leverage is favorable, which contradicts the signal provided by NPV.

Both the financing alternatives provide the same NPV in Figure 1 where the profile of the leveraged case intersects the NPV level of $30,839 obtained from discounting the all-equity cash flows at 12 percent. For Mao, this intersection is a critical value, since it establishes the standard for determining leverage favorability using NPV. The intersection occurs at a 15.13 percent required rate of return on equity. Below 15.13 percent for the leveraged case, NPV and ROR both lead to conclusions of favorable

FIGURE 1. NPV Profiles for Alternative Financing Arrangements

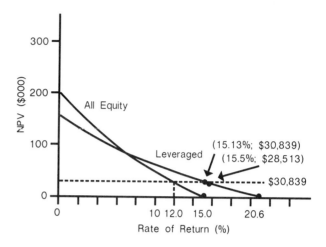

leverage, assuming that a 12 percent rate is appropriate for the all-equity case. For required rates from 15.13 percent to 20.6 percent, however, NPV and ROR yield conflicting indications of leverage favorability.

Routine application of the NPV procedure illustrated in Figure 1 may lead to nonoptimal financing decisions affecting the wealth of an investor under conditions common in real estate investments. First, when one of the alternatives being evaluated includes debt as a significant portion of project financing, the disparity in scale of equity investment is reflected significantly in the comparison of NPVs. Second, real estate investors often face the problem of limited resources in relation to the investments they would like to make. In these cases, an investor must plan carefully how to spread limited equity funds over multiple projects. Disregard of these two factors can lead to nonoptimal financing decisions derived from the NPV comparisons. That this may occur can readily be demonstrated.

The illustrative project, if financed only with equity, requires a $400,000 equity investment but only $200,000 of equity in the debt + equity combination. It would not be unlikely for a real estate investor having the previously described eight-unit apartment project in one location to have alternative projects of roughly comparable cost and profit potential in other locations. If the investor had $400,000 of equity capital, as implied by consideration of the all-equity case, $200,000 of equity could be used for each of two $400,000 projects, the remaining 50 percent of each being financed with debt. The combined leveraged cash flows in such a case would be double those of the single leveraged project:

Year End	Equity Cash Flows
0	($400,000)
1	85,812
2	83,226
3	80,382
4	477,252

Figure 2 shows the NPV profiles of comparably scaled equity investments: two leveraged projects versus a single all-equity project. As indicated in Figure 2, if the investor's required return rises to the 15.5 percent level hypothesized by Mao because of leverage-financing risk, the investor's expected NPV totals $57,026 (2 x $28,513) for the two $200,000 equity investments. An NPV of only $30,839 is expected from the all-equity $400,000 investment, evaluated at the unleveraged 12 percent required return. Thus, after equalizing the sizes of the equity investments, we observe that financial leverage appears favorable at a required return of 15.5 percent, which previously (in Figure 1) had been shown as leading to a conclusion of unfavorable leverage in Mao's NPV illustration.

NPVs of large investments (e.g., $400,000) are often large in comparison to NPVs of small investments (e.g., $200,000). Moreover, the size of equity investments in real estate projects can vary greatly because of substantially different financial arrangements. The analyst should take care to nullify the effect of disparate sizes of equity investments before making conclusions on the favorability of financial leverage.[6] In cases where the investor faces a rationing of capital, the comparison of multiple leveraged projects to a single unleveraged project provides insight and a basis for the analyst's judgment.

In the present illustration, we have assumed that the multiple projects are of comparable risk and profitability. Hence, the applicable discount rates are the previously assumed 12.0 percent for an unleveraged investment and 15.5 percent for the more

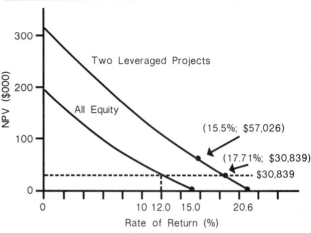

FIGURE 2. NPV Profiles When Scale Disparity is Nullified

risky leveraged equity investment. When equity funds are distributed over multiple projects, one might consider discounting the cash flows at lower rates. If project returns are less than perfectly positively correlated, the diversifiable business risk is lowered by spreading equity over several properties. In turn, the present value of expected bankruptcy costs would be lowered. If expected bankruptcy costs are negligible, the diversifiable business risk would have no impact on the investor's required rate of return; only the nondiversifiable risk would be relevant. In either case, financial leverage adds substantially to nondiversifiable risk, and the required return should be increased to accommodate the increased risk. Use of the 15.5 percent rate conveniently permits continuation of the numerical example. A smaller percentage would not alter our conclusions. Analysis of larger percentages is presented in the next section.

Additional Analysis

What is the critical value to which the investor's required return on equity may rise because of financial risk before the wealth of the investor is impaired? Figure 1 shows the critical value to be 15.13 percent when a single leveraged project is compared to the all-equity case. If two leveraged projects are compared to the all-equity case to nullify the scale disparity, however, the critical rate rises to a higher level.

As shown in the NPV profiles of the comparably scaled equity investments of Figure 2, if the required rate of return on the leveraged projects reaches 17.71 percent, the NPV of the leveraged projects equals the $30,839 NPV of the all-equity case evaluated at a 12 percent rate. For all rates below 17.71 percent, the critical value, both the NPV and ROR procedures indicate favorable financial leverage. From 17.71

[6]The scale disparity might also be nullified by other methods. The analyst could consider the investor as buying half of the unleveraged project for $200,000, assuming that the other half would be taken by another investor who also evaluates the project at an unleveraged rate of 12 percent. In this case, each equity investor's expected NPV would be $15,419 (1/2 x $30,839); but this amount is below the NPV of $28,513 expected from leveraging the project even though the required return rises to the leveraged return requirement of 15.5 percent. Additionally, the analyst might evaluate the alternatives by means of a profitability index (PI) reflecting the project's present value per dollar invested. For example, the PI for unleveraged $400,000 investment at the postulated 12 percent required return is 1.077 (30,839/400,00 + 1). For the leveraged $200,000 investment at a required return of 15.5 percent, the PI is 1.143 (28,513/200,000 + 1), which supports the choice of the leveraging opportunity despite the higher required return.

percent to 20.6 percent, the procedures produce conflicting conclusions, with NPV indicating unfavorable leverage. Thus, even with the scale disparity alleviated, the NPV and ROR procedures may provide opposite signals on the favorability of financial leverage. Whether a conflict will exist depends on the size of the premium added for financial risk stemming from leverage. In the present illustration the premium must exceed 5.71 percent (17.71 minus 12) before conflict arises.

As a practical matter, the ROR procedure has an advantage over the NPV procedure. The advantage arises because of the separation of the cash-flow mathematics of leverage from the premium added for the financial risk of leverage. Under the ROR procedure, the first step states: if the internal rate of return on leveraged equity exceeds that on unleveraged equity, then leverage is favorable in terms of the cash flows but ignores increased risk.[7] The second step, to account for added risk, can be stated as follows after equalizing the scale of alternative equity investments if the investor's required rate of return on leveraged equity is less than the critical value (for example, the 17.71 percent illustrated in Figure 2), then leverage is favorable despite the added risk exposure. If, however, the investor's required rate of return on leveraged equity exceeds the critical rate then leverage is unfavorable considering the added risk of leverage.

The one-step NPV procedure requires a risk-adjusting discount rate for assessing the favorability of leverage. If NPV indicates that leverage is unfavorable, the analyst does not know whether the unfavorability stems from the reduced cash flows to the investor or to the premium added for risk. Since the risk premium itself is subject to some uncertainty, the analyst might wish to know from whence the

---

[7]The first step for evaluating favorability of financial leverage was spelled out in ZEC's 1977 article, *op.cit*; its validity remains unimpeached.

negative signal has come. The two-step procedure provides a convenient basis for sensitivity analyses of the cash flows and the risk-adjusted required return. Although not developed here, the NPV procedure might be disaggregated into a two-step procedure, similar to the ROR procedure, to assist the analyst in evaluating financial leverage.

Implications

In capital budgeting, discounted-cash-flow procedures frequently produce conflicting signals on the ranking of projects. The same problem of ranking may occur in the comparison of alternative financing arrangements for real estate investments. Yet, comparisons must be made if the analyst is to assess the favorability of financial leverage.

A fundamental reason for the conflicting ranking produced by ROR and NPV is the difference in size of equity investment. Perhaps in no other business decision is the problem of scale disparity more common than in the assessment of financial leverage. The problem is especially prevalent in real estate, where substantial financial leverage is customary. Comparison of the favorability of leveraged equity to that of unleveraged equity must be done with caution.

If the analyst uses NPV to evaluate leverage, the size of the equity investments should be equalized by considering feasible, multiple leveraged projects versus the unleveraged project. Otherwise, nonoptimal decisions affecting investor wealth may result. In terms of cash flows but ignoring risk differentials, leverage is favorable if ROR on leveraged equity exceeds that on unleveraged equity. Consideration of risk premia requires additional analysis as explained earlier. In general, for the real estate investor with limited funds, the two-step ROR procedure provides an excellent basis for evaluating the merits of financial leverage.

A look at real estate duration

Duration is a function of lease contracts and market conditions.

David J. Hartzell, David G. Shulman, Terence C. Langetieg, and Martin L. Leibowitz

The analysis of duration, or the sensitivity of an asset's value to changes in interest rates, has followed an interesting path since the development of duration concepts for investments outside the fixed-income area. The duration concept has been extended to common equities, liability structures, and the management of the pension surplus. In this article, we use the effective duration concept to analyze real estate, with a look toward consolidating the contractual differences between real estate holdings and the equity duration model.[1] This topic is particularly relevant in the measurement of total portfolio duration for portfolios with a significant real estate content.

Real estate duration can be determined using methods similar to those for common stocks, such as the dividend discount model (DDM). As with common equity, however, empirical estimates of duration vary considerably between the traditional dividend discount model and newer techniques. We analyze these differences, using examples that differ in their ability to pass through inflation to net income. In particular, we model the speed of adjustment to inflation in lease contracts. This factor determines how quickly total returns adjust to inflation-induced changes in interest rates and, hence, the effective duration of the asset class.

We analyze duration under a number of scenarios, which differ by inflation adjustment assumptions. First, we define real estate as an investment vehicle, with a particular focus on the microfactors affecting real estate performance. Second, we describe the different rental adjustment processes used as inputs to duration calculations. The results show that different lease rollover assumptions result in different durations. Third, we discuss the impacts of a change in real interest rates. Finally, we present our conclusions and implications of the analysis.

REAL ESTATE DEFINED

Equity real estate has the same attributes as common stock and can be viewed as an industry segment within a broad securities index. As a result, the equity duration model is applicable. An investor receives a stream of payments called net rents and holds a claim on the residual value of the asset.

Real estate is also characterized by three factors that differentiate it from common stock. Real estate represents an unusually large segment of the economy, which is subject to its own cycle and is a major factor of production in all industries. Hence, investors can diversify within real estate with relative ease, which is not possible for other given industry groups. For example, it is easier to diversify away unsystematic risk in real estate than in almost any of the S&P industry groupings. Even though there is a general real estate "cycle," the heterogeneity of local markets, as well as the different lease and economic characteristics of the various property types, creates the potential for risk reduction through diversification within the real estate portfolio (Hartzell et al., 1986).

Second, the contractual nature of the cash flows, which are determined by the property's leasing

DAVID J. HARTZELL is a Vice President, DAVID G. SHULMAN is a Director, TERENCE C. LANGETIEG is a Vice President, and MARTIN L. LEIBOWITZ is a Managing Director, all at Salomon Brothers Inc in New York (NY 10004).

structure, means that equity real estate embodies some debt aspects. We can generate differing maturities and bond-like cash flows by altering the terms of the portfolio of leases.

Finally, real estate rents and values are determined by replacement costs that approximate inflation. This offers investors the long-term potential to receive rates of return indexed to inflation.

Three factors affect the indexation of returns and, therefore, the duration of real estate: the lease structure, the supply and demand cycle for real estate, and product deterioration or enhancement over time. The two polar extremes for lease structure are fully-indexed leases and non-indexed leases. The former allows the full pass-through of inflation into rents on a periodic basis. The pass-through can be accomplished contractually by indexation clauses in leases or by rolling over short-term leases in markets where real estate supply and demand conditions remain unchanged. From this perspective, hotel leases provide the ultimate inflation sensitivity, because they can be adjusted overnight; such leases also create vacancy risk, because these short-term contracts are typically not renewed.

At the other extreme are financing leases, where lease rates remain unchanged for a decade or more. The only way to pass inflation through to the investor with this type of lease structure is to release the space at the expiration of the lease, at which time the capital value of the asset would adjust to reflect the new level of rents. The trade-off here is between a non-indexed rent stream and a guaranteed occupancy level for the term of the contract. Reality in the real estate marketplace is somewhere between the two extremes; even with indexed leases, there is sufficient friction to prevent a full pass-through of inflation.

Superimposed on the lease structure are market risks generated by real estate supply and demand conditions that historically have been more of a national, rather than local, phenomenon. These market risks require a fully-diversified real estate portfolio to have a time diversification dimension, as well as product and geographic diversification dimensions. Real rents fluctuate in response to local supply and demand conditions, which are influenced by national economic conditions.[2] Consequently, rents may increase at rates higher or lower than the underlying rate of inflation in the short run. This obviously influences the ability of real estate to pass through inflation-based returns to its owners. In the long run, however, competition erodes abnormal returns, as long-term supply adjusts to long-run demand. As a result of recent overbuilding, "long-term" in real estate could be very long indeed.

The third aspect of real estate risk lies in the notion of product obsolescence and enhancement. Although many financial models of real estate transactions make assumptions concerning these risks, obsolescence and enhancement exist and ultimately affect the residual value of the asset. If the product maintains its attractiveness over time, then its value in equilibrium will be its replacement cost. If there is obsolescence or deterioration, however, its value would be lower than its replacement cost, preventing the residual value from fully passing through the inflation increases. Conversely, if the product improves over time because its site value is enhanced, its replacement cost would increase at a rate faster than that of inflation (Corcoran, 1987).

RELATION TO PREVIOUS RESEARCH

The adjustment in real estate returns as a result of changing inflation rates has been discussed in prior studies (Hartzell et al., 1987; Brueggeman et al., 1984). A fundamental problem with these studies concerns the quality of data that they employ, and, in a more general sense, the unavailability of real estate return data with which to analyze theoretical finance issues.

The ability of real estate to provide hedges against inflation can be determined by testing for the empirical reaction of real estate returns to changes in the expected and unexpected components of inflation. In general, studies have found that real estate provides a strong hedge against expected inflation. On the other hand, only the Hartzell, Hekman, and Miles study (1987) found a strong hedge against unexpected inflation. This study categorizes the data sample by different property characteristics, which leads to similar conclusions for various property types (office, retail, and industrial) and property sizes. Most studies do not shed light on the way changes in inflation affect real estate returns, beyond a discussion of methodology and empirical results.

One problem in previous studies is the use of appraisals to calculate the holding-period returns. The typical appraisal process that commingled real estate funds — the source of data — follow includes at least annual external appraisals, with in-house employees updating these values in the quarters between reappraisal. It is likely that the in-house appraisers merely adjust for inflation in the values of the properties, which would lead to an obvious inflation hedge finding. Such a problem is inherent in the use of any data series that uses appraised values as proxies of transaction values to calculate holding-period returns. In tests of duration, with real estate returns measured by appraisals, we find duration levels of zero.

Returns exhibited by equity real estate investment trusts (REITs) have been suggested as proxies for measuring the performance of real estate portfolios. Given the possibility of induced stock-like price volatility and the use of financial leverage for this type of security, though, most observers believe that these returns are not an accurate reflection of the nature of the underlying properties. Estimates of duration using equity REIT returns over the 1980s range from two to four years, about two-thirds of the duration of the S&P 500 over the same time period.

Given the limitations of existing real estate data sources, we propose an analytical approach to measuring effective duration. Using a realistic valuation model of market rents and lease contracts, we analyze the impact of changing inflation rates on duration and real interest rates for several different contracting regimes.

THE VALUATION OF REAL ESTATE

We begin with the premise that the rate of increase in real estate income is a function of the inflation rate modified by lease structure, real supply and demand conditions, and the degree of product enhancement or deterioration that occurs over time. *In this form, real estate can be viewed as a bond whose principal is inflation-indexed and whose coupons range from zero to full indexation.* Thus, the price of real estate can be reduced to the following equation:[3]

$$\begin{pmatrix} \text{Current} \\ \text{Property} \\ \text{Value} \end{pmatrix} =$$

$$\begin{pmatrix} \text{Present Value of} & \text{Present Value of} \\ \text{Net Rents Over} & + \text{Expected Market Price} \\ \text{Next T Years} & \text{in T years} \end{pmatrix}$$

$$P_0 = \sum_{t=1}^{T} \left(\frac{\overline{NR}}{(1 + k_0)^t} \right) + \qquad (1)$$

$$\frac{E[NR_0(1 + g_0 + \breve{u}_1)(1 + g_0 + \breve{u}_2) \ldots (1 + g_0 + \breve{u}_T) \times \overline{M}_T]}{(1 + k_0)^T}$$

where:

P_0 = present value of future cash flows generated by the property;

T = term of lease;

$\overline{NR}$ = net rental income on lease (fixed over T years);

NR_0 = current level of market rents;

g_0 = current expected growth rate in property value, which reflects the expected economywide inflation rate;

$\breve{u}_t$ = unexpected growth rate in rents in year t that reflects unexpected inflation, local supply and demand imbalances, as well as obsolescence and enhancements, which are interrelated with local market conditions;

$\overline{M}_t$ = price-to-rent multiple in year T;

k_0 = current required rate of return; and

$E[\cdot]$ = expected property value in T years.

The net rent variable in the equation is determined by the interaction of the structure of the contracts underlying the real property, the supply and demand conditions within local markets, and inflation. For the former, net rents will rise or fall depending on the ability of the landlord/property-owner to roll over leases, thereby adjusting for inflation. In our annual model, for example, the interval for which lease payments are fixed can range from one year to more than twenty years. At the short end, rents adjust as announcements of inflation are made. Over the long term, rents do not adjust at all to inflation and are held constant for the entire lease term. At lease renewal, rents adjust to "catch up" for all previous inflation during the fixed contract period. Thus, the interaction of inflation rates and speed of adjustment determines the effective duration of the asset class.

With this valuation equation, we can calculate the effective duration of real estate by measuring asset price changes in response to changes in interest rates under varying types of lease contracts. In this context, an asset with an effective duration of five years would experience a 5% decrease in value in response to a 1% increase in interest rates. We assume that there is direct and instantaneous transmittal of changes in the expected inflation rate to the discount rate. Initially, we assume that the expected real rate of return is constant and that there is no unanticipated rent growth. Later, we allow changes in the underlying real rate or real estate risk premium to cause changes in the nominal interest rate.

ALTERNATIVE LEASE STRUCTURES: PERFECT MARKETS VERSUS MARKET FRICTIONS

The limited availability of appropriate data to use in empirical tests of duration requires us to use an analytical valuation model. Our duration calculations are based on Equation (1), with five alternative contract terms:

- Continuous rent adjustment to the prevailing market rent;
- Rent adjustments every two years;
- Rent adjustments every five years;
- Rent adjustments every ten years; and
- Rent adjustments every twenty years.

In all five cases, we assume a ten-year holding period, which is typical for most real estate investment managers. In the case of a twenty-year lease, we have assumed a sale at the end of the tenth year, by discounting the net rents from years 11–20 and the residual value at the end of the period.

Our analysis assumes a 6% real rate of return for real estate, a rate real estate investment managers use frequently for quality assets. The real return consists of a general economic real interest rate plus a risk premium appropriate for real estate.[4] An initial 5% expected inflation rate is also assumed for the base case. This translates into an initial discount rate (k) of 11.3%. The expected growth rate of the rental stream at the beginning of the holding period is equal to the expected inflation rate.

With continuous rent adjustment, inflation over the next year is fully embedded into next year's rents and in every subsequent year's rents during the holding period, as well as in the terminal value of the property. For fixed-rent contracts, the adjustment to the new rate of inflation takes place at the end of the contract term. With a contract term of ten years, for example, there is no rent adjustment to inflation during the next ten years. Nevertheless, inflation is embedded in the growth of the property value, as represented by the second term in Equation (1). This case is similar to a ten-year bond with a fixed coupon and an indexed principal.

We analyze two generic types of leasing contracts. Both types assume that the contracting term is held constant throughout the holding period. That is, at the end of an initial lease term, a new lease is put into effect with the same term as the initial one. From that point forward, the contract rolls over every T years until the end of the holding period. Further, the property, after the assumed ten-year holding period, is sold under the condition that leases have been contractually set so that their maturities will equal T in the future.

The first contract regime, which we call the "market frictions regime," assumes an equal rent for all lease terms. Contracts with different terms are not present value equivalents unless the expected inflation rate is equal to zero, but the market frictions regime is typical of existing rent contracts in major markets where there is often little difference between rents on contracts with different terms. One explanation for this is the possible presence of substantial periods of vacancy, leasing commissions, and other contracting costs. The potential cost of those market frictions is much greater with short-term leases than with long-term contracts. Consequently, benefits arising from inflation may be reduced with a long-term

fixed-rent contract, but substantial costs resulting from market frictions are avoided.

The second contract type, which we call the "perfect markets regime," sets the fixed rent such that the present value of the rent payments until the leases roll over is equal to the present value of the expected inflation-indexed rent payments over the same time period. At the end of the investment horizon, the property value is equal to the market value of a fully-indexed cash flow stream, which is also the value of a perpetual floating-rent contract. The assumption is that the two contracts have equivalent present values. Given information asymmetries and market frictions related to local market supply and demand conditions, as well as inflexibility in setting lease terms, this case is more theoretical than real.

A graphic example serves to clarify this cash flow generation process. Figure 1 shows the cash

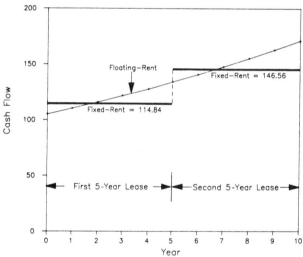

FIGURE 1

CASH FLOWS FOR A FIVE-YEAR LEASE —
PERFECT MARKETS REGIME

flows earned by the property for a floating-rent contract and a five-year fixed-rent contract in the perfect markets regime. Assuming the base case, where expected inflation is 5% throughout the holding period, the present value of the five-year fixed-rent contract is $114.84, which is equal to the present value of a five-year rental stream starting at $105 that increases annually at the 5% expected inflation rate. After the initial five-year contracting period, the fixed rent is increased to $146.56. The present value of this second five-year annuity is equal to the present value of the floating-rent contract, which starts at $134.01 in year six ($105 × 1.05⁵ = $134.01), and is again indexed to the 5% expected inflation rate. A similar process is employed for leases with terms not equal to five years.

Figure 2 shows the rents for the fixed-rent and

FIGURE 2

CASH FLOWS FOR FIVE-YEAR LEASE —
MARKET FRICTIONS REGIME

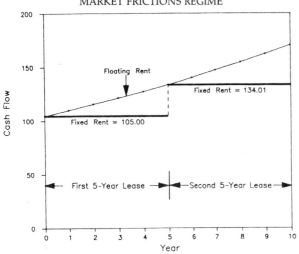

floating-rent leases in the market frictions regime. The fixed-rental stream is equal initially to the initial year's indexed-rent flow of $105. For the sixth year, the indexed rent rises to $134.01, and the fixed rent is set equal to this amount for the remaining five years of the holding period.

To illustrate the effect of a change in expected inflation, suppose that the rent contract is determined on the basis of a 5% inflation rate, and a shock occurs causing inflation expectations to increase to 6%. The effect of this change on the rental stream depends on the lease term, which determines how long it takes until rents can adjust to the inflation rate.

Figure 3 shows the rental stream for the market frictions regime before and after the instantaneous increase in inflation expectation from 5% to 6%. As

FIGURE 3

CASH FLOW EFFECT FROM AN INCREASE IN THE INFLATION
RATE FROM 5% TO 6% — MARKET FRICTIONS REGIME

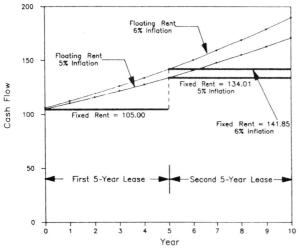

the five-year contract is put into place prior to the shock, the base rent remains at $105 for the first five years. In year six, the new fixed rent — given that inflation has been rising at 6% — is $141.85. This is obviously higher than the fixed rent of $134.01, because the new contract adjusts to catch up to 6% versus 5% inflation. A similar adjustment takes place in the perfect market regime to preserve the "present value equivalence" in years 6–10.

PRICE SENSITIVITY TO CHANGES IN THE EXPECTED INFLATION RATE

A floating-rent or fully-indexed contract has a base payment in year zero of $100. With an expected inflation rate of 5%, the first-year payment is expected to be $105, the second-year payment $110.25, and so forth. The property value with a perpetual floating-rent contract is $1667 for our example, with a 5% expected inflation rate and 11.3% discount rate.[5] This translates into a capitalization rate — equivalent to a dividend yield — of 6.3% on income in year one.

An instantaneous increase in the expected inflation rate to 6% after the lease contract is entered into would have no effect on value, because the lease is assumed to be fully and immediately indexed to inflation. This automatically increases income in year one to $106 and the discount rate to 12.36%. Consequently, there is no effect on asset value from a 100 basis point change in inflation, and the value of the property remains at $1667. Thus, the effective duration in the fully-indexed case is zero in both simulations.

A ten-year fixed-rent lease obviously leads to a different conclusion. In this case, the lease income remains unchanged at $105 during the life of the lease, but the residual value at expiration increases at the rate of inflation. This implies an initial value of the asset of $1383 and a residual value of $2253. The loss of coupon indexation results in a 17% diminution in value. We derive these values by assuming the capitalization rate in year ten is the same as in year zero.

If the expected inflation rate increases to 6%, the lease contract rents remain unchanged, but the discount rate increases by 106 basis points, and the resulting value falls to $1324. This represents a 4.26% drop in value and an effective duration of approximately 4.02 years for the market frictions case.[6] By contrast, the change in value for a ten-year lease contracting period in the perfect markets case is 1.8%.

DEVELOPING AN EQUIVALENT MEASURE OF INFLATION PASS-THROUGH

The inflation sensitivities that we find in these calculations can also provide some insights regarding the flow-through of inflation for real estate with different leasing structures. Given the indicated inflation sensitivities and the extension of the DDM incorporating inflation sensitivity, we can estimate an implied pass-through parameter. The price sensitivity of a floating-rent contract to a change in the expected inflation rate is equal to:[7]

$$\begin{pmatrix} \text{Price Sensitivity} \\ \text{to a Change} \\ \text{in the Expected} \\ \text{Inflation Rate} \end{pmatrix} = -D_{DDM}(1 - \lambda)\Delta I \quad (2)$$

where:

$$D_{DDM} = \frac{1}{k - g} = \begin{array}{l}\text{duration of the dividend}\\ \text{discount model;}\end{array}$$

ΔI = change in the expected inflation rate; and

λ = inflation flow-through parameter.

D_{DDM} represents the duration in the traditional sense. It measures the price sensitivity to a change in the discount rate, holding the cash flow stream constant. A change in interest rates caused by a change in the expected inflation rate will also increase rents. For the floating-rent lease, we have assumed complete pass-through of inflation, hence λ is equal to one, and the price sensitivity to a change in the expected inflation rate is zero.

For the fixed-rent lease, we determine the price sensitivity to a change in the expected inflation rate as discussed above. Having determined the left-hand side of Equation (2), we then solve for λ to obtain a measure of the imputed inflation pass-through. Thus, we can determine an equivalent measure of inflation pass-through, which we then can use to compare contracts with level payments for fixed terms with contracts in which rents continuously adjust to reflect all or part of inflation.

Estimates of Inflation Sensitivity and Effective Duration

Given the methodology and assumptions underlying the valuation equation, the percentage change in value resulting from a 1% inflation-induced change in interest rates can be obtained for both the market friction and perfect markets cases. As mentioned above, estimates of the inflation flow-through measure are implied in these effective durations.[8]

The results, presented in Table 1 and Figure 4, are intuitively appealing. They show that effective duration, or the price change arising from a 1% increase in inflation rates, increases with the lease term. In what we consider our typical leasing arrangement, with a five-year term, the duration of real estate is 2.1 years in the more realistic market frictions case. By

TABLE 1

Changes to Value and Duration When a Discount Rate Increase Results From 1% Increase in the Expected Inflation Rate

	Market Frictions Regime		Perfect Markets Regime	
Inflation Rate	5%	6%	5%	6%
Discount Rate	11.3%	12.4%	11.3%	12.4%
Term	Value	Effective Duration[a]	Value	Effective Duration[a]
1 Year	$1,667	$1,667 0	$1,667	$1,667 0
2 Years	1,628	1,617 0.6	1,667	1,664 0.1
5 Years	1,524	1,490 2.1	1,667	1,656 0.6
10 Years	1,383	1,324 4.0	1,667	1,635 1.8
20 Years	1,191	1,114 6.1	1,667	1,592 4.2

[a] See Footnote 6 for the calculation of effective duration.

FIGURE 4

EFFECTS OF A CHANGING LEASE TERM ON DURATION

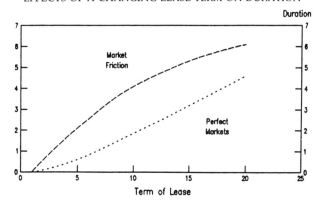

contrast, under the assumption of perfect markets, the duration of real estate is only 0.6 year. This number is higher than what was found for appraisal-based returns, but at the low end of the range when REIT data were used to measure returns.

Next we look at the equivalent inflation pass-through, λ^*, of a fixed-rent lease, which is defined as follows:

$$\begin{pmatrix} \text{Equivalent} \\ \text{Inflation} \\ \text{Pass-Through } (\lambda^*) \end{pmatrix} = 1 +$$

$$\begin{pmatrix} \text{Price Sensitivity} \\ \text{to a Change in the} \\ \text{Expected Inflation Rate} \end{pmatrix} / D_{DDM}$$

As an example, in the market frictions regime the current property value for the five-year lease is $1524. If the expected inflation rate increases from 5% to 6%, the price drops to $1490, a drop of 2.23%. Using Equation (2), this results in an equivalent inflation pass-through of:

$$\lambda^* = 1 - (2.23/16.67) = 0.87.$$

In other words, a five-year fixed-rate lease has an inflation pass-through that is equivalent to a floating-rent lease that passes through 87% of inflation. Figure 5 illustrates the inflation pass-through

FIGURE 5

ESTIMATES OF EQUIVALENT INFLATION PASS-THROUGH

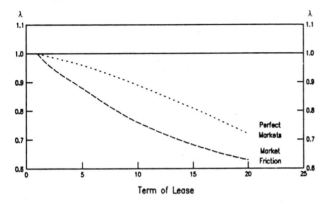

for leases of different terms. Obviously, the amount of implicit pass-through decreases as the length of the adjustment period, or lease term, increases. Furthermore, the decrease occurs at a declining rate. The pass-through is also higher under the perfect markets assumption, because fixed-rent leases are assumed to compensate investors partially for expected inflation at the beginning of the lease term.

**Price Sensitivity to Changes
in the Real Rate of Return**

In theory, the discount rate for real estate has three components: the expected inflation rate (I), the expected real interest rate (R), and the real estate risk premium (H). Up to now we have been concerned only with inflation sensitivity. The underlying real interest rate and real estate risk premium, however, can change as well, and these effects can be far more powerful than changes in the inflation premium. For the floating-rent contract, the price sensitivity to changes in the expected real interest rate is equal to:

$$\begin{pmatrix} \text{Price Sensitivity} \\ \text{to a Change in the} \\ \text{Expected Real Rate} \end{pmatrix} = -D_{DDM}(1 - \gamma)\Delta R \quad (3)$$

where:

ΔR = change in the expected real interest rate, and

γ = sensitivity of rents to changes in real interest rates.

In a similar way, we can determine the price sensitivity to changes in the risk premium, H:

$$\begin{pmatrix} \text{Price Sensitivity} \\ \text{to a Change in the} \\ \text{Risk Premium} \end{pmatrix} = -D_{DDM}\Delta H \quad (4)$$

where:

ΔH = change in the risk premium.

The real interest rate directly affects the discount rate and also may affect the level of rents as represented in the sensitivity parameter. On the other hand, a change in the risk premium affects only the discount rate. Together, the real interest rate plus the risk premium represent the expected real rate of return on real estate. Combining Equations (4) and (5), the price sensitivity to a change in the expected real rate of return is equal to:

$$\begin{pmatrix} \text{Price Sensitivity} \\ \text{to a Change} \\ \text{in the Expected} \\ \text{Real Rate of Return} \end{pmatrix} = -D_{DDM}[(1 - \gamma)\Delta R + \Delta H] \quad (5)$$

where:

$R + H$ = expected real rate of return.

In our calculations, the expected real rate of return is 6%. If a change in either the real interest rate or the risk premium caused the expected real return to increase from 6% to 7%, the value of our hypothetical real estate asset would fall from $1667 to $1429, a drop of 14.3%. As a result, changes in the discount rate caused by changes in the real rate introduce the potential for very high interest rate sensitivity or duration.

Furthermore, both floating-rent and fixed-rent contracts in either market regime have very high price sensitivities when the interest rate change is due to a change in the real interest rate or the risk premium. By comparison, a duration of 14.3 years is far higher than durations in the one-to-six range reported in Table 1 for interest rate changes caused by changes in expected inflation. In either case, however, real estate has a positive duration.

In addition, the level of real interest rates and the risk premium have implications for inflation pass-through. Table 2 and Figure 6 illustrate the impact of an inflation pass-through at 4%, 6%, and 8% real rates

TABLE 2

Estimates of the Equivalent Inflation Pass-Through with
Varying Real Rates and Lease Contract Terms

Term	Market Frictions Regime Expected Real ROR[a]			Perfect Markets Regime Expected Real ROR[a]		
	4%	6%	8%	4%	6%	8%
1 Year	1.00	1.00	1.00	1.00	1.00	1.00
2 Years	0.97	0.96	0.95	0.99	0.99	0.98
5 Years	0.92	0.87	0.83	0.98	0.96	0.94
10 Years	0.84	0.76	0.68	0.94	0.89	0.83
20 Years	0.76	0.63	0.51	0.85	0.74	0.63

[a] The expected real rate of return (ROR) consists of the real interest rate plus the risk premium.

FIGURE 6

ESTIMATES OF THE EQUIVALENT INFLATION
PASS-THROUGH — MARKET FRICTIONS REGIME

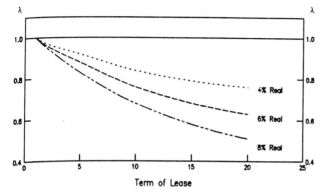

Term of Lease

in the market frictions case. The higher the real expected rate of return, the lower the inflation pass-through for a given lease term, because the real rate has an inverse relation to D_{DDM}. A lower inflation pass-through is a result of discounting a given inflation-indexed residual value at a higher discount rate. Thus, a higher real rate per se diminishes the attractiveness of real estate as an inflation hedge.

CAN REAL ESTATE DURATION BE NEGATIVE?

Our analysis has shown that an increase in interest rates caused by an increase in the expected inflation rate or the real interest rate leads to a decline in real estate prices. Although this result is characteristic of a positive duration investment, it appears to be counterintuitive because real estate seemed to increase in value in the face of rising interest rates during the late 1970s and early 1980s. Two factors can explain this apparent contradiction.

First, although the economywide real interest rate increased during that time, the risk premium for real estate actually declined as investors switched from financial assets to other assets, such as real estate, that offered the potential for a high inflation flow-through. High and uncertain inflation increases the importance of assets that have a high inflation pass-through. The effects of rising real interest rates and declining risk premiums tend to offset one another to some degree. The net effect could even be a reduction in the expected real rate of return. This decreased return would cause investors to bid up the price of real estate as a result of their willingness to accept a lower real return. There can be a very significant price increase associated with declines in expected real rates of return.

Second, these events occurred during the period when net rents were increasing faster than the inflation rate because of very tight real estate markets. Thus, in the short run, real estate offered a pass-

through factor in excess of one, which empirically gives the appearance of a negative duration. Consequently, two factors were at work that resulted in a price increase in the face of rising interest rates.

Rising real rents, rising real estate prices, and the willingness of investors to accept lower real returns became a clear signal to create more real estate. In the late 1970s and early 1980s, the development community responded with the greatest commercial real estate building boom in history. Within our framework, this reduces the growth rate of rents below expectations, thereby lowering the value of real estate and limiting the ability of the asset to permit the flow-through inflation. The negative duration aspects of real estate during the late 1970s and early 1980s were eroded by increased supply, which lowered both net rents and residual value. To protect themselves, both renters and owners also moved toward longer lease contracts, effectively lengthening the duration of real estate.

IMPLICATIONS AND CONCLUSIONS

This analysis has two implications. First, given market conditions, real estate investors have some control over the duration of the asset through the lease contracting process. Second, the duration of real estate is not always as low as investors implicitly assume it to be. Duration is a function of lease contracts and market conditions. The longer the lease contract (excluding indexed leases), the longer the duration of the asset. Real estate investors who hold assets with long leases in reality own annuities with a claim on an inflation-indexed residual.

Market conditions influence the duration of real estate in two ways: The length of the lease term contract is market-determined to some extent, and the residual value of the asset, which affects inflation sensitivity, is determined not only by the cumulative inflation over the lease term but also by market conditions at the end of the lease. To the extent that the real estate investor can control the term of the lease, the investor has some control over the duration of the position. The management of real estate duration is further augmented by the ability to structure real estate financing in conjunction with the underlying lease contract.

REFERENCES

Brueggeman, W., A. Chen, and T. Thibodeau, "Real Estate Investment Funds: Performance and Portfolio Considerations." *AREUEA Journal,* Fall 1984.

Corcoran, Patrick. "Explaining the Commercial Real Estate Market." *Journal of Portfolio Management,* Spring 1987.

Hartzell, D., J. S. Hekman, and M. Miles. "Diversification Categories in Investment Real Estate." *AREUEA Journal*, Fall 1986.

——. "Real Estate Returns and Inflation." *AREUEA Journal*, Spring 1987.

Hartzell, D., D. G. Shulman, T. C. Langetieg, and M. L. Leibowitz. *A Look at Real Estate Duration*. Salomon Brothers Inc, December 1987.

Rent Projections in the Context of a Rent Cycle. Salomon Brothers Inc, October 22, 1986.

Smith, Lawrence B. *Adjustment Mechanisms in Real Estate Markets*. Salomon Brothers Inc, June 1987.

A Total Differential Approach to Equity Duration. Salomon Brothers Inc, September 1987.

[1] See *A Total Differential Approach to Equity Duration*, Salomon Brothers Inc, September 1987.

[2] See *Rent Projections in the Context of a Rent Cycle*, Salomon Brothers Inc, October 22, 1986, and *Adjustment Mechanisms in Real Estate Markets*, Lawrence B. Smith, Salomon Brothers Inc, June 1987.

[3] We discuss the valuation model in detail in the Appendix to *A Look at Real Estate Duration*, Salomon Brothers Inc, December 1987.

[4] We initially assume the expected real return is invariant to the lease structure, which may not necessarily be the case;

however, we examine the effects of changes in the expected real return later in this article.

[5] For a floating-rent contract, the price can be calculated from the familiar Gordon–Shapiro model

$$P_0 = \frac{NR_0(1 + g)}{k - g} = \frac{105}{0.113 - 0.05} = \$1667$$

[6] The effective duration is equal to:

$$\frac{-\delta P/\delta k}{P} = \frac{-\Delta P/\Delta k}{P} = -\frac{(1324 - 1383)/0.0106}{1383} = 4.02$$

[7] Equation (2) shows the price sensitivity for a floating-rate contract with continuous, rather than discrete, rent payments. In this context D_{DDM} is equal to $1/(k^c - g^c)$, where k^c and g^c are interpreted as continuous rates. We set $k^c = 0.11$ and $g^c = 0.05$, which produces a property value of $1667 and a D_{DDM} of 16.67 for the continuous floating-rent case. We focus on the continuous case so that our estimate of inflation pass-through is consistent with the concept of inflation pass-through developed for common stocks in *A Total Differential Approach to Equity Duration*, Salomon Brothers Inc, September 1987. For more detail, see the Appendix to *A Look at Real Estate Duration*, Salomon Brothers Inc, December 1987.

[8] The implied λ^* is not an instantaneous pass-through parameter. Rather, it is a pass-through equivalent parameter implied under the varying lease terms used in the simulations. The actual pass-through comes at the rollover of the leases.

REVIEW OF THE CHICAGO
REAL ESTATE MARKET

Mark Lauritano
Director of Real Estate Research

Jennifer Peterson
Assistant Real Estate Research Officer

NOTE

Written as part of the ongoing real estate research at John Hancock Properties, Inc. (JHPI), this report is intended to provide a current assessment of the fundamental forces that govern the Chicago real estate market. It is based on independent research and a series of interviews with economists, planners, and real estate professionals in the Chicago area. The report is organized into the following sections: Executive Summary, Economic Environment, Political Environment, and Real Estate Markets.

The geographic definition of the Chicago metropolitan area is subject to a variety of opinions. Unless otherwise noted, this analysis is based on the six-county metropolitan area, the former Standard Metropolitan Statistical Area (SMSA), encompassing Cook, DuPage, Kane, Lake, McHenry, and Will Counties. This particular definition captures the bulk of economic activity in the Chicago area and is used by most local professionals. Data from some sources constrained us to report figures for the Chicago Primary Metropolitan Statistical Area (PMSA), which consists of Cook, DuPage, and McHenry Counties.

EXECUTIVE SUMMARY

During the mid-1980s, economic growth in the six-county Chicago metropolitan area surpassed the national rate for the first time in over twenty years. This expansion was largely a function of the strength of the Midwest economy in general and the Great Lakes region in particular.

Chicago's growth, however, has been neither stable nor uniform. Although wholesale trade and transportation services are booming, other sectors of the market have performed at or below the U.S. average. Recent employment growth has been sluggish. Of particular concern to city planners, suburban development has occurred at the expense of urban neighborhoods.

There are other signs that the economy may be weakening. Though the decline in manufacturing employment forced a much-needed diversification, the production sector has not participated in the region's recovery. Thousands of jobs were lost when two local banks ran into trouble, but recent restructuring may allow employment growth in this industry to keep pace with the rest of the economy. The inferior quality of the Chicago public school system, rated among the nation's worst, is a serious deterrent to corporate relocations. Whether current efforts to decentralize the bureaucracy will improve educational standards remains to be seen.

In this increasingly uncertain economic environment, the performance of Chicago's real estate markets has been lackluster. In our analysis of the office, industrial, apartment, and retail markets, frequent reference is made to real estate returns derived from the John Hancock Real Estate Market Indicator (JHREMI). This is a measure of market condition used to compare a particular market with the U.S. or other areas. The JHREMI can be translated into an estimate of the rate of return that is based on the fundamental conditions of supply and demand in the market. The JHREMI-Return represents the annualized total nominal return that a market may provide over history and through the forecast period.

The office market recently enjoyed a rate of return above the U.S. average for the first time in more than a decade, the result of a lull in completions following the building boom of the late 1980s. This market remains healthy, but is expected to begin a decline by mid-1990 as supply outpaces demand.

The industrial market, which likewise enjoyed a recent boom, also shows signs of slowing. Nearly 40 million square feet of space became available in 1988, pushing vacancy rates to 7.7 percent from 7.3 percent a year earlier. Returns in this market have historically demonstrated more volatility than the national average. Continued additions to supply in the face of weakening demand should hold returns marginally below the U.S. average through 1992.

The apartment market, after being fueled through the mid-1980s by expectations of tax reform, suffered a sharp setback following the financial shocks of 1987. This deterioration should continue through the end of 1990. The return on multifamily residential properties should resume an upward trend in 1991, yet returns will linger well below the U.S. average throughout the projection period.

The retail market, historically a poor performer relative to other metropolitan areas, was devastated when the 1982 drop in spending pushed returns close to zero. A healthy recovery soon followed, with returns soaring to nearly twenty percent in 1985. This hiatus was short-lived, however, and returns have since returned to their historical position somewhat below the U.S. rate. With retail markets likely to suffer from the introduction of new space over the next two years, returns are expected to hover below the national average through 1992.

It is unlikely that the Chicago economy can sustain the pace of the past six years. During that time, the city's jobless rate fell to roughly the U.S. average. With such low unemployment, continued rapid economic growth would require steady additions to the labor force. As employment growth slows, however, opportunities for better jobs and higher incomes are insufficient to draw new workers to Chicago from other areas.

Accordingly, we expect the Chicago economy to grow at a modest pace in 1990, well below its recent performance. Over the long term, a more vigorous forecast is justified only if Chicago either reverses decades of below-average growth or expands from a regional to a national economic role.

ECONOMIC ENVIRONMENT

Chicago is the nation's third largest metropolitan area and the economic capital of the Great Lakes region. After a steady drop in economic activity from 1980 to 1982, Chicago rebounded sharply in 1983. Much of the recovery was fostered by the turnaround in trade, which is considered to be critical to the Midwest economy. As the falling dollar improved the region's competitive position in international markets, Chicago's economic growth surpassed the U.S. average rate for the first time in more than twenty years. Employment gains in Chicago had typically exhibited a pattern of steep declines during recessions, followed by modest recoveries. Since 1983, the Chicago economy has kept pace with rapid national growth, but has fallen short of U.S. performance during weaker periods.

TOTAL NONAGRICULTURAL EMPLOYMENT
(1969 to 1989:2)

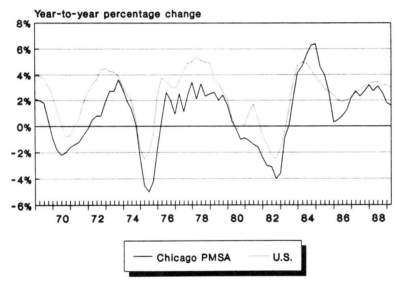

Source: Bureau of Labor Statistics

A careful review of the area's key employment sectors reveals several factors that help to explain Chicago's exceptional economic performance during the recovery. The sectors responsible for the turnaround in Chicago illustrate the area's dependency on the economic region that it serves. The strength of the recovery was based not on any significant improvement in Chicago's manufacturing sector, but on the rebound of the Midwest economy. The sectors that clearly outperformed the national economy in terms of job growth were the sectors that provide essential services to the region. In particular, wholesale trade and transportation services exceeded the gains made in the U.S. economy by a wide margin.

While many industries enjoyed rapid growth over this period, the only other sector to outperform the nation was construction. The Chicago area experienced a tremendous increase in nonresidential and residential investment during the recovery. The six-county metropolitan area has added roughly 75 million square feet of office space and 84,600 units of multifamily housing since the recovery began.

Employment Concentration and Growth - Chicago PMSA vs. U.S.

| Employment Sector | Share of Total | | Relative Concen- tration | Compound Annual Growth | | | |
| | Chicago | U.S. | | 1983-87 | | 1987:4-89:2 | |
				Chicago	U.S.	Chicago	U.S.
Total	100.0%	100.0%	1.0	3.2%	3.3%	2.0%	3.1%
Manufacturing	18.1	18.4	1.0	0.0	1.3	0.8	1.6
Food Processing	1.6	1.5	1.1	-2.5	0.2	0.9	1.4
Printing & Publishing	2.5	1.5	1.7	1.6	3.8	0.5	3.4
Chemicals	1.1	1.0	1.1	-0.4	-0.1	3.5	3.3
Fabricated Metals	2.3	1.4	1.7	0.4	1.1	2.1	1.9
Electrical Machinery	2.8	2.0	1.4	-0.4	1.2	-2.5	-0.6
Instruments	0.7	0.7	0.9	-2.5	0.9	0.9	5.0
Nonmanufacturing	81.9	81.6	1.0	4.1	3.8	2.2	3.4
Construction	4.2	4.9	0.9	9.3	6.0	5.5	3.3
Finance, Ins, & RE	8.7	6.3	1.4	3.3	4.4	2.0	1.9
Banking	1.9	1.6	1.2	-1.5	0.9	1.4	1.3
Commodities	1.1	0.4	2.5	9.3	10.1	3.9	-2.9
Government	11.8	16.5	0.7	1.4	1.7	1.8	2.0
Trans, Comm, & Util	6.1	5.3	1.2	3.8	1.9	-0.4	3.2
Trucking	1.6	1.5	1.1	5.0	5.2	2.9	6.6
Air Transportation	1.1	0.6	1.9	9.2	7.3	-2.9	5.5
Services	26.2	24.2	1.1	4.4	5.4	3.2	5.5
Health	6.4	6.8	0.9	1.2	3.3	1.0	6.3
Business	7.3	5.3	1.4	9.9	10.2	5.7	5.4
Legal, Accting, & Misc	8.3	6.8	1.2	2.9	4.2	2.9	5.9
Trade	24.9	23.8	1.0	4.3	3.9	1.9	3.0
Retail	16.8	18.1	0.9	4.3	4.3	2.4	2.8
Wholesale	8.2	5.7	1.4	4.3	2.7	1.1	3.6

Note: Relative Concentration is the ratio of Chicago share to U.S. share.
Source: Bureau of Labor Statistics

Two sectors that failed to share in the rebound of employment during much of the recovery were banking and manufacturing. Both sectors have undergone significant restructuring. Two of the area's leading banks were forced to cut back employment and write off a sizeable portion of their energy loan portfolio. The manufacturing sector in the Chicago PMSA witnessed a decline of 200,000 jobs during the 1982 recession. In order to compete once more in international markets, producers have closed inefficient plants, shed unprofitable business lines, and invested in new plant and equipment. However, this restructuring has done little to boost Chicago manufacturing employment, which remains near its recession trough.

The most significant effect of the recovery is that the Chicago economy is now more diversified. In particular, the manufacturing sector's share of total employment has fallen from 25.6 percent in 1980, well above the national average, to 18.1 percent in 1988, slightly below average. Late Mayor Harold Washington viewed the city's diversity as "a series of emporiums that have enabled us to be self-contained." Along with many Chicagoans, he believed that the economy diversified itself through strategic restructuring. However, the new diversity is far more likely the forced result of extremely hard times for the city's mainstay production industries. Like other mature cities, Chicago is following the evolutionary pattern of development from manufacturing to finance to transportation and distribution. Several consequences of this evolution should be noted:

- While diversification appears to have improved insulation from cyclical downturns, it has also tempered the benefits of the recovery in manufacturing.

- A former tenet of regional economic theory held that the primary determinant of a region's economic base is the production sector (manufacturing, mining, or agriculture), which provides goods to export and a derived demand for services. Most economists now recognize that thriving financial and trade sectors can also provide a stimulus for employment growth in other sectors.

- The economic restructuring has led many planners and business leaders to overestimate Chicago's insulation from future downturns in manufacturing. The area's service industries are still largely tied to the performance of manufacturing industries in Chicago and the Great Lakes Region.

Manufacturing

Local manufacturing remains concentrated in printing and publishing, chemicals, fabricated metals, electrical equipment, instruments, and food processing. Local development groups have formulated plans to retain and attract these target industries by accentuating the competitive advantages of Chicago: a growing business service sector, an expanding transportation infrastructure, and affordable housing for workers.

Chicago is not as heavily concentrated in automobile manufacturing as its Midwest neighbors, but the weakness in this industry is likely to take a toll on production of related capital goods, a local mainstay. Chicago is also far less dependent on the defense industry than the production sectors of the two coasts; the area should thus be insulated from the repercussions of defense cuts felt elsewhere.

Chicago's economy is closely linked to the trade-sensitive industries of the Great Lakes region. After enduring the wave of import substitution during the dollar's strength in the early 1980s, the region's firms are now acquiring market share abroad. Although the world seems to be realizing that the U.S. is not the only place where food can be grown, the commodities markets will continue to provide a source of export expansion. U.S. exports improved as the dollar declined, but its recent strength indicates that the U.S. trade deficit may deteriorate by up to $1 billion per quarter in 1990, according to economists at the First National Bank of Chicago.

The Free Trade agreement with Canada should have a positive impact, since most trade with our northern neighbor flows directly south. However, it has been suggested that the upper Midwest may have less of a comparative advantage than the South since the region's agricultural and industrial production is so similar to that of Canada. The Midwest is also at a disadvantage in trade with other areas, particularly the Pacific Rim, since less expertise has been necessary in dealing with Canada, and transportation costs are higher than on the coasts.

Financial Services

The city's financial sphere is dominated by the four exchanges: Chicago Board of Trade, Chicago Mercantile Exchange, Chicago Board of Options Exchange, and Midwest Stock Exchange. The Commercial Club of Chicago reported in 1988 that the exchanges provide $4 billion on deposit in local banks, $1 billion in annual expenditures on goods and services, and over local 100,000 jobs. Exchange-related legal billings (estimated at $30 million in 1986) and accounting fees ($40 million) have continued to grow.

Recently, however, the Board of Trade and the Merc, the two commodity futures exchanges, have been wracked by a government investigation of trading practices that may have cheated customers out of millions of dollars. Potential abuses of dual trading, in which a pit broker executes trades simultaneously for customers and his own account, had long been recognized, but were tolerated in order to maintain high trading volumes at the two exchanges. Undercover FBI agents working in the pits for two years have gathered evidence of shady dealings and 46 traders have been indicted so far. A likely outcome of the inquiry is increased regulation, which would constrain the operation of the formerly free-wheeling exchanges.

The investigation and possible reform comes at a critical time, just as the Chicago exchanges fight to maintain their share of the increasingly competitive futures and options market. Still relying on the colorful but corruption-prone open outcry system, Chicago exchanges are facing stiff competition from foreign exchanges using computerized trading. With the new technology, commodities and financial instruments can be traded 24 hours a day from anywhere in the world. The rapid growth of the foreign exchanges demonstrates that they can efficiently handle large volumes of transactions. Hoping to stem the erosion of their competitive advantage in trade volume, Chicago exchanges are forming joint ventures with firms such as Reuters Holdings to develop their own electronic trading systems.

Chicago retained its share of corporate headquarters (an estimated 46 Fortune 500 industrial corporations and 31 Fortune 500 service corporations) even after production facilities left the area. Borg-Warner, Amoco, and Beatrice are among the major firms that remain. Management consulting, accounting, advertising, and public relations, the attendant or allied services to these headquarters operations, are thriving. This consolidation as a regional service center began in the late 1970s, and has become even more visible in the 1980s. A few firms are even exporting services to other regions.

Financial and business service firms claim to have no trouble recruiting young professionals, particularly those who were educated locally, to work in the Chicago area. The high quality of life and relatively low costs are cited as reasons for this attraction.

Relocation opportunities have been limited by financial sector constraints, however. For its size, little banking is being done in Chicago. Most financing of projects still originates on the East Coast since many perceive that the big money is in New York and that the local banks are too small to bear risk. The major investment banks have a presence in Chicago, but their branches are small.

MAJOR FINANCIAL CENTERS IN THE U.S.

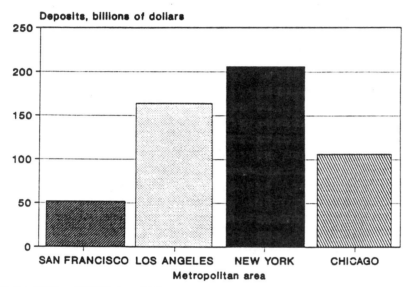

Source: FDIC and FSLIC, June 1988

Nevertheless, commercial banks such as Manufacturers Hanover and Citicorp are expanding operations in the city to capitalize on growing demand for retail banking services. After helping to finance construction of the elevated train system and Midwest railroads in the late nineteenth century, the New York banking firm that became Citicorp played an indirect role in Chicago until opening its first local office in 1981. With the purchase of ailing First Federal Savings and Loan of Chicago in January 1984, Citicorp accelerated the pace of its expansion into the market. Now, with a work force of nearly 3,000 in 30 subsidiaries, Citicorp is the third largest financial services employer in the city.

Japanese banks are beginning to penetrate the Chicago market. Between 1986 and 1988, six of the seven foreign-bank branches opened in the city's financial district were Japanese, including one trust bank with the power to act as a stock transfer and stock dividend agent. Many Japanese firms such as Canon, Mitsubishi, and Sony have established operations in Chicago, and the banks have followed to serve them. Japanese banks are also interested in capturing the business of the many large U.S. corporations headquartered in Chicago. The city's futures and options markets, extensive transportation infrastructure, and reputation as a regional financial center have been attractive factors in the location decision.

The federal bail-out at Continental Illinois Bank was unable to preserve thousands of banking jobs. Both Continental and First Chicago were hurt by foreign loan defaults and untimely oil-related investments, but have since developed topnotch appraisal and diversification policies. First Chicago is now competing on a national scale. Local banks are becoming more aggressive and taking on the risk of larger deals; more construction loans and interim financing are being originated locally.

Without a major money center bank, Chicago remains a regional rather than a national or international financial center. First Chicago and Continental are making a comeback in the region, but have failed to fully penetrate national and international financial markets. Nevertheless, many local financial professionals feel that a regional focus may be adequate for maintaining financial services expansion. The managing partner of one Chicago-based investment bank considers regional to be anything outside of New York, although this may only be a rationalization for Chicago's third place status behind New York and Los Angeles. Over the last four quarters, sluggish financial services employment growth of 0.8 percent, lagging the national rate of 2.0 percent, indicates that business opportunities are developing more slowly than might be desirable.

As local possibilities dwindle, attendant service firms are feeling an urgency to attract new business beyond regional borders. A Chicago advertising agency determined that over two-thirds of the city's top 150 companies either use in-house agencies or have little or no advertising budget; half of those remaining are clients of out-of-town or specialized agencies. New billings have failed to keep pace with the loss of many national advertising accounts, prompting layoffs and resignations among agency employees. According to an industry executive, Chicago firms are "offering 1970s advertising to answer 1990s marketing problems." (Advertising Age, July 25, 1988) In advertising, as with all business services, Chicago firms must gain a competitive edge in national and increasingly global markets.

Distribution Services

Chicago's central location and easy access to agricultural areas through vast transportation networks have made it a national center for distribution operations. The area's role as a transportation hub has also been an important source of local employment. Wholesale trade industries employ over 250,000 workers in the Chicago PMSA. In addition to wholesale trade, employment in the air transportation, trucking, and warehousing industries totals over 85,000. The number of jobs in each of these industries as a share of all Chicago employment is well above the U.S. share.

Since a significant amount of the region's cargo is transported by truck, maintaining and improving Chicago's extensive network of interstate, state, and local highways is essential to prevent the trucking industry from migrating to another city. To relieve traffic on the Tri-State Tollway (Interstate 294), the major north-south artery in the metropolitan area, Highway 53 is being extended south beyond the East-West Tollway (Interstate 88) to as far as Interstate 55 in Bolingbrook. In Spring 1989, the 2010 Transportation System Plan recommended several other projects to improve the area's highway system, but warned that even under cautiously optimistic funding scenarios, resources would be inadequate for maintaining the current system.

Tourism

As the largest city of an historic and centrally located state, Chicago attracts many visitors throughout the year. Annual expenditures from business and pleasure visitors were estimated at over $5 billion in 1987. In 1986, 83,000 tourists, including 14,000 foreigners, visited the exchanges. Hosting over 900 major conventions, trade shows, and fairs each year has earned Chicago a reputation as the convention and trade show capital of the U.S. With 1.6 million square feet, McCormick Place is the largest temporary exhibition center in North America. In mid-August 1989, the center easily housed the National Hardware Show, the largest trade show in the U.S., with exhibit space totalling 790,000 square feet, the size of seventeen football fields. The O'Hare Expo Center in Rosemont has 500,000 square feet of display space. The Chicago Convention and Visitors Bureau has recorded continuous increases in the number of conventions, trade shows, and meetings held in the area since 1985. To meet the demand, city hotels are planning to add nearly 5,000 rooms to the current stock of 18,400 by 1991. As many as 11,000 rooms may also be added in the suburbs.

Prospects For Future Economic Growth

When considering the outlook for future economic growth, it is critical to keep in mind Chicago's role as the provider of business, financial, and distribution services to the Great Lakes Region. If the Midwest manufacturers slip into a recession, Chicago's high-flying services firms will also suffer. In the current environment of slow national economic growth, there are signs that Chicago's economy is weakening. Over the first half of 1989, employment in the six-county Chicago metropolitan area grew at a mere 0.9 percent annual rate, compared with a national rate of 2.9 percent. Gains in industrial production have leveled off and improvements in U.S. export activity have diminished. If the dollar remains stable and the Fed guides the economy to a soft landing in 1990, we expect that the Chicago economy will grow at a modest pace, well below its performance over the last two years.

In the long term, there are few scenarios in which the Chicago economy can expand at rates approaching those of the last six years. During this recovery, Chicago managed to bring its jobless rate down to the national level. When unemployment is low, rapid economic growth requires steady additions to the labor force. In order to generate these gains, Chicago must draw workers from other areas by offering superior employment and income opportunities. This will happen only if the Great Lakes Region can reverse decades of below-average economic growth, or if Chicago can expand beyond a regional center into a national center of economic activity.

Average Annual Employment Change - Chicago PMSA
(Thousands of Jobs)

	History		Level in	Forecast	
	5-Year	2-Year	1989:2	2-Year	5-Year
Nonmanufacturing					
JHPI	77.0	59.1	2588.9	28.0	34.2
DRI	77.0	59.1	2588.9	33.1	31.4
WEFA	77.0	59.1	2588.9	34.5	40.6
Manufacturing					
JHPI	-5.8	6.7	566.5	-6.9	-5.9
DRI	-5.8	6.7	566.5	-6.0	-3.7
WEFA	-5.8	6.7	566.5	-0.4	-1.0

POLITICAL ENVIRONMENT

Mayor Richard M. Daley is viewed as a mover by business and real estate professionals. He has acquired a good background as a state senator and Cook County prosecutor, and has worked quickly to change the city's image as a political machine. Where unqualified appointees once held responsible offices, experienced candidates are now chosen. Back taxes and water revenue are being collected to expand the city's financial resources. Even Mayor Daley's backers are surprised at how quickly he is moving to develop task forces of local business leaders, but he has much to prove in a short time. Having been elected to serve out late Mayor Washington's term, Daley's first bid for re-election comes in April 1991.

Education

While still Secretary of Education in 1987, William Bennett rated Chicago's public school system as the nation's worst, with a dropout rate of 45 percent and average test scores at many schools in the bottom one percent in the U.S. Chicago has the lowest level of public education in the nation and Illinois education expenditures per capita rank 46th in the nation. Education is universally believed to be a major deterrent to relocations by corporations and families; some even claimed that the Sears move was prompted by the low literacy level of the downtown labor force. Attempts at redevelopment through Enterprise Zones may be hindered by residents who are underqualified for back-office jobs in business services.

The poor quality of public education is at the top of the mayor's agenda. The magnet school plan has helped some students, but many others have applied and are waiting to be placed on the priority lists. In order to break up the omnipotent central bureaucracy that many believed was crippling the schools, Chicago has instituted a radical decentralized system. Each school will be run by a council of six parents, two community residents, and two teachers with the authority to approve budgets, recommend curricula, and dismiss formerly tenured principals. While there is a risk that the councils will become the domain of individuals with little experience as educators, they provide a way to ensure the involvement of those with the greatest stake in the schools.

Yet the Chicago metropolitan area is a center for higher education, with the University of Chicago, Northwestern University, DePaul University, Loyola University, Illinois Institute of Technology, and the Chicago campus of the

University of Illinois all within its boundaries. The area has been home to many pioneering scientists, including the University of Chicago physicists who performed the experiment that produced the world's first controlled nuclear reaction. Now the Fermi National Accelerator Laboratory and Argonne National Laboratory provide an incubator for future breakthroughs.

Racial Concerns

Considered the most segregated city in the U.S., Chicago is still plagued by the perception that racial tensions are strong. West and South Side neighborhoods look worse than ever, illustrating that many residents have failed to share in the recovery. Prospects for ameliorating the situation may not improve with Daley as mayor. Political fragmentation remains a problem in Chicago.

Economic Development

Differential rates of growth in the greater Chicago area have led to what has been called a "dumbbell economy," with rapid growth in the Loop and suburbs matched by declines in the city's neighborhoods. In fact, suburban development has historically taken growth away from the downtown. In particular, DuPage County to the west is one of the fastest growing counties in the country. The county government is noted for its conservative stance on taxation, zoning, and provision of services, particularly low-cost housing. DuPage County introduced development impact fees in 1989 under a statewide enabling law, so other counties may follow suit. Revenue on the fees, which range from $600 for a single-family house to nearly $7,000 per 1,000 square feet for a busy retail establishment, have been earmarked for transportation. Naperville is currently booming, but the effects of impact fees and other growth restrictions on the horizon have yet to be seen.

As the slow- or no-growth sentiment continues to take hold of community groups and local governments, the development outlook nationwide will become more tightly controlled, according to a survey of real estate journalists conducted earlier this year by the National Association of Real Estate Editors. George Arquilla III, president of the Home Builders Association of Greater Chicago, believes that "the number one issue in our region is impact fees and the growth versus no-growth debate." (Chicago Tribune, February 12, 1989)

The more affordable areas near Joliet in Will County are expected to benefit from growth controls in DuPage County. The expansion of a transportation infrastructure in the southwest has permitted the development of this area, the last of the greater Chicago submarkets to take off. The new Interstate 55 corridor and commuter rail line to Midway Airport have boosted land prices from $20,000 per acre in 1985 to $80,000 in 1989. Office complexes are being built with forest preserves, golf, and other recreational amenities nearby. Burr Ridge and Hinsdale are joining Naperville as good addresses.

As suburban rents rise and out-of-city commutes become more difficult, firms are looking for alternatives to the northern, western, and, more recently, southwestern drift that has taken place. In response, the city is trying to clean up its act. Already known for the entertainment value of its retail areas, museums, and sports franchises, Chicago is becoming more accessible and safe for workers who are moving into the city to live. Neighborhood festivals, the legacy of former mayor Jane Byrne, run throughout the year and exhibit the rich cultural mix in the city. Chicago hopes to capitalize on its reputation as an "open, burly, and friendly" city.

Incentive programs such as enterprise zones and tax increment financing have been established in urban neighborhoods to encourage area banks to locate back office operations there. Yet the effectiveness of these programs may be limited by high illiteracy rates among the labor force. In a widely publicized maneuver, the Illinois General Assembly passed legislation to loosen restrictions on these incentive programs originally intended for blighted urban areas. Communities with at least 320 acres of contiguous vacant land need only demonstrate that proposed developments would bring private investment of $100 million and 2,000 jobs to qualify for tax increment financing. Applications for the tax subsidies need no longer prove that the development would not occur without the incentives.

The legislation was amended to lure Sears into staying in the Chicago area after the sale of the Sears Tower. In addition to an incentive package of $61 million from the state, Sears received 786 acres of land that will be acquired with tax-exempt bonds. Of the estimated $11 million in annual taxes over twenty years, 80 percent will be applied to retiring the bonds. Critics claim that Hoffman Estates, the prosperous northwestern suburb chosen for the relocation, can hardly be considered blighted and that tax increment financing should be reserved for the needy inner city. Proponents of the deal counter that the departure of Sears, the state's largest private employer, would have cut $400 million in salaries, $19 million in taxes, and as many as 7,600 jobs.

Few would argue that the state and city have worked aggressively to keep the corporations already headquartered in the city and to encourage the relocation of new firms. Representatives of Southern cities and even Mayor Ed Koch of New York have made raids on Chicago. Some feel that since Governor Thompson has already announced that he will not run again, he is no more politically motivated to take action than are the political appointees in development positions who "don't take the job seriously." The atmosphere has changed since Mayor Daley brought in Joe James as the Commissioner for Economic Development. With experience in Austin and Philadelphia, the new commissioner has quickly changed the style of development to be more proactive and to focus on retention, since existing business generates 80 to 85 percent of growth. Retention teams comprised of representatives from major corporations and utilities have been formed to make trade missions and open offices overseas.

Transportation Infrastructure

Growth discrepancies could be addressed with the location of a third airport in one of the weaker neighborhoods. The mayor has recommended the south side of the city, but this site is unlikely to be chosen since there is not enough open acreage available to build even a small airport. Sites farther south, some on the Illinois state line and some in Indiana, are being given more serious consideration.

It has been recommended that the third airport be restricted to air freight and cargo usage, as in the successful Fort Worth, Texas airport. Distribution services continue to play a major role in the Chicago economy, while passenger traffic out of busy O'Hare Airport is showing signs of reversing its trend of rapid growth. Passenger volume during the first quarter of 1989 was over seven percent lower than the same period last year. In contrast, Midway Airport reported an increase of 28 percent. For the two airports, passenger volume was four percent lower than in 1988. These declines may indicate a response to higher fares rather than any long-term trend, since traffic was only slightly up in Dallas-Fort Worth and down ten percent in Atlanta, two comparable hub airports.

Congestion, already a major problem on the West and East Coasts, is becoming a constraint in Chicago. While short and hassle-free by coastal standards, commutes are getting

longer and becoming more of a factor in the location
decisions of individuals and businesses. The commuter lines
and elevated rail (known as the "El") are adequate on the
north shore. The El was recently extended to O'Hare and
construction through the southwest part of the city to
Midway Airport is ongoing. However, the interstates to the
west and south move slowly throughout the day; what was once
a 45-minute commute can stretch to two hours during rush
hour. A growing number of commutes lie entirely in the
suburbs rather than between residential areas and the
downtown. Municipalities cannot solve their congestion
problems alone; a consolidated approach is needed.

Taxes

Real estate taxes, as a percent of gross rent, are among the
highest in the U.S. Tax assessments are controlled by the
County Assessor. Until the early 1970s, appraisals were
based on standard depreciation rates for similar properties.
Since the mid-1970s, when assessors began to consider sales
price, their assessments have been closer to fair market
value. In Cook County, assessments must be 38 percent of a
commercial property's fair market value by law, down from a
high of 40 percent. In contrast, single-family homes and
multifamily buildings with no more than six units are
assessed at only 16 percent, while multifamily with seven or
more units are assessed at 33 percent.

By state law, each county must be assessed in aggregate at
one-third of fair market value. Since the valuation of
single-family homes varies widely, particularly among older
homes, an equalization factor of nearly two must be applied
to all properties to reach the 33 percent community
assessment. These valuation discrepancies have encouraged a
booming business in tax appeal litigation, and the community
assessment law has proved to be unpopular with county
governments.

Under the current system, rates are held steady, so
reassessment is the only way to raise tax receipts. Local
government has alternative sources of revenue, such as
uncollected water taxes and parking and traffic violations,
or even imposing a city income tax. More farfetched
proposals such as river gambling and a casino on Navy Pier
have also been contemplated. Yet real estate is considered
the easiest way to generate revenue quickly. With
reassessments, higher rates, and a larger multiplier, the
total billed property taxes in Cook County increased 12.5
percent in 1989.

To ward off impending budget shortfalls for schools and other public services, the frequency of reassessments is being accelerated from quadrennial to triennial. Property owners fear that more frequent reassessments will boost tax payments. In fact, this year's assessments on Chicago's North Side increased by an average of 30 percent. Political pressure is mounting to hold assessments down and to raise revenue more equitably through higher tax rates.

In spite of the protests, the State of Illinois spends a meager one percent of revenue on administration of the tax system. The national average allotment for administering property tax collections is four percent.

Zoning

With abundant land and prime sites for redevelopment, Chicago is not as constrained for space as other cities. Meeting zoning requirements still involves knowing lawyers and "greasing the right wheel," but zoning is not a critical issue. It was claimed that the government's laissez-faire attitude towards zoning has forced developers to become more educated about the interaction of supply and demand; they ask "Should we?" rather than "Can we?" when the free market is allowed to work. Responding to recent increases in downtown office vacancy rates, one observer explained that new office construction is outpacing absorption because of the availability of financing; "as long as the money is out there and developers are willing to use it, they are going to build more buildings [than we need]." (Chicago Tribune, July 4, 1989)

To avert a steady deterioration of real estate markets both downtown and in the suburbs, construction lending requirements are becoming tougher. Investors demand that a larger percentage (up to 40 from close to zero percent) be pre-leased before financing. Postures such as that of one local developer who claimed that "pre-leasing is for sissies" are quickly being modified. However, many buildings are still being completed with 60 percent of space to fill.

REAL ESTATE MARKETS

Office Market

There are six principal office submarkets:
- Downtown: West Loop, Central Loop, East Loop, North Michigan Avenue, River North. Stock of 110 million square feet.
- East/West Corridor: Oak Brook, Downers Grove, Naperville, Aurora. Stock of 26 million square feet.
- Northwest: Schaumburg, Arlington Heights, Rolling Meadows, Itasca, Hoffman Estates, Palatine, Buffalo Grove, Elgin. Stock of 20 million square feet.
- North: Edens/Tri-State Corridor, Deerfield, Lake County. Stock of 13 million square feet.
- O'Hare: Rosemont, Schiller Park, Park Ridge, Des Plaines. Stock of 12 million square feet.
- South: Hinsdale, Burr Ridge, Bolingbrook, Joliet.

The downtown office market is stabilizing from the rollover of leases in 1984 to 1986 just as over eight million square feet of new space came on line. Many tenants traded up, badly hurting the low-end, and signed ten-year leases to take advantage of the concessions. Net effective rents in Class A properties range from $10 to $20 per square foot, with expenses and taxes ranging from $11 to $15 per square foot. Concessions, including 12 to 18 months of free rent on a ten-year lease and tenant improvement allowances of $30 to $40 per square foot, trim base rents by 25 to 35 percent. The Chicago market shares its psychology with other reasonably healthy markets: since development financing often requires a minimum base rent, landlords prefer to keep base rents high and compete for tenants with more attractive concession packages. When the market tightens, landlords have more flexibility to reduce the concessions than to raise the base rent in existing leases. In effect, the ubiquitous concessions become part of the rent.

The Building Owners and Managers Association of Chicago (BOMA/Chicago) recently surveyed the management of 330 buildings accounting for 107.5 million square feet, or 95 percent, of the central business district office market. As 4.0 million square feet of space came on line between October 1988 and May 1989, 3.4 million square feet in the last six months alone, only 1.5 million square feet were absorbed. For six years through Spring 1988, absorption had averaged around three million square feet annually. The rate of leased and occupied space declined 1.5 percentage points from 87 percent, pushing the vacancy rate to 14.5 percent. The survey also reported that 7.5 million square feet of new office space will be completed by 1991. With the relocation of the Sears Merchandise Group leaving two million square feet vacant in the Sears Tower, occupancy rates are likely to deteriorate even further if the pace of absorption does not accelerate.

Other surveys report more favorable conditions because they use less restrictive definitions of occupancy, including space that is leased but vacant (tenant still holds lease but has moved out) and space that is vacant but leased (tenant has yet to move in but has signed lease). Coldwell Banker reports a downtown office vacancy of 11.0 percent in June 1989, up only slightly from 10.9 percent in March 1989. Frain Camins & Swartchild finds 13.1 percent vacancy in an existing stock of 104.5 million square feet.

In 1990, one-quarter of downtown lease contracts will expire into what is likely to still be a tenant's market of aggressive leasing. In the mid-1990s, an even larger number of leases signed during the mid-1980s building boom will be up for renewal. Meanwhile, demand for office space is still growing as law and accounting firms, local insurance companies, and other business service firms expand. Brokers are beginning to wonder how much longer the demand growth will continue.

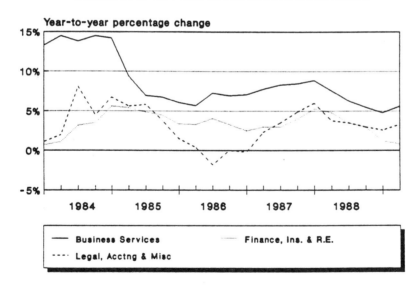

CHICAGO PMSA EMPLOYMENT GROWTH
SELECTED OFFICE INTENSIVE INDUSTRIES

Source: Bureau of Labor Statistics

Japanese investors entered the downtown office market in late 1985, long after they had begun to play a major role in coastal real estate markets. By 1988, they had participated in transactions involving roughly ten percent of the office market, two major hotels, and a highly visible mixed-use project. Major institutional players have been life insurance, private real estate, finance, and trust companies, and banks. A preference has been demonstrated for large transactions in the $100 million range with potential for economies of scale in management. Buildings must also be of high quality with a strong tenant mix. As the Japanese become more comfortable with the Chicago market, the pace of investment is likely to accelerate. Most observers believed that Japanese firms would be involved in the Sears Tower sale, either to provide long-term financing for the acquisition or to take an ownership interest, but the Japanese Ministry of Finance encouraged investors to stay out of the bidding to mitigate concerns that they are "buying up America."

Chicago is the city of master planner Daniel Burnham, who urged future builders to "make no little plans." Following his advice, developers Lee Miglin and J. Paul Beitler are planning a 1,914-foot skyscraper that would rise 15 stories above the Sears Tower, currently the world's tallest building. David Sharpe of the Illinois Institute of Technology in Chicago claims that the proposed skyscraper manifests the "bigger, taller, wider, deeper kind of syndrome. Chicagoans don't want just a convention center -- they want the world's biggest convention center. They don't want just a building -- they want the world's tallest building." (New York Times, June 4, 1989)

Breaking away from Chicago's tradition of big and brawny skyscrapers, architect Cesar Pelli designed the building with graduated tiers, prompting Robert Bruegmann of the University of Illinois at Chicago to call it "a romantic spire capping the skyline." With only 10,000 to 18,000 square feet on each floor of the 1.2-million-square-foot skyscraper, it should attract smaller tenants than those usually found in trophy buildings. Estimating its cost to be $300 to $400 million, the developers hope that their project will be easier to finance and market than the Sears Tower only three blocks away. The building, known as Madison Plaza II, has already received zoning approval and should be ready for occupancy in 1993 or 1994.

The East/West Corridor, the largest suburban market at 26 million square feet, has grown from less than ten million square feet in 1981. Over two million square feet were absorbed in 1988, bringing vacancy down to 17.7 percent from 20.5 percent in 1987. (Coldwell Banker, <u>Chicago</u> <u>1989</u>, <u>The</u> <u>Commercial</u> <u>Real</u> <u>Estate</u> <u>Market</u>) The area's residential neighborhoods provide an indigenous labor force that office developers find attractive. This market may see rent inflation as the DuPage County transportation impact fee takes effect.

Healthy absorption of 1.4 million square feet in the Northwest suburbs brought vacancy below 20 percent for the first time in two years. Already more overbuilt than any other suburban market, much more supply is likely to be added over the next several years, dominated by the Sears-backed development in Hoffman Estates. Concessions of 30 percent are restricting returns, particularly among Class B buildings.

In the North market, vacancy also declined from 18.9 percent in 1987 to 16.8 percent in 1988, as only 510,000 square feet came on line. Builders have fled to Lake County to escape from high Cook County taxes, but plans for a county-wide impact fee may make the North market less attractive.

O'Hare has become the tightest suburban market, with vacancy at 15.9 percent in 1988, down from 21.7 percent in 1987. As fewer developable sites remain, concession packages are shrinking relative to other areas. Rehabilitation is supplanting new construction as a source of office space, especially for larger tenants.

As residential development moves south, a few pioneers are locating office buildings there. Still in its infancy, the South suburban area has yet to be recognized as a major office submarket.

In the six-county metropolitan area, JHPI expects completions of new office buildings to taper off from their heady pace of 15 million square feet annually between 1986 and 1988. Additions to the office stock should average 9.3 million square feet over the next four years.

OFFICE COMPLETIONS
Chicago SMSA

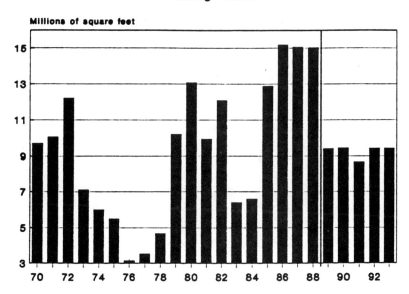

In the face of this relatively restrained supply behavior, demand is expected to slow dramatically. The rebound in services employment has run its course, and growth in this sector is likely to stabilize at a moderate rate. Through 1993, average annual gains of only 37,000 in nonmanufacturing employment are expected.

NON-MANUFACTURING EMPLOYMENT, ANNUAL CHANGE
Chicago SMSA

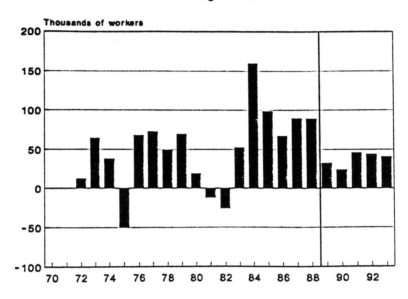

Chicago office returns have historically trailed the national average, achieving much lower rates in the heyday of the late 1970s than other metropolitan markets. During the building boom of the late 1980s, when pent-up office demand needed to be satisfied, the rate of return climbed above the national average for the first time in a decade. This upward trend should continue through early 1990, before reversing into a more rapid descent than will be experienced nationally as supply outpaces demand. Returns will level off in 1992 at around two percentage points below the U.S. rate.

OFFICE MARKET ANNUAL RETURNS

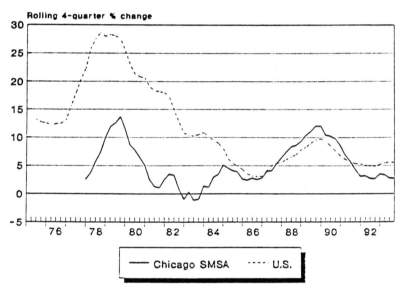

John Hancock Properties, Inc. (October 1989)
The JHREMI-Return represents the annualized total nominal return that a market may provide over history and through the forecast period, based on supply and demand.

A comparison of returns by county indicates the relative performance of the office submarkets. By far, the largest share of office space is in Cook county, so returns closely mirror the metropolitan area. Office properties in rapidly growing DuPage County had outperformed those in high-tax Cook County in the first half of the 1980s, as supply barely kept up with phenomenal demand growth. From 1985 to 1987, developers rushed in to capitalize on the opportunities and added nearly 13 million square feet just as demand was waning. Office returns in DuPage County have since demonstrated the consequences of overbuilding. With nonmanufacturing employment growth tapering off over the forecast period, returns are unlikely to recover soon.

OFFICE MARKET ANNUAL RETURNS

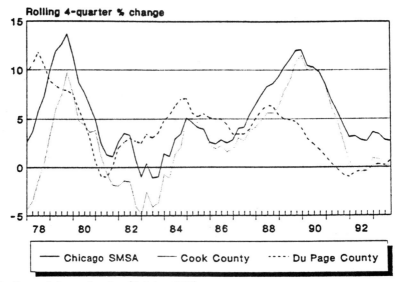

John Hancock Properties, Inc. (October 1989)
The JHREMI-Return represents the annualized total nominal return that a market may provide over history and through the forecast period, based on supply and demand.

Industrial Market

The greater Chicago industrial market has been enjoying a boom over the past four years. Institutional investors have discovered that Midwest industrial properties, which were considered unattractive five or six years ago, now add extremely desirable diversification benefits to their portfolios. With a record 36 million square feet of absorption in 1988 boosting lease rates and sale prices a dramatic 20 percent over 1987, Chicago has come to be considered one of the most robust industrial markets in the U.S.

The competition between owner-users and institutional investors has encouraged many potential sellers to hold onto properties until prices rise even further. Both buyers and sellers are eager, but have reached a stalemate.

Recent evidence indicates that the industrial market may already have peaked, however. Nearly 40 million square feet of space became available during 1988, pushing industrial vacancy to 7.7 percent from 7.3 percent in 1987. Even in the "healthy" Chicago industrial market, some submarkets have experienced falling rental rates and limited concessions are starting to appear.

Industrial submarkets mirror the location of suburban office development. The O'Hare market has historically been the most active. Because the airport handles more air freight tonnage than any other in the U.S., most of the area near O'Hare is distribution space. Land prices are climbing, to $15 to $20 per square foot in Rosemont, for example. As the supply of new buildable sites dwindles, more properties will be obtained through rehabilitation and in-fill; environmental issues may become a factor as old industrial space is redeveloped.

With the extension of the Northwest Tollway to Elgin, interest is growing in Elk Grove, Bensenville, and Wood Dale, neighbors to the northwest of the airport. Kensington, the prototypical industrial park, is in Mount Prospect. Buffalo Grove, on the border of Lake County, is the northern frontier of the Northwest market. Rents range from $2.30 to $3.00 per square foot in Cook County and $3.25 in DuPage County.

Developable sites are abundant in Lake County, but there are not enough people to work in industrial settings. Land prices range between $3.75 and $4.50, with shell rents at $4.25. The typical product in the North market is relatively small, with 30,000 to 60,000 square feet, one-third office finish, 140-foot turning radius, and an interior loading dock protected from harsh winter weather.

South of the city in Cicero, Berwyn, Bedford Park, and Alsip, older in-fill space dominates the industrial market. Land prices are low for redevelopment, but the area is subject to Cook County taxes, which are 30 to 50 percent higher than in either DuPage or Lake counties. At around $2.50 per square foot, net rental rates are subsequently lower than in other submarkets. Along the Interstate 55 corridor to the southwest, developers are taking advantage of an abundant supply of land and easy access to major distribution networks. Lemont, near the Argonne National Laboratory, is the site of substantial additions to the inventory of distribution space. Further into Will County, tax advantages furnish an extra spark for development.

Along the East/West Tollway, major developers are building industrial parks between Aurora and Naperville, where land is $3.00 and rent is $4.00 per square foot. Office finish in this market ranges from five to thirty percent. Further north, West Chicago has a reputation as a major distribution center derived from the days of the railroads. Since nearby Highway 59 has frequent traffic lights and only two lanes, rent is merely $3.00 per square foot, inviting the location of large warehousing facilities.

Builders of industrial space have gradually responded to improving market conditions over the second half of the 1980s. Additions to industrial inventory have stepped up from 2.5 million square feet in 1983 to nearly 7.3 million square feet in 1988, and will continue to climb through 1990. Supply will then stabilize at less than seven million square feet per year through the end of the forecast.

INDUSTRIAL COMPLETIONS
Chicago SMSA

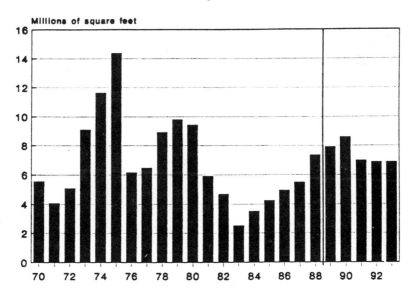

Growth in the industrial work force fails to represent the
forces driving the Chicago warehouse boom, since much of the
demand has been derived from institutional investors rather
than end-users of industrial product. In the longer term,
however, owners of industrial stock require a steady influx
of potential tenants to generate revenue. Chicago's
production sector was badly hit by the last recession, and
has since secured more insulation from cyclical downturns.
Manufacturing and trade employment experienced healthy gains
in 1987 and 1988, but has still failed to recoup the losses
of the 1982 recession. Over the forecast, the production
sector is expected to continue its gradual erosion, with
declines offsetting modest increases.

POTENTIAL INDUSTRIAL OCCUPANTS, ANNUAL CHANGE
Chicago SMSA

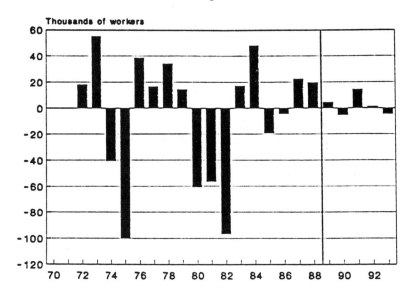

Reflecting highly cyclical industrial demand, returns have historically demonstrated more volatility than the U.S. average. Continued additions to supply in the face of weakening demand should hold industrial market returns below the national rate through the end of the forecast.

INDUSTRIAL MARKET ANNUAL RETURNS

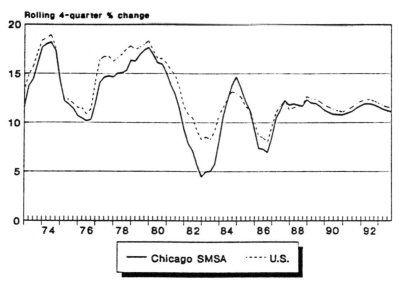

John Hancock Properties, Inc. (October 1989)
The JHREMI-Return represents the annualized total nominal return that a market may provide over history and through the forecast period, based on supply and demand.

A comparison of industrial submarkets suggests that the smaller, more rapidly growing counties have exhibited the strongest returns since 1980. DuPage County has clearly performed robustly, both on a mean and risk-adjusted basis. With returns never dipping below 12 percent, this industrial submarket weathered the 1982 slump far better than either the six-county metropolitan area or the U.S. Industrial returns in Lake County experience turning points earlier than the rest of the Chicago market. Returns in this submarket are currently two percentage points higher than in the metropolitan area. Both of these counties continue to outperform the six-county area over the forecast. Aside from a more moderate decline during the last recession, Kane County has closely tracked the SMSA market. Will County, on the other hand, was clobbered by job losses in 1986 and has been slow to recover. The outlook for this submarket is subject to the most uncertainty, bringing risk-adjusted returns down to nine percent.

Industrial JHREMI Returns - History and Forecast

| | 1980-89:2 | | 1989:3-91:2 | | 1989:3-94:2 | |
	Mean	Risk-adj	Mean	Risk-adj	Mean	Risk-adj
Chicago SMSA	10.8%	10.8%	11.2%	9.0%	11.4%	9.2%
Cook County	9.5	10.5	11.1	8.7	11.2	8.8
DuPage County	12.8	11.7	11.4	9.5	11.7	9.9
Kane County	10.8	10.8	11.5	9.3	11.3	9.4
Lake County	11.9	11.3	11.3	9.4	11.4	9.6
Will County	10.5	10.7	11.6	9.0	11.2	9.0
U.S.	11.9	11.2	11.6	9.5	11.8	9.7

Apartment Market

The Chicago apartment market survived a watershed year in 1987. The Tax Reform Act of 1986 eliminated tax-exempt financing, a crucial motive for investment in multifamily housing. Nationally, permits for the construction of apartment buildings dropped by nearly one-half in 1988. More specific to Chicago, Cook County's quadrennial reassessments of 1987 hiked property taxes for some owners by as much as 200 percent. Property values and income plummeted. Demand was feeble and vacancy was high, reducing the capacity to pass the charges on to tenants through increased rents. To attract tenants in this weak market, some owners were compelled to market more aggressively, offering concessions such as free rent and interior upgrades just as in the office market.

The multifamily housing market soon recovered from these impacts, however. Investors looked for alternatives to the stock market after Black Monday. Despite the loss of tax incentives, investing in the apartment market was judged to yield relatively stable and predictable returns. The supply glut in the suburban office market also limited opportunities for institutional investors. Many entered the apartment market, seeking properties with conversion potential.

Snapshot demographics for the multifamily housing market are exceptional. The population of the eight-county consolidated metropolitan area is young: according to the 1986 Current Population Survey, 32.1 percent are under the age of 35, compared with 29.3 percent nationally. Nearly thirty percent of all downtown dwellers are single, six percentage points above the U.S. average. The population of the metropolitan area is particularly well educated and affluent; 15.6 percent of Chicago residents have college degrees and 18.4 percent of households have annual income exceeding $50,000, compared with national averages of 11.8 percent and 14.7 percent, respectively. Unfortunately, demographic dynamics have been less favorable. Population growth has been sluggish, averaging only 0.5 percent annually between 1983 and 1988, and lagging even the slow national rate of 1.0 percent.

While there is little potential for a wholesale expansion of the apartment market, some niche markets deserve attention. After a period of little expansion during the wave of condominium conversions in the late 1970s and early 1980s, the downtown multifamily housing market is gaining momentum. Among affluent empty-nesters, a propensity to move in from the suburbs has boosted demand for luxury units. The number of Loop residents has grown to 100,000 from 25,000 ten years ago. The development of this market may be constrained by the poor quality of urban schools, however. Despite the many advantages of living in the central city, it may be less attractive to households with children.

The Near North area is predominantly residential and its properties are of high quality. Nevertheless, the poor school system restricts demand in this area as well. With the availability of affordable single-family housing in suburbs with higher standards of public education, families are reluctant to compromise on education for location.

Aside from shortages in northwest Indiana, the suburban Chicago residential market is currently in balance, with plenty of available and affordable housing. Even Hoffman Estates, the destination of the proposed relocation of over 5,000 Sears Merchandise Group employees, has an adequate stock of rental apartments. Allstate, Ameritech, and Siemens have already brought 7,000 workers to the Schaumburg area. With occupancy in multifamily units rising to 95 percent, rents are increasing by five to seven percent. One local developer believes that these areas will see "a run on land" suitable for single-family housing.

Demand for multifamily units in suburban markets has been limited by the relatively low cost of single-family housing. At $105,000 in the second quarter of 1989, the median sales price of an existing single-family home is above the national average of $93,200, but is less than half that of most West Coast markets. The housing price spiral that has already hit the coastal cities is sweeping into Chicago, albeit more meekly than elsewhere. In 1988, the median home price increased more than ten percent over the previous year. With the rate of growth moderating to six percent in 1989, Chicago may be able to elude the affordability crunch that has wracked other metropolitan housing markets.

The pattern of apartment building completions demonstrates the market's response to the demographic and legislative changes noted above. Stagnating population growth in the early 1970s induced a sharp contraction in additions to supply. As the population of the city of Chicago declined by 360,000 over the decade of the 1970s, apartment construction was concentrated in rapidly growing suburban areas. In anticipation of impending tax reform, developers rushed to obtain financing and permits before the incentives were suspended. The twenty million square feet of supply added in both 1987 and 1988 surpassed the average of the previous ten years by six million square feet. Staggered completions of apartment projects through the end of the forecast should prevent an oversupply of multifamily housing.

APARTMENT COMPLETIONS
Chicago SMSA

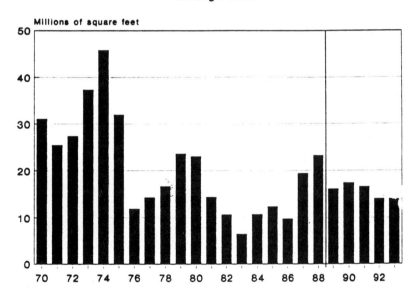

Chicago clearly suffered from the shifting migration trends of the last two decades. Rapid population growth in the first half of the 1970s was fueled by the expansion of the suburbs, especially DuPage County, whose population increased by 70,000 between 1970 and 1976. The area continued to attract new residents from throughout the industrial Midwest and agricultural Plains states as it had since its incorporation. The influx halted in 1978, however. The demise of the Rustbelt manufacturing sector and the downscaling of farms generated a new migration to the Southwest; Texas, Arizona, and southern California became the new destinations. Chicago has now experienced ten years of modest population gains, and the outlook is for a continuation of this trend.

ESTIMATED MULTIFAMILY DWELLERS, ANNUAL CHANGE
Chicago SMSA

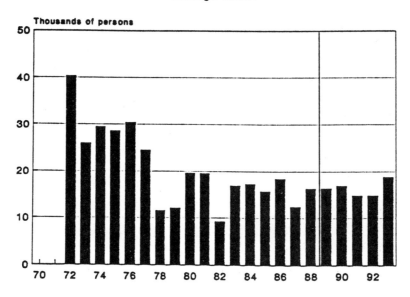

While the return on investing in apartment properties peaked across the nation, Chicago's declining share of the U.S. population restrained the performance of this market. When the 1982 recession hit, the Chicago apartment market actually improved while most areas suffered falling returns. The activity in expectation of tax reform propelled the Chicago market above the national average through the mid-1980s, but the shocks of 1987 contributed to a 75-percent decline in returns. After sustaining more moderate deterioration through the end of 1990, the return on multifamily residential properties should resume an upward trend.

APARTMENT MARKET ANNUAL RETURNS

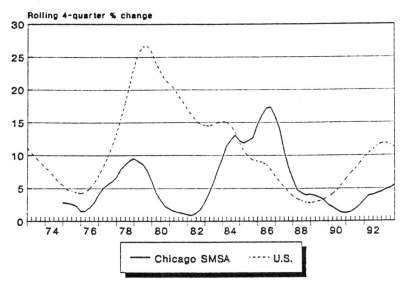

John Hancock Properties, Inc. (October 1989)

The JHREMI-Return represents the annualized total nominal return that a market may provide over history and through the forecast period, based on supply and demand.

Retail Market

With retail completions averaging less than three million square feet annually during the first half of the 1980s, Chicago was perceived as being understored relative to other major markets. (Salomon Brothers, Chicago Real Estate Market, October 1987) After four years of rapid development, however, the Chicago retail market has more than caught up. Now excess supply is putting pressure on vacancy rates. Retail vacancy in the six-county metropolitan area is up two percentage points to ten percent in 1988. In particular, the wrong product has been added; small strip centers that were constructed without feasibility studies are suffering from low occupancy. The downtown Chicago vacancy rate climbed to fifteen percent in 1988 from eight percent in 1987. (The REIS Reports, Retail Market Service: Chicago, Illinois, First Half 1989) Among downtown submarkets, vacancy ranges from five percent along the Magnificent Mile to 20 to 30 percent in the River North, West Loop, and South Loop areas. Given languid employment and population growth, income is unlikely to expand at a rate that would support the current pace of retail construction.

In spite of this, there is a widely held perception that changing residential patterns and novel retailing approaches are creating areas of opportunity. As the office market expands and high-income workers become downtown residents and shoppers, there will be scope for continued urban retail development. Hoping to create an "18-hour downtown," city planners actively encourage builders to include ground-floor retail in their plans for new and rehabilitated office space. The declining manufacturing sector has left vacant large industrial sites on Chicago's North Side. As demand grows for retail, office, research and development, and residential space in this market, the number of conversions will increase.

Many believe that the currently rising vacancy rates merely reflect the simultaneous completion of several large projects and that demand is bound to catch up soon. Others fear that the new competitive environment is here to stay and that old-time Chicago retailers will need more than their established reputations to contend with new arrivals such as Bloomingdale's. Marshall Field's has already decided to undergo a $110-million, decade-long renovation of its flagship store on State Street.

In the metropolitan Chicago area, Cook County houses the largest share of all retail classes, with nearly half of its stock in regional centers. In the early 1970s, Homart developed suburban malls in empty fields around major interchanges. What was once the periphery is now centrally located, and these regional malls are thriving. Since 1986, however, over ten million square feet of community and neighborhood space came on line in the county, compared to only three million square feet of regional centers. With demand for large centers satisfied and the supply of available sites drying up, little new supply of this type is being added outside of the rapidly developing southwestern parts of Cook and DuPage counties.

Retail fads include the power center, a hybrid of regional and community malls, and the hypermarket, modeled after the French concept of one-stop shopping. The power center has dominated recent retail construction since it can attract as many shoppers as a regional mall, but is built on far less space. This retail category is prone to huge vacancy rates if only one anchor tenant is lost, however. The hypermarket has been less successful in Chicago than in other areas, partly because the concept of the store is misunderstood and partly because of adverse reactions to the non-union hiring policies of the French parent company. Auto-oriented retail is being developed downtown; in the auto-dominated Midwest, this is not as unusual as it might seem for a major city.

Retail construction was slow to recover from the last recession, when retail spending fell by as much as $1 billion in 1981 alone. By 1986, however, nearly eight million square feet were added annually as developers acted on the widespread perception that the supply of stores was inadequate. Contract awards for retail construction indicate that new supply will skyrocket to almost twelve million square feet in 1990, before slipping to six to seven million square feet each year through the end of the forecast.

RETAIL COMPLETIONS
Chicago SMSA

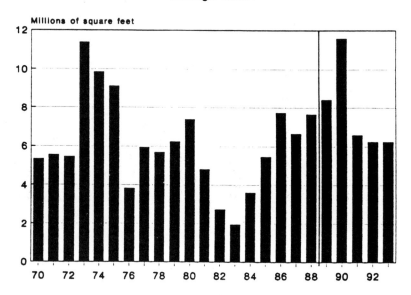

Growth in retail spending suggests why North Michigan Avenue has acquired a reputation as one of the premier shopping districts of the world. After suffering through the tumultuous 1970s and early 1980s, Chicago shoppers revelled in the buoyant recovery and pumped the economy with their consumption dollars. The spending rebound reached a peak of $4 billion dollars in 1985. Subsequent gains have been more modest, averaging $2.2 billion through 1988. The outlook is for continued moderation, with retail spending ranging between $1 billion and $2 billion through 1993.

ESTIMATED RETAIL SPENDING, ANNUAL CHANGE
Chicago SMSA

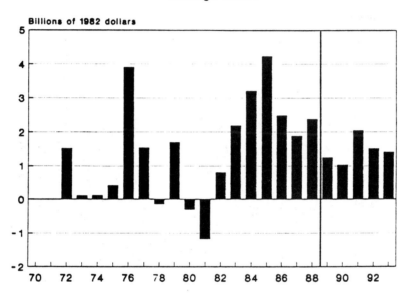

Chicago stores have historically underperformed other metropolitan markets, as evidenced by chronically weak retail returns. Unprecedented spending declines during the 1982 slump pulled returns down to almost zero. The market quickly responded to the consumption-driven recovery, however, and returns soared to over eighteen percent. As retail spending dissipates while the inventory of stores swells, returns are likely to tumble below the national average and hover around seven percent through the forecast period.

RETAIL MARKET ANNUAL RETURNS

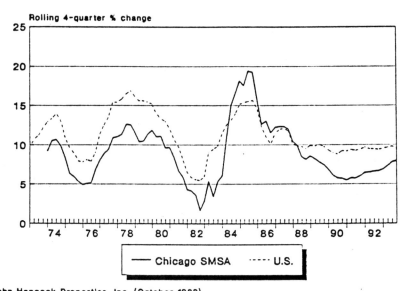

John Hancock Properties, Inc. (October 1989)
The JHREMI-Return represents the annualized total nominal return that a market may provide over history and through the forecast period, based on supply and demand.

SOURCES

Interviews

Nancy Braund Boruch, Senior Principal, Laventhol & Horwath

Michael E. Crane, Attorney, Crane and Norcross

James Crowley, CAE, Crane and Norcross

Eleanor Erdevig, Economist, Research Department, Federal Reserve Bank of Chicago

Stephen B. Friedman, Principal, Laventhol & Horwath

Kenneth I. Galvin, Frain Camins & Swartchild

Dr. John MacLennan, Economist, City of Chicago Department of Economic Development

Hubert Morgan, Assistant Planner, Northeastern Illinois Planning Commission

John Norcross, Attorney, Crane and Norcross

Robert B. Rosen, President, Frain Camins & Swartchild

William T. Ryan, Economic Development Coordinator, Commonwealth Edison

Bruce J. Sherman, Frain Camins & Swartchild

Diane C. Swonk, Regional Economist, First National Bank of Chicago

William A. Testa, Senior Economist, Federal Reserve Bank of Chicago

Wim Wiewel, Director, Center for Urban Economic Development, University of Illinois at Chicago

John I. Wrzesinski, MAI, Senior Vice President and General Manager, Landauer Associates, Inc.

Jim Zemezonak, Financial Services, Frain Camins & Swartchild

Publications

Bennett, Andrea, "Influx of Japanese Banks Continues,"
American Banker, May 13, 1988.

Bennett & Kahnweiler Incorporated, _Industrial Real Estate
Market Update_, 1988 and 1989.

Building Owners and Managers Association of Chicago,
Occupancy Survey, June 1989.

Byrne, Harlan S., "Some Questions Dog the Proposed Sale of
the World's Tallest 'Trophy,'" _Barron's_, November 7,
1988.

Cawthorne, David M., "Illinois Offers a Hub of Rail, Truck,
Air and River Transport Services," _Journal of Commerce_,
January 17, 1989.

"Chicago Market Facts," _Crain's Chicago Business_, July 3-9,
1989, pp. F1-F30.

City of Chicago Department of Economic Development, _Chicago:
The City That Works_, 1989.

Civic Committee of The Commercial Club of Chicago, _Chicago!_,
1989.

Coldwell Banker Commercial, _Chicago: The Commercial Real
Estate Market_, 1988 and 1989.

_____, _O'Hare Area Industrial Real Estate Market
Newsletter_, August 1989.

_____, _Elk Grove Village Area Industrial Market
Newsletter_, August 1988 and January 1989.

_____, _Office Vacancy Index of the United States_, June
30, 1989.

Commins, Kevin, "Chicago Futures Markets Poised to Continue
Growth," _Journal of Commerce_, January 17, 1989.

Coulter, John, "Positive Gains in Chicago Area Economy,"
Commerce, April 1988, pp. 36-40, 173.

_____, "Outlook for Chicago Employment Is Hopeful,"
Commerce, April 1988, pp. 82-84.

Crawford, Jan and Presecky, William, "Sears move linked to
expressway plan," _Chicago Tribune_, June 28, 1989.

Cushman & Wakefield, Focus on Chicagotrends: Japanese Investment in Chicago Real Estate, January 1988.

Davis, Jerry C., "City Review: Chicago," National Real Estate Investor, April 1988.

_____, "Chicago: City doing well while suburban construction slows," National Real Estate Investor, June 1988.

_____, "Chicago: Foreign interest, strong preleasing keep market strong," National Real Estate Investor, November 1988.

_____, "Chicago: Dwindling supply a good sign for new development," National Real Estate Investor, March 1989.

_____, "More than 4 bids for tower, Sears says, but mum on price," Chicago Sun-Times, June 25, 1989.

_____, "Housing plentiful, realty experts say," Chicago Sun-Times, June 27, 1989.

_____, "City's O'Hare site called 'can't miss,'" Chicago Sun-Times, June 28, 1989.

_____, "Sears, Ameritech make strong suburban market," Chicago Sun-Times, June 29, 1989.

Economic Development Commission of the City of Chicago, Chicago Economic Update, Spring 1989.

Elstrom, Peter J. W., "Cook county hit with property tax wallop," Crain's Chicago Business, July 3-9, 1989, p. 57.

Frisbie, Thomas, "DuPage 'take' in impact fees nears $200,000," Chicago Sun-Times, February 15, 1989.

Gibbons, Tom, "Hynes wants reassessment every 3 years," Chicago Sun-Times, June 20, 1989.

Goozner, Merrill, "Sears picks Hoffman Estates," Chicago Tribune, June 26, 1989.

_____, "The package that landed Sears," Chicago Tribune, June 27, 1989.

_____, "Sears left O'Hare site in spotlight," Chicago Tribune, June 28, 1989.

_____, "Bill to assist Sears' relocation also could aid other businesses," Chicago Tribune, July 2, 1989.

Hayutin, Adele M., Kostin, David J., Drutick, Jill S., and Hopkins, Robert E., Chicago Real Estate Market, Salomon Brothers, Inc., October 1987.

"High-minded: Skyscraper plan gives Chicago second thoughts," Milwaukee Journal, June 6, 1989.

Hornung, Mark, "TIFs for the rich: Sears deal just the start?" Crain's Chicago Business, July 3-9, 1989, pp. 3, 58.

Hume, Scott and Erickson, Julie Liesse, "City of Big Shoulders Slumps," Advertising Age, July 25, 1988, p. 12.

Ibata, David and Szymczak, Patricia, "Boom, not gloom, seen in move," Chicago Tribune, June 27, 1989.

Johnson, Robert, "Sears Mulls 16-Floor Addition To Fend Off Challenger For 'World's Tallest' Title," Wall Street Journal, July 7, 1989.

Kerch, Steve, "No-growth movement is growing," Chicago Tribune, February 12, 1989.

_____, "Office market surges in the suburbs," Chicago Tribune, June 18, 1989.

Linden, Fabian, "The Windy City," American Demographics, February 1988, pp. 6-8.

McCarron, John, "Plan Commission OKs 2 projects, but stalls State Street building," Chicago Tribune, June 9, 1989.

McCormick, John, "In Chicago, It's Back to the Future," Newsweek, February 6, 1989, p. 26.

Manofsky, Carl M., "Industrial Revival Leads To Strong Demand," Commerce, April 1988, pp. 98-101.

Moberg, David, "Can Chicago Be Saved?" Inc., March 1988, pp. 84-91.

Northeastern Illinois Planning Commission, Population, Households and Employment in Northeastern Illinois, 1980 to 2010, Data Bulletin 88-1, May 1988.

_____, The Components of Population Change in Northeastern Illinois, 1980 to 1986, Data Bulletin 88-2, May 1988.

_____ and Regional Transportation Authority, 2010 Transportation System Development Plan, Spring 1989.

Pauly, David and Padgett, Tim, "More Shoes Drop in the Pits," Newsweek, February 6, 1989, p. 26.

Real Estate Research Corporation, "Chicago Metropolitan Area," ULI Market Profiles, 1989.

"Real Estate Review," River North News, August 15, 1989, p. 12.

Recktenwald, William, "Navy Pier bill a plum for Daley," Chicago Tribune, July 3, 1989.

The Reis Reports, Inc., Retail Market Service: Chicago, Illinois, First Half 1989.

Ringer, Richard, "Exchanges Are Lifeblood of Chicago's Financial Image," American Banker, November 18, 1987.

_____ and Bennett, Andrea, "Retailers Nab Space on LaSalle Street as Financial Industry Changes," American Banker, October 14, 1988.

Schrodt, Anita, "New Markets Open Up For State's Industries," Journal of Commerce, January 17, 1989.

_____, "Chicago Expects to Match '88 Volume," Journal of Commerce, January 31, 1989.

Siegel, Daniel R., "Chicago Must Modernize or Perish," New York Times, August 13, 1989.

"Show Aisles Packed," Hardware Show News, August 15, 1989.

Strahler, Steven R., "The Sears moooove: A real estate windfall," Crain's Chicago Business, July 3-9, 1989, pp. 1, 54.

_____, "Chicago-area industrial space up 4.4% in 2nd qtr.," Crain's Chicago Business, July 3-9, 1989, p. 14.

Swonk, Diane C., "The Great Lakes Gear Up for a Slowdown in Auto Sales," First Regional Report, First National Bank of Chicago, Summer 1989.

Tamarkin, Bob, "Chicago: 150 Years of Financial Innovation," *Fortune*, Fall 1987.

Weiner, Lisabeth, "Manufacturers Hanover Corp. Reaches New Heights in Chicago," *American Banker*, April 3, 1988.

_____, "Brokers Fear Dual-Trading Bank Would Hurt Exchanges, *American Banker*, February 10, 1989.

_____, "Exchanges Bring Jobs, Money, and Civic Benefits, Study Finds," *American Banker*, July 8, 1988.

Wiewel, Wim, *The State of the Economy and Economic Development in the Chicago Metropolitan Region*, Center for Urban Economic Development, University of Illinois at Chicago, October 1986.

Wilkerson, Isabel, "Chicago Rival Wll Look Down on Sears Tower," *New York Times*, June 4, 1989.

_____, "What Illinois Gave to Keep Sears," *New York Times*, August 27, 1989.

_____, "New School Term in Chicago Puts Parents in Seat of Power," *New York Times*, September 3, 1989.

Ziemba, Stanley, "Sears pushing $1 billion-plus bid for Tower," *Chicago Tribune*, June 23, 1989.

_____, "Japanese steer clear of Sears Tower sale," *Chicago Tribune*, June 29, 1989.

_____, "Second deal in works for Tower bidder," *Chicago Tribune*, June 29, 1989.

_____, "City shows signs of office glut," *Chicago Tribune*, July 4, 1989.

_____, "Olympia & York resists keeping the Sears name," *Chicago Tribune*, July 6, 1989.

The historical perspective of real estate returns

And a comprehensive review of the literature.

G. Stacy Sirmans and C. F. Sirmans

This study provides a review of the literature on the risk and return performance of real estate relative to alternative assets. The paper also examines the ability of real estate and these other assets to serve as a hedge against expected and unexpected inflation.

In summary, results of studies examining real estate returns and risk relative to other assets have found that, in general, when variation in return is used as the measure of risk, equity investments such as common stocks have been riskier than debt securities such as corporate or government bonds. The comparisons of real estate returns and risk to other assets is mixed. More than half the studies find that absolute returns on real estate have been higher than returns on either stocks, bonds, or other assets. Some studies show that real estate outperformed debt securities but not common stocks on an absolute rate of return basis. On a risk-adjusted basis (return divided by risk), most of the studies indicate that real estate earned a higher return per unit of risk than common stocks and the other assets included in the studies.

In examining the absolute risk of the asset returns, the results are mixed. Most of the studies show a higher standard deviation for common stocks than for real estate, while only a few studies show a higher variation for real estate. One study reports equal standard deviations for real estate and common stocks. In several cases, the reported standard deviations for real estate are even less than those reported for either corporate or government bonds. Later sections of this study will discuss the problems that are encountered in measuring real estate returns and risk and the smoothing and inaccuracy that may result from measurement error.

We also discuss several studies that examine real estate and other assets as hedges against inflation. Some studies find that real estate has been a good hedge against both expected and unexpected inflation. Other studies show that some types of real estate have provided an excellent hedge against expected inflation but not against unexpected inflation. The results of studies examining the value of financial assets as an inflation hedge are also mixed.

MEASURING RETURNS ON REAL ESTATE

The results of studies to measure the historical rate of return on real estate are shown in Table 1.

Miles and McCue (1982) examine the unleveraged rates of return on properties held by sixteen REITs over the period 1972–1978. They find average returns ranging from 8.44% to 9.62% for different types of properties.

A study by Webb and Sirmans (1982) presents expected returns on various types of real property over the period 1966–1976. These returns are shown in Table 1 and Table 4. The lowest average annual return is 9.54% for office buildings, while the highest return is 9.64% for retail properties. Risk for the properties is similar with the standard deviations ranging from 0.74% for non-elevator apartments to 1.05% for shopping centers.[1]

1. Footnotes appear at the end of the article.

G. STACY SIRMANS is Associate Professor of Finance in the College of Commerce and Industry at Clemson University in Clemson (SC 29631). C. F. SIRMANS is Professor of Finance at Louisiana State University in Baton Rouge (LA 70803). The authors are grateful to an anonymous referee for helpful comments.

TABLE 1

Studies Examining Returns on Real Estate Investment

Author(s)	Title	Source	Time Period	Summary
M. Miles and T. McCue	Historic Returns and Institutional Real Estate Portfolios	*Journal of the American Real Estate and Urban Economics Association,* Summer 1982	1972-1978	Examines property values of properties held by sixteen REITs. Return estimates are derived for the unlevered cash yields by property size, type, and location. REIT portfolios are compared to commingled fund portfolios. Using a regression equation to estimate the cash yield of the portfolios, the study finds the average returns on office, residential, and retail properties to be 8.62%, 9.62%, and 8.44%, respectively. Comparison of REIT and CREF portfolios would suggest that CREF portfolios should contain more residential property.
J. R. Webb and C. F. Sirmans	Yields for Selected Types of Real Property vs. the Money and Capital Markets	*The Appraisal Journal,* April 1982	1966-1976	Using real estate data from the American Council of Life Insurance, the study calculates investment yields of specific property types for fifteen companies. The average overall yields by property type were: elevator apartment, 9.57%; non-elevator apartment, 9.59%; retail, 9.64%; shopping center, 9.56%; office building, 9.54%; and medical office building, 9.63%.
D. G. Edwards	Rates of Return from S & L Investments in Service Corporations, 1979-83	Research Working Paper, Office of Policy and Economic Research, Federal Home Loan Bank Board, November 1984	1979-1983	Data from over 1,000 S & Ls with investments in service corporations are analyzed to obtain estimates of the rates and variability of returns from these investments. Many investments by service corporations are in areas such as unimproved land, land development, commercial properties, etc. In December 1983, real estate comprised 31.4% of service corporation assets with the remainder being cash and securities, receivables, fixed assets, first mortgage loans, other loans, and unconsolidated subsidiaries. The annual rates of return on service corporations for the sample S & Ls averaged 17.4% with a standard deviation of 40% over the 1979-1983 period. Of the sample firms, 67% reported returns below the industry's average rate on new conventional single-family mortgage loans closed for the period (13.35%).
National Council of Real Estate Investment Fiduciaries	The NCREIF Report	National Council of Real Estate Investment Fiduciaries and the Frank Russell Company	1978-1983	The Frank Russell Company publishes real estate returns on an index of income-producing properties that are completed and non-leveraged. As of December 1983, there were 845 properties in the index. The returns are based on net operating income plus change in property value. Changes in property value are determined by appraisal where appropriate. The average annual returns by index and type of property over 1978-1983 are: index, 15.6%; apartments, 18.28%; retail, 11.58%; hotels, 24.62%; industrial, 14.97%; office, 18.02%.

Edwards (1984) indirectly measures the return and risk on real estate investments by examining the performance of wholly-owned service corporations of savings and loan associations. As of December 1983, real estate, such as unimproved land and commercial properties, comprised 31.4% of service corporation assets. Edwards measured the average annual return for service corporations to be 17.4% over the 1979–1983 period. The standard deviation of the service corporation returns was 40%.[2]

The National Council of Real Estate Investment Fiduciaries in conjunction with the Frank Russell Company provides an index of returns on various types of income properties. The index begins in 1977.

As of December 1983, 845 properties are included. Table 1 and Table 4 (the NCREIF report) show the average annual returns over the 1978–1983 period. The returns range from 11.58% for retail properties to 24.62% for hotels, with hotels being riskiest.

At this point, the limitations and problems of a real estate return series such as the Frank Russell Company (FRC) series should be acknowledged. The index uses appraised values to measure the "capital gain" component of returns. The use of appraised values rather than actual observed market values may produce inaccuracies and smoothing of returns, thereby underestimating standard deviations. For example, the FRC properties are appraised independently once a year. This appraisal value is used to calculate the rates of return and can obviously vary from the actual market value were the property to be sold. Also, indexes, such as the FRC index, include a diversified group of properties from various geographic regions throughout the United States. Rates of return on an index of this type may not be representative of returns prevalent in a specific geographical area.

Returns on Real Estate and Other Assets

A number of studies have attempted to measure return and risk on real estate investments relative to other assets. These studies are presented in Tables 2 and 3. The results are mixed, in that real estate performs sometimes better, sometimes worse than other assets in a risk–return analysis. Brueggeman, Chen, and Thibodeau (1984), for example, show that

TABLE 2

Studies Examining Returns on Real Estate Relative to Other Assets

Author(s)	Title	Source	Time Period	Summary
C. Froland, R. Gorlow, and R. Sampson	The Market Risk of Real Estate	*Journal of Portfolio Management*, Spring 1986	1970-1984	Constructs an index of returns and risk based on valuation of average NOI using an average market capitalization rate for office buildings in four major cities. Results show that the office index outperformed the S&P 500. The variability of real estate was much greater than the S&P 500 index. Washington had the lowest absolute return for real estate while San Francisco had the highest. On a risk-adjusted basis, Washington and San Francisco outperformed the stock index. Results also show in general that negative correlations exist between cities and the index. This implies certain benefits for real estate of geographical diversification as well as diversification across other assets.
W. B. Brueggeman, A. H. Chen, and T. G. Thibodeau	Real Estate Investment Funds: Performance and Portfolio Considerations	*Journal of the American Real Estate and Urban Economics Association*, Spring 1984	1972-1983	Estimates rates of return on two CREFs using cash returns and unit values. Unit values are proxies for market values of the underlying real estate. Unit values are based on appraisals. Results show an average annual yield of 11.73% for the entire period. Subperiods of 1972-1977 and 1978-1983 show average annual yields of 8.37% and 15.09%, respectively. When measuring return relative to risk, the real estate investment funds performed very well compared to common stocks and corporate bonds.
J. W. Hoag	Toward Indices of Real Estate Value and Return	*Journal of Finance*, May 1980	1973-1978	Examines returns based on income and price changes (as determined by a valuation model) for 463 industrial properties that are primarily warehouses with some light manufacturing and distribution. The average returns are weighted by property size and are unleveraged and pretax returns. The average annualized return over the study period was 14.2%.
R. G. Ibbotson and C. L. Fall	The United States Market Wealth Portfolio	*Journal of Portfolio Management*, Fall 1979	1947-1978	Examines returns based on income and changes in index values (USDA and Home Purchase Indexes) for farm real estate and residential housing. The returns are weighted by component size. The average annual return for farms was 11.7% and 6.9% for housing over the study period.

TABLE 2 *(Continued)*

H. R. Fogler	20% in Real Estate: Can Theory Justify It?	*Journal of Portfolio Management*, Winter 1984	1915-1978	Estimates the returns on various assets over a long time period by adding historical risk premiums to the prevailing Treasury bill rate. Two proxies for real estate returns are estimated — Proxy 1 follows the Ibbotson and Fall study above, and Proxy 2 was calculated using a construction cost series and a rent series. The mean return on real estate is shown to be 11%. In a portfolio context, the results make a strong case for a 20% minimum investment in real estate.
R. G. Ibbotson and L. B. Siegel	Real Estate Returns: A Comparison with Other Investments	*Journal of the American Real Estate and Urban Economics Association*, Fall 1984	1947-1982	Examines the return and risk for various types of real estate along with stocks, fixed-income assets (bonds, preferred stocks, commercial paper), government securities (bills, notes, bonds) and municipal bonds. The results show that real estate had an average return of 8.33% and was substantially less risky than other investments. The authors concede, however, that the real estate series may be smoothed thus creating artificially low standard deviations.
J. McMahan Associates, Inc.	Institutional Strategies for Real Estate Equity Investment	*Pension Trust Investment in Realty*, November/December 1981	1951-1978	Examines return based on income and price change as determined by changes in the construction cost index for mortgage commitments on multi-family and nonresidential properties as reported by fifteen life insurance companies. The returns are unleveraged and pretax. The average annual return on real estate over this period was 13.9%.
M. Brachman	Rating Commingled Funds	*Pension World*, September 1981	1970-1979	Examines the return on three commingled funds. Total return is based on income and changes in market value as measured by appraisals. The returns are pretax and are 10.3% for real estate over the study period.
A. A. Robichek, R. A. Cohn, and J. J. Pringle	Returns on Alternative Investment Media and Implications for Portfolio Construction	*Journal of Business*, July 1972	1951-1969	Examines return based on income and changes in market value as indicated by index values for farm real estate. Uses the Department of Agriculture Index of Average Value of Farm Real Estate per acre. Returns are unleveraged and pretax. The average return on real estate over this period was 9.5%.

real estate held in two large commingled real estate funds performed well compared to common stocks and corporate bonds. The Hoag study (1980) shows that real estate outperformed other assets such as stocks and bonds, not only with a higher average return but also with greater return relative to risk. Hoag's conclusions are based on a real estate index using such variables as location, size, age, and demographics.

The Ibbotson and Fall study (1979) shows that, although real estate had a lower average return than common stocks, it substantially outperformed other investments on a risk-adjusted basis. The same is true for the Ibbotson and Siegel study (1984) and the Robichek, Cohn, and Pringle study (1972). Studies that show that real estate performed better than other assets, not only with a higher average return but also

a higher return on a risk-adjusted basis, are McMahan (1981) and Brachman (1981).

On the other hand, the Fogler study (1984) shows that real estate was outperformed by common stocks on an absolute return basis and also on a risk-adjusted basis over the 1915–1978 period. On a risk-adjusted basis, real estate was also outperformed by bonds and Treasury bills.

Returns on Real Estate Measured by REIT Performance

Some of the previous studies use appraised values in determining real estate returns (Brueggeman, Chen, and Thibodeau; Brachman; and Ibbotson and Siegel, for example). Because the use of appraised value instead of actual market value may tend to reduce the variability in real estate returns, these results may be biased in favor of real estate.

TABLE 3

Studies Measuring Real Estate Returns Using Data of Real Estate Investment Trusts (REITs)

Author(s)	Title	Source	Time Period	Summary
W. L. Burns and D. R. Epley	The Performance of Portfolios of REITs plus Common Stocks	*Journal of Portfolio Management*, Spring 1982	1970-1979	Examines the returns on thirty-five REITs relative to other investment trusts (closed-end and mutual funds) and the Standard & Poor's Composite Index. In a portfolio context, results show that portfolios of all assets outperform portfolios of just REITs. The average return on real estate (REITs) is 16% over the study period. In subset time periods, the return is 3% for 1970-1974 and 37.4% for 1975-1979.
H. A. Davidson and J. E. Palmer	A Comparison of the Investment Performance of Common Stocks, Homebuilding Firms, and Equity REITs	*The Real Estate Appraiser*, July/August 1978	1972-1977	Calculates the return and variance on each of eleven equity REITs, the Standard & Poor's 500 Index, and ten homebuilding common stocks. Over the period examined, the equity REITs outperformed both building firms and the S&P 500 on a systematic risk-adjusted basis. On a total risk-adjusted basis, the REITs outperformed the S&P 500. The average annual return on the REITs was 8.8%.
K. V. Smith	Historical Returns of Real Estate Equity Portfolios	*The Investment Manager's Handbook*, 1980	1965-1977	Examines the rate of return based on purchase price, quarterly cash distributions, and the sale price at the end of the holding period for fourteen equity REITs. The returns are pretax. The average return over this study period was 9.8%.

In order to avoid this problem, other studies have used data for real estate investment trusts (REITs). These studies are shown in Tables 3 and 4. The returns on REITs can be calculated using the income accruing to the REITs and the change in the market price of the share. As the principal underlying assets of the REITs are either real estate or mortgages or both, then, to the extent that the market price re-

TABLE 4

Summary Statistics of Returns on Real Estate Relative to Returns on Other Assets

Study	Time Period	Type of Assets	Average Annual* Rate of Return (%)	Standard Deviation (%)
Froland, Gorlow, and Sampson	1970-1984	Office		
		Chicago	25.4	53
		Manhattan	32.9	66
		Washington	19.0	29
		San Francisco	34.8	34
			8.8	15
		Treasury Bills	7.8	3
Miles and McCue	1972-1978	Office Real Estate	8.62	—
		Residential Real Estate	9.62	—
		Retail Real Estate	8.44	—
Webb and Sirmans	1966-1976	Elevator Apartments	9.57	0.76
		Non-elevator Apartments	9.59	0.74
		Retail	9.65	0.80
		Shopping Centers	9.56	1.05
		Office Buildings	9.54	0.78
		Medical Office Buildings	9.63	0.77
Edwards	1979-1983	Investment in Service Corporations by S&Ls	17.4	40
NCREIF Report	1978-1983	Index	15.6	3.91
		Apartments	18.28	6.99
		Retail	11.58	8.08
		Hotels	24.62	24.82
		Industrial	14.97	3.28
		Office	18.02	5.95

TABLE 4 *(Continued)*

Brueggeman, Chen, and Thibodeau	1972-1983	Properties of 2 CREFs (1972-1983)	11.73	8.35
		Properties of 2 CREFs (1972-1977)	8.37	4.14
		Properties of 2 CREFs (1978-1983)	15.09	9.99
		Common Stocks (1972-1983)	9.71	34.99
		Corporate Bonds (1972-1983)	6.54	26.50
Hoag	1973-1978	Real Estate	14.2	17.2
		Common Stocks	3.7	20.8
		Bonds	6.4	8.0
		Treasury Bills	6.2	1.0
Ibbotson and Fall	1947-1978	Real Estate	8.1	3.5
		Common Stocks	10.3	18.0
		Bonds	2.9	5.5
		Treasury Bills	3.5	2.1
Fogler	1915-1978	Real Estate	11	4
		Common Stocks	13	4
		Bonds	8	2.6
		Treasury Bills	6	0
Ibbotson and Siegel	1947-1982	Real Estate		
		Farms	11.32	7.89
		Residential	7.5	3.89
		Business	8.1	3.78
		Total	8.33	3.71
		Common Stocks	12.42	17.52
		Fixed-Income Corporate Securities	3.76	6.47
		U.S. Government Securities	4.09	4.92
		Municipal Bonds	2.24	10.83
McMahan	1951-1978	Real Estate	13.9	3.8
		Common Stocks	11.4	18.3
		Bonds	3.5	6.7
		Treasury Bills	3.9	1.9
Brachman	1970-1979	Real Estate	10.3	4.9
		Common Stocks	4.7	19.6
		Bonds	5.6	8.0
		Treasury Bills	6.3	1.8
Burns and Epley	1970-1979	Real Estate	16.0	28.5
		Common Stocks	4.7	19.6
		Bonds	5.6	8.0
		Treasury Bills	6.3	1.8
Davidson and Palmer	1972-1977	Real Estate	8.8	17.0
		S&P 500	5.5	10.0
		Homebuilding Firm Stocks	9.2	39.0
Robichek, Cohn, and Pringle	1951-1969	Real Estate	9.5	4.5
		Common Stocks	11.9	17.4
		Bonds	1.3	5.0
		Treasury Bills	3.0	1.5
Smith	1965-1977	Real Estate	9.8	22.1
		Common Stocks	4.6	18.4
		Bonds	4.2	8.7
		Treasury Bills	5.4	1.3

* Some rates of return are calculated and presented in R. H. Zerbst and B. R. Cambon, "Real Estate Returns and Risks," *Journal of Portfolio Management* (Spring 1984), pp. 5-20.

flects the true value of the underlying assets, the returns on the REIT may serve as a proxy for the return on the underlying real assets. A caveat is that pension real estate studies usually measure unleveraged (fully-owned) properties; thus, while having REIT market prices instead of appraisals is a plus, one loses in terms of purity of the portfolio.

The studies using REIT data show that real estate has had higher absolute returns than other as-sets such as common stocks and bonds. Burns and Epley (1982), for example, show a 16% average return on thirty-five REITs from 1970 to 1979. On a risk-adjusted basis, this outperforms stocks but not bonds.

Davidson and Palmer (1978) compare the performance of eleven equity REITs to the S&P 500 Index and ten homebuilding common stocks over the period 1972–1977. On an absolute return basis, the REITs outperformed the S&P 500 but not the homebuilding stocks. On a risk-adjusted basis, the REITs outperformed the homebuilding stocks but not the S&P 500.

The Smith study (1980) shows that fourteen equity REITs outperformed stocks and bonds on an absolute return basis. On a risk-adjusted basis, the REITs outperformed common stocks but not bonds over the study period 1965–1977.

The problem in using returns on REITs to measure real estate returns is that, in some periods, the REIT returns in the market may not match actual property returns. In the early 1970s, for example, REITs had poor returns while the underlying property values were relatively robust. Ibbotson and Siegel suggest that a possible reason for this divergence may be that high inflation increases the tax shelter attribute of real estate relative to REITs. Factors such as confidence in management's ability and the effects of leverage on REIT returns also may cause differences to arise.

REAL ESTATE RETURNS AND INFLATION

Real estate has received increasing attention in recent years as one of the few assets that provided an adequate hedge against inflation during the 1970s. To be a complete inflation hedge, an asset must adequately protect the investor from both expected and unexpected inflation. Expected inflation would be reflected in interest rates, while unexpected inflation would not be incorporated in market rates — although it might show up in *changes* in interest rates.

Several studies have attempted to measure the inflation hedge value of real estate relative to other assets such as common stocks and government or corporate bonds. These studies are shown in Table 5,

TABLE 5

Studies Examining the Inflation Hedge Value of Real Estate and Other Assets

Author(s)	Title	Source	Summary
R. G. Ibbotson and L. B. Siegel	Real Estate Returns: A Comparison with Other Investments	*Journal of the American Real Estate and Urban Economics Association,* Fall 1984	Examines the total returns on a general index of real estate and compares those to other asset returns over the period 1947-1982. The purpose is to compare real estate returns to other returns over a long period of time to reduce statistical noise and eliminate temporary trends. Finds that common stocks had the highest return at 11.0% annually. Real estate had an unleveraged average return of 8.3%. All fixed-income securities had average returns below the inflation rate.
			A caveat of real estate returns is that they are based on appraised values. This causes smoothing and inaccuracy, thus reducing standard deviations. Also, real estate is not readily marketable as are stocks and bonds. In the case of these assets, reported returns are close to realized returns. Real estate is different in that it cannot necessarily be sold instantaneously at the quoted (appraised) value.
			Regression of asset returns on inflation shows that the real estate was an excellent, although not perfect, hedge against inflation. The comovement of real estate to inflation was 85%. Stocks and bonds reacted negatively to inflation.
E. F. Fama and G. W. Schwert	Asset Returns and Inflation	*Journal of Financial Economics,* November 1977	Estimates the extent to which private residential real estate, common stocks, Treasury bonds, Treasury bills, and labor income provided hedges against expected and unexpected inflation over the 1953-1971 period. Found real estate to have been a complete hedge against both expected and unexpected inflation. Treasury bills and bonds were complete hedges against expected but not unexpected inflation. Estimation problems made generalization about labor income difficult. Stock returns were found to have been negatively related to expected inflation and also, to a lesser extent, unexpected inflation. Thus, stocks could not be considered an inflation hedge over this period.

TABLE 5 *(Continued)*

R. G. Ibbotson and R. A. Sinquefield	Stocks, Bonds, Bills, and Inflation: Year by Year Historical Returns (1926-1974)	*Journal of Business*, January 1976	Analyzes returns on common stocks, corporate bonds, Treasury bonds, and Treasury bills over 1926-1974 period. Finds that over this period Treasury bills provided a zero real rate of return, i.e., the average nominal return matched inflation at 2.2%. Government and corporate bonds earned nominal rates of 3.2% and 3.6% per year, respectively. Stocks earned an average nominal yield of 8.5% per year.
D. Hartzell, J. S. Hekman, and M. E. Miles	Real Estate Returns and Inflation	Unpublished paper, October 1985	Examines the ability of real estate to hedge against anticipated and unanticipated inflation. Uses quarterly returns for 300 properties of a large CREF over the 1973-1983 period. Develops two models of expected and unexpected inflation: one that uses a constant real rate and one that allows it to vary. The results show that real estate compensated the investor for both types of risk. By proper type for the entire period, industrial and office properties provide complete protection from expected inflation while retail properties were much weaker. Retail properties, however, seemed to be a better hedge against unexpected inflation. For the most recent five years of the sample period, industrial and office properties show complete protection from expected and unexpected inflation.
H. R. Fogler	20% in Real Estate: Can Theory Justify it?	*Journal of Portfolio Management*, Winter 1984	Identifies three types of periods over 1915-1978: inflation, deflation, and normal. Finds eight periods of significant inflation and deflation. Examines what happened to real estate and other assets in these periods. There were six periods when the inflation rate exceeded 5%. Common stocks seemed to do well until the later periods of 1960s and 1970s. Real estate did well in the 1960s and 1970s and also over the period 1915-1919. For other periods between these, real estate increased slightly, and there were mixed returns on stocks.
			In periods of deflation during the 1920s, there were several real estate booms in regional areas. Bonds did well at these times. In deflation in the 1930s, rents dropped, bonds did well, and common stocks did poorly. In normal periods, stock returns averaged higher than bond returns. Real estate returns seemed to be about the same as common stocks.
R. B. Peiser	Risk Analysis in Land Development	*Journal of the American Real Estate and Urban Economics Association*, Spring 1984	Examines risk analysis, including inflation risks, as it relates to land development. Income property development raises a number of risks not present in existing income property such as cost overruns, construction interest rate changes, delays, rent concessions, and absorption rates. Also, land development does not offer the tax benefits of income properties.
			Inflation in construction costs was found to be somewhat higher than average inflation in all commodities as measured by the CPI. Using an internal rate of return model, finds that project returns are significantly more sensitive to changes in sales price, sales price inflation, and sales rates than to changes in construction costs, construction cost inflation rates, and interest rates.

TABLE 5 *(Continued)*

H. R. Fogler, M. R. Granito, and L. R. Smith	A Theoretical Analysis of Real Estate Returns	*Journal of Finance,* July 1985	Estimates inflation betas for real estate, stocks, and bonds over several periods since 1952. While the data provide some support for the hedge demand hypothesis, the results are not strong enough to conclude that a rising inflation beta and declining required return on real estate was a cause of above-normal real estate returns in recent years. Thus the hypothesis cannot be rejected that there has been no change in expected returns on real estate because of an increase in its demand as an inflation hedge. The data used are Census Bureau index on new single-family houses sold, Livingston survey of farm prices, the CPI, S&P 500, and returns on twenty-year U.S. Treasury bonds. The study also addresses the problem of high returns on real estate but low variances. One solution proposed was that high unexpected rates of inflation lead to high realized returns on assets that are highly correlated with inflation such as real estate. The second solution was high realized returns on real estate as a result of changing investor perceptions about the degree of sensitivity of real estate returns to inflation. This could cause investors to bid up real estate prices.
J. B. Kau and C. F. Sirmans	Changes in Urban Land Values: 1836-1970	*Journal of Urban Economics,* 1984	Develops a model for measuring the return to land and examines these returns using a random coefficient estimation procedure for land in Chicago over specific periods from 1836 to 1970. A mean rate of return for land for each time period is derived from the model. The results suggest that the long-term rate of return on land is no higher than the rate of return on high-grade bonds over this period. The results also suggest that the rental income on land does not exceed, on average, the holding costs attached to the property.

where we can see that the results are mixed. Fama and Schwert (1977) find that real estate provided a good hedge against both expected and unexpected inflation from 1953 to 1971. Hartzell, Hekman, and Miles (1985) find that property types such as industrial and office properties provided complete protection from expected inflation but not unexpected inflation. They find that retail properties were a better hedge against unexpected inflation over their study period of 1973–1983.

Fogler examines the reaction of real estate to inflationary and deflationary periods from 1915 through 1978. He finds that real estate did well in the later inflationary periods (1960s and 1970s) and had slight increases in all inflationary periods. Common stocks did well until the later periods of the 1960s and 1970s. In normal periods, real estate and common stocks seemed to average about the same returns with both being greater than bonds.

Fogler, Granito, and Smith (1985) examine inflation betas for real estate, stocks, and bonds over various periods beginning in 1952. Their primary concern was whether there has been a significant change in expected returns on real estate as a result of its increased demand as an inflation hedge. While the data provided some support, the hypothesis that there has been no change could not be rejected.

Ibbotson and Siegel find that, over their study period of 1947–1982, common stocks had the highest annual return of 11% compared to 8.3% for real estate. Fixed-income assets had average returns below the inflation rate. While real estate seemed a good inflation hedge, they find that stocks and bonds reacted negatively to inflation.

While they find real estate to be a good hedge against expected and unexpected inflation over 1953–1971, Fama and Schwert find Treasury bills and bonds to be good hedges against expected but not unexpected inflation. On the other hand, they show common stocks to be negatively related to both expected and unexpected inflation.

Ibbotson and Sinquefield (1976) find that, with

an average inflation rate of about 2.2%, common stocks earned an average return of 8.5% over the 1926–1974 period. Government and corporate bonds earned 3.2% and 3.6%, respectively, while the average Treasury bill yield equaled the inflation rate, thus yielding a zero real rate of return.

A study by Peiser (1984) that analyzes inflation risk and land development finds that inflation in construction costs was higher than average inflation as measured by the CPI. Peiser also finds that the returns on land development were much more sensitive to sales price inflation than to construction cost inflation.

A study by Kau and Sirmans (1984) examines changes in urban land values over the period 1836–1970. Using a model to measure rate of return, they determine that the long-term return to land was no higher than the rate of return on high-grade bonds over this period.

SUMMARY AND CONCLUSIONS

This study has analyzed the literature covering the returns and risk on real estate relative to other assets and the value of real estate as an inflation hedge.

In general, these studies indicate that common stocks have been riskier than debt securities such as government or corporate bonds. The results are mixed for real estate, in that some studies show real estate to be riskier than either stocks or bonds, some say real estate is riskier than bonds only, and others argue that it is less risky than either stocks or bonds. Some studies concede, however, that measurement errors in real estate returns may result in those returns appearing to be less risky than returns on other assets when actually that may or may not have been the case.

On the question of hedging against inflation, all studies found that debt securities were either not a good inflation hedge or allowed protection only for expected inflation. Common stock returns were, in general, negatively related to inflation rates, indicating that this asset did not serve as a good hedge against inflation. Some studies showed real estate has been a good hedge against both expected and unexpected inflation. Taken together, the studies seem to indicate that real estate served as a better inflation hedge over the time periods studied than common stocks and corporate or government bonds.

[1] These results seem a little peculiar. Typically, income returns may be this stable; capital gains returns, however, would be expected to be more variable than these estimates indicate.

[2] It should be noted that the reliability of these data as a source of real estate returns depends on the accuracy of information reported to the regulating agencies.

REFERENCES

Brachman, W. O. "Rating Commingled Funds." *Pension World*, September 1981, pp. 25-38.

Brueggeman, W. B., A. H. Chen, and T. G. Thibodeau. "Real Estate Investment Funds: Performance and Portfolio Considerations." *AREUEA Journal*, Fall 1984, pp. 333-354.

Burns, W., and D. Epley. "Performance of Portfolios of REITs and Stocks." *Journal of Portfolio Management*, Vol. 8, no. 3 (Spring 1982), pp. 37-42.

Davidson, H. A., and J. E. Palmer. "A Comparison of the Investment Performance of Common Stocks, Homebuilding Firms, and Equity REITs." *The Real Estate Appraiser*, July/August 1978, pp. 35-39.

Edwards, D. G. "Rates of Return from S & L Investments in Service Corporations, 1979-83." Research Working Paper Series, Office of Policy and Economic Research, Federal Home Loan Bank Board, November 1984.

Fama, E. F., and G. W. Schwert. "Asset Returns and Inflation." *Journal of Financial Economics*, Vol. 5 (November 1977), pp. 115-146.

Fogler, H. R. "20% in Real Estate: Can Theory Justify It?" *Journal of Portfolio Management*, Vol. 10, no. 2 (Winter 1984), pp. 6-13.

Fogler, H. R., M. R. Granito, and L. R. Smith. "A Theoretical Analysis of Real Estate Returns." *Journal of Finance*, Vol. 40, no. 3 (July 1985), pp. 711-719.

Froland, Charles, R. Gorlow, and Richard Sampson. "The Market Risk of Real Estate." *Journal of Portfolio Management*, Vol. 12, no. 2, (Spring 1986), pp. 12-19.

The Handbook of Basic Economic Statistics. Bureau of Economic Statistics, Inc., Economic Statistics Bureau of Washington, D.C., Vol. 34, no. 11 (November 1985), pp. 97-101.

Hartzell, D., J. S. Hekman, and M. E. Miles. "Real Estate Returns and Inflation." Unpublished paper, October 1985.

Hoag, J. W. "Toward Indices of Real Estate Value and Return." *Journal of Finance*, May 1980, pp. 569-580.

Ibbotson, R. G., and C. L. Fall. "The United States Market Wealth Portfolio." *Journal of Portfolio Management*, Fall 1979, pp. 82-92.

Ibbotson, R. G., and L. B. Siegel. "Real Estate Returns: A Comparison With Other Investments." *AREUEA Journal*, Vol. 12, no. 3 (Fall 1984), pp. 219-242.

Ibbotson, R. G., and R. A. Sinquefield. "Stocks, Bonds, Bills, and Inflation: Year by Year Historical Returns (1926-1974)." *Journal of Business*, Vol. 49 (January 1976), pp. 11-47.

Kau, J. B., and C. F. Sirmans. "Changes in Urban Land Values: 1836-1970." *Journal of Urban Economics*, Vol. 15 (1984), pp. 18-25.

McMahan, J. "Institutional Strategies for Real Estate Equity Investment." *Pension Trust Investment in Realty*, Practicing Law Institute, November/December 1981.

Miles, M., and T. McCue. "Historic Returns and Institutional Real Estate Portfolios." *AREUEA Journal*, Vol. 10, no. 2 (Summer 1982), pp. 184-199.

The NCREIF Report. Published by the National Council of Real Estate Investment Fiduciaries. Washington, D.C.: Issue III (Spring 1984).

Peiser, R. B. "Risk Analysis in Land Development." *AREUEA Journal*, Vol. 12, no. 1 (Spring 1984), pp. 12-29.

Robichek, A. A., R. A. Cohn, and J. J. Pringle. "Returns on Alternative Investment Media and Implications for Portfolio Construction." *Journal of Business*, July 1972.

Smith, K. V. "Historical Returns of Real Estate Equity Portfolios." *The Investment Managers Handbook*. Homewood, Ill.: Dow Jones/Irwin, 1980.

Webb, J. R., and C. F. Sirmans. "Yields for Selected Types of Real Property vs. the Money and Capital Markets." *The Appraisal Journal*, April 1982, pp. 228-242.

Zerbst, R. H., and B. R. Cambon. "Real Estate Returns and Risks." *Journal of Portfolio Management*, Vol. 10, no. 3 (Spring 1984), pp. 5-20.

Real Estate Returns and Inflation

David Hartzell, * *John S. Hekman,* ** *and Mike E. Miles* **

The ability of assets to protect an investor from purchasing power risk due to inflation has received a good deal of attention in the literature recently. The focus of much of this research has been on the properties of common stocks as inflation hedges. Bodie [1976] finds that the real return on equity is negatively related to both anticipated and unanticipated inflation; a similar result is obtained by Fama and Schwert [1977]. Bernard and Frecka [1983] examine individual common stock returns and find that the majority exhibit this negative relationship. This paper uses similar logic to examine the ability of a well-diversified portfolio of real estate to hedge against anticipated and unanticipated inflation.

INTRODUCTION

Real estate has received increasing attention in recent years as an alternative to stocks and bonds. The rapid growth of pension fund assets, accompanied by the passage of ERISA[1] and the relatively poor performance of the stock market through the 1970s, has resulted in an increased interest in real estate investment by institutions, especially through Commingled Real Estate Funds (CREFs). Several authors have tested the relationship of real estate returns and inflation (Ibbotson and Fall [1979]; Ibbotson and Siegel [1983];

*College of Business Administration 6.222, The University of Texas, Austin, Texas 78712. Currently on leave to Salomon Brothers Inc., One New York Plaza, New York, New York 10004.

**School of Business Administration, The University of North Carolina — Chapel Hill, Carroll Hall 012A, Chapel Hill, North Carolina 27514

Date Received: May 29, 1985; Revised: December 3, 1985.

[1]The Employment Retirement Security Act of 1974 redefined the role of the fiduciary and has come to serve as an endorsement for diversification across asset classes.

Fogler [1983]). However, none of these authors has performed a rigorous test of the response of these returns to inflation using a portfolio of real estate assets. Rather, they have used various indices to proxy for returns such as the home purchase price component of the CPI (Fama and Schwert) or home prices plus the USDA farm index (Fogler; Ibbotson and Fall).

This study utilizes quarterly holding-period returns from over 300 properties that comprise the assets of a large CREF.[2] It provides a greater degree of regional and property-type diversity as well as property-specific detail than any data set used to date. Two alternative models of expected and unexpected inflation are estimated over the period 1974-83; the results indicate that real estate returns compensate the investor for both types of inflation, and that a portfolio composed of real estate and default-free bonds can reduce inflation risk substantially below that of a bonds-only portfolio. Finally, the nature of this inflation protection is investigated by looking briefly at the degree of hedging available by property type, property value, and urban growth rate.

ASSET RETURNS AND INFLATION

The literature on stock market returns and inflation has found that monthly, quarterly and annual comparisons do not produce the presumed positive relationship (Fama and Schwert [1977]; Bodie [1976]). Schwert [1981] finds that stock prices react negatively, albeit modestly, to new information on inflation.

Interest rates are also presumed to provide inflation protection through the Fisher effect. Fama [1975] provides evidence that the bill market is efficient over the period 1953-71 in the sense that the market correctly uses all historic information in setting nominal rates of interest. However, this study assumed a constant real rate of interest. Subsequent work (Fama and Gibbons [1982]) has concluded that the expected real rate of interest is not independent of the expected rate of inflation, so that Treasury bills do have some amount of inflation risk.[3]

Studies of the Fisher effect have tended to show low and insignificant coefficients for the effect of inflation on nominal interest rates when periods before the 1970s were used. When the early 1970s are included, the effects are often unstable, suggesting that the equation has been misspecified by omitting important variables. More re-

---

[2] This CREF currently constitutes approximately 30% of pension fund equity investment in real estate.

[3] Note that the data for these studies is pre-DIDMCA (1980) which is widely believed to have increased real returns.

cently, Peek and Wilcox [1983] estimated a reduced-form equation for the nominal rate which included the effects of changes in effective marginal tax rates and aggregate supply shocks. They were able to reduce the instability of the expected inflation coefficient by a considerable amount over the postwar period 1952-1979. Fama and Gibbons [1983] adopted the alternative strategy of modeling expected inflation by allowing the real rate of interest to vary using a moving average process. As the period covered by this paper is considerably shorter than that covered by Peek and Wilcox, the approach used here is the Fama and Gibbons technique (which allows the use of pre-sample data to model the expected rate of inflation). Two measures of expected and unexpected inflation are presented, one with a constant real rate (following Fama and Schwert) and the other with a real rate that is allowed to vary using the Fama and Gibbons framework.

If the expected real interest rate is assumed to be constant, then nominal rates would increase on a one-to-one basis with expected inflation, and these nominal rates would provide an index of expected inflation. The one-period nominal interest rate realized in period t is that which is determined in the market at the end of period t-1, or

$$R(t\text{-}1) = r(t\text{-}1) + EI\,(t\text{-}1) \tag{1}$$

and so

$$EI(t\text{-}1) = -r(t\text{-}1) + R(t\text{-}1) \tag{2}$$

The inflation rate in period t, $\Delta(t)$, is the sum of the expected rate $EI(t\text{-}1)$ and the unexpected rate. Assuming the expected real rate of interest $r(t\text{-}1)$ to be a constant means that $R(t\text{-}1)$ is an index of expected inflation, and unexpected inflation ($UI(t)$), is the difference between actual inflation in t and the measure of expected inflation, $R(t\text{-}1)$. Thus, following Fama and Schwert, the equation to be estimated for an asset return R_j as an inflation hedge becomes

$$\tilde{R}_j\,(t) = \alpha_j + \beta_j\,R\,(t\text{-}1) + \gamma_j\,(\tilde{\Delta}(t) - R(t\text{-}1)) + \tilde{z}_j\,(t) \text{ where } \tilde{z}_j\,(t) \tag{3}$$

is the random disturbance term.

Alternatively, if the real interest rate embedded in $R(t\text{-}1)$ is not constant over time, then $R(t\text{-}1)$ is not an accurate reflection of the market's expected rate of inflation. The procedure used here to allow for a non-constant real rate is that adopted Fama and Gibbons [1983]. A Box-Jenkins model is used to forecast the real rate using moving average parameters. First the ex-post real rate of return series is calculated as

$$r(t) = R(t\text{-}1) - \Delta(t). \tag{4}$$

Applying the integrated moving average process and generating forecasts of the expected real return yields a time series resembling a random walk.[4] The expected rate of inflation is then the difference between the nominal interest rate and the forecast real rate $\hat{r}$:

$$EI(t) = R(t\text{-}1) - \hat{r}(t) \qquad (5)$$

Unexpected inflation is the difference between actual inflation and expected inflation:

$$UI(t) = \Delta(t) - [R(t\text{-}1) - \hat{r}(t)] \qquad (6)$$

The regression model to test for the inflation hedging ability of an asset j is

$$\tilde{R}_j(t) = \alpha_j + \beta_j[R(t\text{-}1) - \hat{r}(t)] + \gamma_j[\Delta(t) - (R(t\text{-}1) - \hat{r}(t))] + \tilde{z}_j(t) \qquad (7)$$

The models represented by (3) and (7) provide two alternative tests of an asset as an inflation hedge.

The effectiveness of assets such as real estate in providing protection from inflation is determined by the extent to which they can be used to reduce the purchasing power risk of an investor's portfolio.[5] Default-free Treasury bills are free of all risk except that from purchasing power, so the effectiveness of real estate as an inflation hedge can be measured by the proportionate reduction of the variance of return on Treasury bills by the addition of a diversified portfolio of real estate.

Following Bodie and Bernard and Frecka (1983), two measures are used in the empirical work to gauge the diversification benefits of real estate. The first is W_1, the proportion of real estate which should be held in a portfolio of government bonds and real estate in order to minimize the variance of the portfolio. The other is S_1, the proportionate reduction in the variance of the portfolio gained by holding the fraction W of the portfolio in real estate.[6]

---

[4] See Box and Jenkins (1970), pp. 123-44, 144-46.

[5] Other possible definitions of an inflation hedge cited by Bodie are: (a) elimination of the possibility that the real rate of return will fall below some set minimum (see Reilly, Johnson and Smith [1971]); (b) the real rate of return on an asset is independent of the rate of inflation (see Branch [1974]; Fama and Schwert[1977]). Definition (b) is consistent with the tests employed here, whereas (a) has not received a great deal of attention in the debate over inflation hedging, since it requires quite restrictive assumptions in any useful application.

[6] $W = [(1+R)(1+R+\alpha)]/[(1+r+\alpha)^2 + \text{var}(\tilde{\epsilon})/\text{var}(\tilde{UI})]$ and $S = [1+\text{var}(\tilde{\epsilon})/(1+r+\alpha)^2 \text{var}(UI)]^{-1}$, where $\alpha = \text{cov}(1+\tilde{r}_H, \tilde{UI})/\text{var}(\tilde{UI})$, $\tilde{r}_H = $ real return on portfolio of real estate and bonds, $\tilde{\epsilon}$ is the part of the real return $(1+\tilde{r}_H)$ which is uncorrelated with inflation

RELATIONSHIP TO PREVIOUS STUDIES

Most previous studies of real estate returns and inflation have used indices of the value of real property or portfolios which were limited in terms of the number of properties or property type.[7] The main problem involved with the use of an index is that it does not represent actual portfolio returns available to an investor. Further, it is not possible with a general index to estimate the diversification benefits of real estate by number of properties in the portfolio, property size, type, region or other characteristics.

The use of actual real estate portfolios in the literature is rather limited due to the lack of available data. Wendt and Wong [1965] look only at California apartment properties. Friedman [1970] uses a sample of 50 properties selected from two separate sources. Brueggeman, Chen and Thibodeau [1984], using commercial real estate, show no significant hedge against unexpected inflation. They use a two-factor CAPM to show low and insignificant correlations on their market index and significantly positive coefficients on inflation (the second factor). Following Fama, they derive a second two-factor model with expected and unexpected inflation and find no significance to the unexpected inflation factor. Unfortunately, they use two commingled funds' total return (non-property-specific data). Miles and McCue [1984] employ quarterly return data for a highly diversified portfolio of individual income properties for the period 1973-3 to 1981-3. Using the same method as Fogler [1981] to estimate the relationship of real estate returns to expected and unexpected inflation, they find a strong response to expected inflation as proxied by the average annual commercial paper rate and a weak relationship to unexpected inflation. One shortcoming of this study is the use of an annual interest rate with quarterly real estate returns, which tends to reduce the variation displayed by the expectations variable compared with the use of a quarterly interest rate. In addition, the sample period used may be unrepresentative, as the inflation rate rose more or less steadily from 1973 to 1981, so that the calculated

---

[7] Ibbotson and Fall use an index of residential and farm properties. Miles and McCue [1982] use portfolios of REIT properties. Fogler [1983] uses Ibbotson and Sinquefield data (in later years a combination of three indices) to show strong correlations of real estate returns with unexpected inflation.

Fogler uses annual commercial paper rates and constructs a proxy for unexpected inflation following Fama. In addition to the problems associated with annual data (note that Fama and Schwert had progressively better fits for real estate with longer time periods), the Ibbotson real estate index is a composite of three other composites: (1) Commerce Department residential homes (the rent component is typically neglected), (2) The Agriculture Department farmland series, and (3) The Frank Russell index.

real estate returns cover what could be considered a single period, and one which is far shorter than the spans used by Fama and Schwert, and Fogler.

THE DATA

The data set used in this study provides an opportunity to examine more closely the problem of measuring the potential of real estate investment as a hedge against expected and unexpected inflation. These data were supplied by a large financial institution from its commingled real estate fund. This portfolio begins with 113 properties in the fourth quarter of 1973, rises to a peak of 411 in 1982, and includes 382 properties in the last available quarter, 1983-3. The time period of analysis is a ten-year quarterly sample which exhibits both the increasing inflation of the late 1970s and the slowing inflation of the early 1980s.

In order to examine the response of returns to inflation by property type and other characteristics, holding period returns were developed directly from quarterly cash flow data and quarterly appraisals for individual properties. Previous studies (e.g., Brueggeman, Chen and Thibodeau) have used actual holding period returns calculated from CREF's unit values, i.e., from portfolios including near cash investments. In a strict sense, the property-specific data used here represent hypothetical holding period returns which could have been earned on portfolios formed from the total number of properties held by the CREF. However, these hypothetical returns bear a close relationship to the returns actually earned by pension fund investors in that the CREF's unit values (at which purchases and sales are made) are derived from the same cash flow and appraisal data. The use of property-specific CREF data yields a larger and more diverse sample of properties than has been available in previous studies. (Of course, it is possible that there are institutional biases in property selection which reduce the diversity of this particular CREF's portfolio despite its large aggregate size.)

Holding period returns (HPR) are calculated for each of the properties in the sample for each quarter in the sample period as follows

$$R_i(t) = \frac{MV_i(t+1) + C_i(t)}{MV_i(t) + I_i(t)} - 1$$

where $R_i(t)$ is the HPR for the ith property in the tth period. $MV_i(t)$ and $MV_i(t+1)$ are beginning-of-period and end-of-period market value. $C_i(t)$ is the cash flow earned in period t, and $I_i(t)$ is any change in cash investment which occurred in period t. The cash flow variable is total cash revenues net of operating expenses and property taxes. For properties which were purchased or sold during the sample period, no partial quarters of cash flow are included; the first full quarter for new properties and the last full quarter for sold properties are those used for the first and last quarters in the data set.[8]

Market values are determined by sales price when a property is sold and by appraised value for all other quarters. Pension funds can buy into or withdraw from the open-ended CREF at what is termed the net asset value. This value is determined each quarter, at which time market value estimates are made for each property and summed over all properties. Total market value is divided by the number of units held by the pension funds to arrive at the net asset value per unit, which serves as a price at which the units can be bought or sold.

Appraisals are done by an outside appraiser in each quarter for very large properties and annually for smaller properties. These small property estimates are updated quarterly by in-house staff. The income approach to valuation is used, meaning that an estimate of stabilized income is developed, and the net present value of this income stream is calculated using an appropriate capitalization rate. The resulting net asset value per unit is a market price in that pension fund trades are made on this basis.

A test of the accuracy of the appraised values can be obtained by comparing actual sales prices with the appraised value in the sale quarter. For the 89 properties that were sold over the sample period, the average premium of sales prices over appraised value was 8.7%. This indicates that the calculated holding period returns may be biased slightly downward. However, the recorded sales prices do not include all the costs to the fund of the sales, so that this difference may be overstated somewhat. Also, it is not known at what point in the quarter the appraised values are done. A lag

---

[8] The assumption is that investment (which was paid for during the quarter) actually occurred near the beginning of the period but that the initial market value did not include the impact of said investment. In the case of "earnouts" and tenant finishes, which were the largest additional investments, this assumption is fairly reasonable. In the case of major repairs (new roof), such investments should be treated as a cash outflow in the numerator. The database did not always distinguish the types of incremental investment and we have thus chosen to go with the formulation which fits the bulk of the incremental investments.

Cash flows were taken to a separate account as received and the interest income not included in the numerator, so no adjustment in the denominator is required for these interperiod flows.

between the appraisal and the time at which the sale price is determined may also explain part of the premium.[9,10]

Two samples have been constructed from the CREF data. The first contains data from all properties in the fund for all 40 quarters from 1973-4 to 1983-3. The fund grew from 113 to 382 properties over this period, and many of the acquisitions were new rather than existing structures. As a result, cash flow for many acquisitions is artificially low for some time during the absorption period. In the latter half of the sample period a much smaller proportion of the sample was in this absorption stage, so the cash flow portion of the return is a better reflection of the long-run income-producing ability of the portfolio. To test for the influence of this acquisition bias, the second sample is composed of those properties for which data are available in all of the last 20 quarters of the period, from 1978-4 to 1983-3. This produces a sample of 220 properties that were neither sold nor acquired during this time (only 78 properties with this characteristic are available for the entire 10-year period). The two samples are referred to hereafter as the 40-quarter sample (with 113 to 411 properties per quarter) and the 20-quarter sample (with the same 220 properties in each quarter).

These two portfolios of real estate are used to evaluate the relationship of real estate returns to expected and unexpected inflation. The quarterly default-free interest rate used for this comparison in the models outlined in the previous section is the yield on 3-month Treasury bills. Prices for these pure discount instruments are taken from quotes provided in the *Wall Street Journal.* The rate for quarter t is the yield implied by the market price 92 days prior to the end of that quarter. The inflation rate in period t is the percentage change in the Consumer Price Index (CPI) from t-1 to t. The next section of the paper describes the results of the inflation tests for the entire 40-quarter and 20-quarter samples, as well as for portfolios differing by property type, property size and SMSA growth rate.

---

[9] Clearly the use of appraised values is not ideal; yet, appraisals (with some corroborating sales) are the best data available for this important asset class. The engagement letter to the outside appraiser clearly states that the estimate desired is "market value" according to the definition given in the eighth edition of the American Institute of Real Estate Appraisers' text. Therefore such risk factors as an increase in the probability of future vacancies is included and the market value estimated should be a function of all the factors affecting a typical investor.

[10] With any database, the estimation of appropriate transaction costs is a problem. With commercial real estate the problem is most difficult because there is no standard commission and related costs may vary dramatically depending on the particular situation. We admit the limitation, yet an examination of the sales from this database indicate that while transaction costs varied substantially across properties, they were never over 3% of the sales price.

EMPIRICAL RESULTS

A test of the ability of real estate to hedge against inflation depends on a method of measuring expected and unexpected inflation, as described above. Fama and Schwert estimate the degree to which Treasury bills reflect expected inflation by testing the following model:

$$\tilde{\Delta}(t) = \alpha_0 + \alpha_1 R(t-1) + \tilde{\epsilon}(t)$$

Their results for the period 1953-71, using 3-month bills are

$$\Delta(t) = -0.0023 + 0.93\, R(t)\ R^2 = 0.48$$

which suggests that the T-bill rate compensates fully for inflation ($\alpha_1 \cong 1.0$), and the autocorrelations of this regression equation are insignificant.

The economic situation since 1971 has been considerably more turbulent, encompassing periods of low or even negative realized real returns during the inflation of the 1970s as well as the post-October 1979 period of fluctuating rates and higher realized returns. Table 1 presents estimates of the Fama-Schwert test for the 3-month bill rate as a measure of expected inflation over the period covered by this study.

TABLE 1

3-Month Treasury Bills as Measures of Expected Inflation

$$\Delta(t) = \hat{\alpha}_0 + \hat{\alpha}_1 R(t-1) + \hat{\epsilon}(t)$$

	α_0	α_1	R^2	Durbin-Watson
1. 1973-4/1983-3	0.013 (2.98)	0.338 (1.84)	0.08	0.89
2. 1976-1/1983-3	0.010 (2.05)	0.393 (1.93)	0.11	0.89
3. 1978-4/1983-3	0.007 (0.62)	0.500 (1.31)	0.09	0.78

t-statistics are in parentheses beneath estimated coefficients

Regression (1) shows that the fit is much poorer over the entire period than for the Fama-Schwert period, suggesting that the real rate of interest was not constant; this is also shown by the Durbin-Watson statistic, which suggests positive autocorrelation of the residuals. Regression (2) estimates the same relationship from the end of the wage and price controls period; the results here are substantially the same. Regression (3) covers the 20-quarter sample period from 1978-4 to 1983-3. Here the α_1 coefficient rises somewhat, but it is still insignificant, and there is still autocorrelation. It appears that real interest rates were low in the early part of the 1974-83 period and high at the end, so that this test, which assumes a constant real rate, produces estimates of α_0 which are biased upward and estimates of α_1 biased downward.

The alternative measure of expected inflation as outlined above allows the real rate of interest to wander using the integrated moving average process. Expected inflation is measured as the difference between the T-bill rate and the modeled real rate; unexpected inflation is then calculated as actual inflation less this alternate measure of expected inflation. The results of the moving average estimation process indicate a highly significant positive coefficient, suggesting a good fit for the model. This model allows the real rate of interest to be lower during the mid and late 70s when unexpected inflation was running quite high, and on the other side of the cycle it has the real rate increasing in the early 80s. These two sets of estimates thus allow for two distinctly different sets of assumptions about the behavior of the capital market under which to test the ability of a real estate portfolio to hedge against the two components of inflation.[11]

INFLATION HEDGE RESULTS: ALL PROPERTIES

The first tests were performed on the entire portfolio of properties in the 40-quarter and 20-quarter samples with quarterly holding period returns, value-weighted using the market value of each property in that quarter. Table 2 presents the results of the hedge regressions for both samples and both measures of expected and unexpected inflation. The Bodie measure of the optimal proportion of the asset to be combined with the Treasury securities (W) is reported along with S, the percentage reduction of the bond portfolio inflation risk. Finally, the ratio W/S measures the efficiency of inflation risk reduction.

Using either the constant real rate assumption (hereafter Fama-Schwert) or the variable real rate (a variation of Fama-Gibbons), real estate appears to have provided complete protection from expected inflation over both periods ($\alpha_1 > 1.0$). The α_2 coefficients for unexpected inflation are greater than 1.0 for the 20-quarter sample and are within one standard error of one in the 40-quarter sample. All coefficients are significant at the 5% level except for the co-

---

[11] A table showing quarterly estimates of expected and unexpected inflation rates with the moving average real interest rate is available from the authors.

TABLE 2

Results of Inflation Hedge Regressions for
Expected and Unexpected Inflation

Inflation Expectation Measures	α_1 (Expected)	α_2 (Unexpected)	W	S	W/S	R^2
40-Quarter Sample, 1973-4 to 1983-3						
1. *EI1, UI1* (Constant real return)	1.44 (4.85)	0.76 (3.24)	32.7	19.1	1.71	.40
2. *EI2, UI2* (Moving average real return)	2.23 (3.83)	0.98 (1.97)	14.6	6.3	2.31	.36
20-Quarter Sample, 1978-4 to 1983-3						
1. *EI1, UI1*	1.09 (1.69)	1.77 (4.67)	34.8	59.1	0.59	.56
2. *EI2, UI2*	1.65 (4.26)	1.63 (2.95)	20.7	24.8	0.84	.53

t-statistics in parentheses beneath estimated coefficients

efficient on the Fama-Schwert expected inflation measure in the 20-quarter sample. The measures of W and S vary widely, but it seems that real estate offers about a 20% reduction in inflation risk with a 20% share of real estate in the portfolio. These values are higher for the 20-quarter sample (1978-83) than for the entire 10-year period.

These results contrast markedly with the inflation hedge results reported by others for common stocks (Bodie; Fama and Schwert). The results continue to hold for the more recent years, a turbulent period for interest rates in which old relationships have broken down in the wake of the Federal Reserve System's move away from interest rate targeting in 1979 and the deregulation of capital markets in the 1980s. In fact, the evidence presented here suggests that the ability of real estate to hedge against the risk of inflation has been greater since 1978 than before.[12]

RESULTS BY PROPERTY TYPE

The market value of real property and its cash flow may respond differently to inflation across property types. Many retail leases

[12] Tests using equally-weighted portfolios produced substantially the same result.

contain provisions tying rent to a percentage of gross revenue, so that lease revenues tend to vary directly with the general price level. In several types, there may also be a "pass-through" of operating expenses specified in the lease so that gross (but not net) revenue will increase automatically with cost.[13] Obviously, the response of occupancy rates to the causes of the unexpected inflation will also have a major bearing on the quality of the inflation hedge.

For the tests performed here, the samples are divided into portfolios by three property types: industrial, office and retail.[14] Differences in inflation protection by type are an indication of the degree to which property revenues and expected future revenues respond to inflation and on a quarterly basis. A priori, properties whose income is based directly on the sale of goods and services (which include retail in this sample) should provide better protection than those properties whose rents are not tied directly to the firm's sales (here, industrial and office).

TABLE 3

Results of Inflation Hedge Regressions
by Property Type

Property Type	40-Quarter Sample, 1973-4 to 1983-3					
	α_1	α_2	W	S	W/S	R^2
Industrial						
1. EI1, UI1	3.57 (1.65)	2.07 (1.26)	2.52	1.63	0.94	.07
2. EI2, UI2	3.16 (1.87)	0.80 (0.37)	-0.20	0.005	-3.78	.09
Office						
3. EI1, UI1	1.45 (3.70)	0.55 (1.84)	16.37	6.50	2.52	.27
4. EI2, UI2	1.12 (3.73)	-0.03 (0.07)	-1.07	0.05	-23.50	.31
Retail						
5. EI1, UI1	0.54 (1.21)	0.75 (2.18)	24.39	22.55	1.08	.11
6. EI2, UI2	0.57 (1.62)	0.98 (2.21)	17.04	20.42	0.84	.13

[13] A major difference among property types can occur through variation in the average length of leases. Properties with longer leases which do not have CPI escalator clauses will clearly not see their cash returns increase immediately as inflation rises.
[14] See the Appendix for a complete description of these portfolios.

TABLE 3 (Continued)

Property Type	20-Quarter Sample, 1978-4 to 1983-3					
	α_1	α_2	W	S	W/S	R^2
Industrial						
1. *EI1, UI1*	0.94	1.56	20.62	31.53	0.65	.28
	(0.92)	(2.59)				
2. *EI2, UI2*	1.41	1.61	11.93	15.83	0.75	.27
	(2.33)	(1.89)				
Office						
3. *EI1, UI1*	1.34	2.81	19.05	50.09	0.38	.48
	(1.11)	(3.96)				
4. *EI2, UI2*	2.53	2.65	8.48	13.75	0.62	.43
	(3.44)	(2.53)				
Retail						
5. *EI1, UI1*	-0.04	1.14	19.43	25.12	0.77	.20
	(0.04)	(1.95)				
6. *EI2, UI2*	0.92	0.97	10.13	10.26	0.99	.13
	(1.53)	(1.13)				

t-statistics are in parentheses

Table 3 presents the results of the two inflation tests by property type for the 40-quarter and 20-quarter samples. In the 40-quarter sample the overall results are weak as indicated by the low R^2. Industrial and office properties provide complete protection from expected inflation (coefficients greater than 1.0), while retail properties are much weaker. Conversely, the retail properties appear to provide a better hedge against unexpected inflation (coefficients approximately equal to 1.0) presumably due to the prevalence of expense pass-through and percentage rents in retail leases.

For the 20-quarter sample (which uses the same 220 properties throughout), the results are stronger. Industrial and office properties show complete protection from expected and unexpected inflation, with generally significant coefficients and much higher R^2 values than those for the 40-quarter sample. This is consistent with a change in leasing strategy toward shorter leases with more expense pass-through which occurred as investment managers/property managers reacted to continued high inflation.

The modified Fama-Gibbons form of the equation (*EI2, UI2*) seems to result in markedly higher estimates of expected inflation protection. This *EI2* measure allows the real rate of interest to change from quarter to quarter, and this feature is most useful in this period

(1978-1983) when nominal interest rates were so volatile. However, retail properties do not show strong inflation protection using either the Fama-Schwert or the Fama-Gibbons measures, although the results are much stronger than for the 40-quarter sample. Overall, the results by property type tend to confirm the results for all properties together: real estate, as measured by the properties in this CREF, produced impressive inflation protection over the period 1973-1983.

TESTS BY PROPERTY SIZE

Property size may have an effect on inflation risk mainly through both the nature of the tenant and the type of lease used. The relative proportion of single to multi-tenant properties decreases as property size increases. For the two largest size categories, 97% of the properties leased to more than one tenant.

If there is some variation in the effects of inflation on individual firms, then this will be transmitted to real estate returns through their demand for space. This factor appears to be borne out by the results of hedge regressions by property size reported in Table 4. The coefficients of expected and unexpected inflation generally rise with property size. The two smallest categories, representing properties under $2.5 million, provided less-than-complete protection (coefficients less than 1.0), the third category is mixed, and categories 4-6 (over $5 million) in general show more-than-complete protection against expected inflation and stronger protection against unexpected inflation. These results suggest that portfolios made up of larger properties are superior inflation hedges. (Naturally this conclusion must be tempered by the possibility of selection bias inherent in a database whose properties were selected by one investment manager.)

TEST BY URBAN GROWTH RATE

Tests for inflation protection by city (SMSA) growth rate were also performed. Properties in fast-growing cities may have a greater potential to hedge against inflation because of the higher growth rate of demand for office space. Many slow-growing cities are burdened with unfavorable industrial structures that may lag behind the growth of the country as a whole and suffer disproportionately in recessions. Property owners, employing a strategy of writing short-term leases and incurring possible vacancy losses, may find it easier to locate new tenants in rapidly-growing areas. Some support for this idea is given in Table 5, which shows the lease maturity distribution by fast- and slow-growth SMSAs. Faster-growing SMSAs have a

TABLE 4

Inflation Hedge Regressions by
Property Value

Property Value (000)	40-Quarter Sample, 1973-4 to 1983-3					
	α_1	α_2	W	S	W/S	R^2
$0 - 999						
1. $EI1$, $UI1$	0.85 (1.65)	0.51 (1.26)	3.89	2.24	1.74	.02
2. $EI2$, $UI2$	0.61 (0.78)	0.54 (0.54)	2.62	1.96	1.34	.02
$1000 - 2499						
1. $EI1$, $UI1$	1.18 (2.35)	0.66 (1.72)	14.98	9.07	1.65	.14
2. $EI2$, $UI2$	0.94 (2.36)	0.43 (0.86)	16.15	24.44	0.66	.13
$2500 - 4999						
1. $EI1$, $UI1$	1.07 (3.27)	0.07 (2.92)	34.86	24.86	1.40	.26
2. $EI2$, $UI2$	0.89 (3.42)	0.63 (1.91)	19.95	13.92	1.43	.24
$5000 - 9999						
1. $EI1$, $UI1$	1.19 (4.41)	0.58 (2.81)	39.73	20.90	1.90	.35
2. $EI2$, $UI2$	0.91 (4.22)	0.30 (1.11)	17.26	6.54	2.64	.33
$10000-19999						
1. $EI1$, $UI1$	1.16 (1.97)	0.29 (0.64)	5.22	1.37	3.81	.10
2. $EI2$, $UI2$	0.70 (1.48)	0.04 (0.07)	2.42	0.59	4.12	.07
> $20000						
1. $EI1$, $UI1$	2.06 (3.54)	1.18 (2.58)	12.97	9.82	1.32	.28
2. $EI2$, $UI2$	1.66 (3.55)	0.79 (1.29)	4.28	1.84	2.32	.27

higher than average proportion of short-term leases, suggesting that leases may be written with the expectation that growth will continue and new tenants willing to pay higher rents will be found when leases expire.

On the other hand, the vacancy risk from shorter leases might dominate the price flexibility factor, so that returns on net may not

TABLE 4 (Continued)

Property Value (000)	20-Quarter Sample, 1978-4 to 1983-3					
	α_1	α_2	W	S	W/S	R^2
$0 - 999						
1. EI1, UI1	-2.22	1.46	8.39	16.39	0.51	.22
	(1.21)	(1.35)				
2. EI2, UI2	0.60	1.68	4.86	9.15	0.53	.06
	(0.56)	(1.00)				
$1000 - 2499						
1. EI1, UI1	0.62	0.95	11.55	11.57	1.00	.09
	(0.50)	(1.28)				
2. EI2, UI2	1.02	0.41	3.19	1.36	2.34	.11
	(1.40)	(0.39)				
$2500 - 4999						
1. EI1, UI1	1.87	1.22	27.52	29.21	0.94	.41
	(2.60)	(2.88)				
2. EI2, UI2	1.48	0.78	10.29	5.11	2.01	.43
	(3.58)	(1.32)				
$5000 - 9999						
1. EI1, UI1	2.10	1.34	34.09	38.85	0.88	.55
	(3.53)	(3.83)				
2. EI2, UI2	1.50	1.37	22.08	23.14	0.95	.51
	(4.13)	(2.64)				
$10000-19999						
1. EI1, UI1	2.29	0.67	10.42	4.88	2.14	.29
	(2.58)	(1.28)				
2. EI2, UI2	1.08	0.46	5.55	2.44	2.27	.19
	(1.94)	(0.57)				
> $20000						
1. EI1, UI1	0.58	3.33	14.08	45.54	0.31	.43
	(0.36)	(3.48)				
2. EI2, UI2	2.73	3.29	6.15	12.90	0.48	.34
	(2.68)	(2.26)				

t-statistics are in parentheses

compensate for inflation. In the older slow-growth areas, leases may be written to provide inflation protection for the lessor, passing the risk on to the lessee, whereas in fast-growth areas lease rate speculation may dominate inflation concerns. Thus the hypothesis to be tested is whether properties in fast-growth areas actually provide a better hedge against inflation (given the limitations imposed by the tendency toward shorter leases in these areas). The results of the hedge regressions for fast- and slow-growing areas are presented in Table 6, using the 20-quarter sample. Using any of the criteria — the

TABLE 5

Lease Maturity For High-Growth
And Low-Growth SMSAs*

Lease Maturity	Low Growth		High Growth	
	Number	Percent	Number	Percent
0-2 years	27	36	64	44
2-5 years	27	36	62	43
Over 5 years	21	28	19	13
Total	75	100	145	100

*High-growth areas (more than 2.5% per year employment growth): Anaheim, Houston, Denver, Miami, Dallas, Atlanta, Seattle, Washington, D.C., Minneapolis, New Orleans, Los Angeles, San Francisco; low-growth areas (less than 2.5% per year): Indianapolis, Stamford, Cincinnati, Boston, Newark, St. Louis, Philadelphia, Chicago, Detroit, Cleveland, Pittsburgh, New York.

TABLE 6

Hedge Regressions by Growth of SMSA
20-Quarter Sample

Growth Rate	α_1	α_2	W	S	W/S	R^2
Inflation Measures: $EI1$, $UI1$						
Fast	1.47 (1.73)	1.36 (2.71)	24.47	30.68	0.80	.33
Slow	0.63 (0.57)	2.18 (3.36)	20.59	44.30	0.46	.40
Inflation Measures: $EI2$, $UI2$						
Fast	1.42 (2.85)	1.23 (1.73)	13.18	12.71	1.04	.33
Slow	1.88 (2.77)	2.00 (2.06)	9.67	13.49	0.72	.33

t-statistics are in parentheses

estimated coefficients, reduction in inflation risk (S) or relative efficiency of risk reduction (W/S) — the slow-growing cities show themselves to be a somewhat better hedge, but both groups of cities provide more or less complete inflation protection. The differences between them are not large enough to draw any firm conclusions about which group is necessarily superior. Since slow-growing cities appear to provide, if anything, better inflation protection, there is no support for the idea that fast-growing cities perform better.

CONCLUSIONS

Real estate has become an increasingly popular vehicle for providing a new source of diversification in investor's portfolios. By the end of 1983, pension funds had placed over 20 billion of their nearly 1 trillion dollar aggregate portfolio in commercial real estate equities (see *Pension and Investment Age* [1984]). An important motivation for this trend has been the desire to provide protection from expected and unexpected inflation. The academic literature on inflation and real estate returns has not provided a clear answer about the degree of protection which can be afforded. In particular, tests for protection against unexpected inflation have obtained generally weak results.

The results reported here provide strong evidence that diversified portfolios of commercial real estate have been a complete hedge against both expected and unexpected inflation over the period 1973-83. The database supporting these conclusions is superior to those used in previous studies for a combination of reasons including diversification of property type, size and location; property-specific information; consistent accounting and relevant time period. The inflation rate was 5% or greater over this entire period, but real estate experienced both rising and falling values as the inflation rate accelerated and subsequently decelerated.

Returns by property type also show strong inflation protection with industrial properties holding an inconclusive edge. Larger properties performed better than smaller ones in this sample, which may have been due to the diversification which results from the positive relationship of size and number of tenants. Separating the sample into two portfolios by the growth rate of the SMSAs in which they are located did not reveal any advantage for rapidly-growing markets in hedging against inflation.

Several questions remain in judging the performance of real estate as compared to common stocks in inflationary periods. Quarterly holding period returns are a relevant measure to use for a CREF in that pension funds are allowed to buy and sell based on unit values calculated each quarter. However, one wonders if inflation protection is properly estimated on a quarterly basis. More needs to be done on the measurement of expected and unexpected inflation. Peek and Wilcox [1983] have shown that interest rates are affected by taxes and supply factors. This means that neither the Fama and Schwert nor the Fama and Gibbons approach to expected inflation correctly deals with the complex interaction of taxes, inflation and the real interest rate. Until some expected inflation formulation is generally agreed upon, it will not be possible to measure the risk-reduction benefits of commercial real estate precisely. Finally, the use of appraised values and difficulties with the return calculation continue to be troubling issues.

APPENDIX

TABLE ONE
Number of Properties in the 40-Quarter Data Set*

Quarter	Industrial	Office	Retail	Residential	Hotel-Motel
Q473	95	9	4	2	3
Q174	97	9	5	4	3
Q274	99	14	5	4	4
Q374	105	15	7	4	4
Q474	114	17	8	5	4
Q175	123	18	8	5	4
Q275	129	21	9	6	5
Q375	130	23	9	6	5
Q475	134	26	10	6	5
Q176	139	31	11	6	5
Q276	141	31	11	6	5
Q376	140	32	11	6	5
Q476	143	32	24	6	5
Q177	144	36	24	6	5
Q277	143	37	26	6	5
Q377	144	37	26	6	5
Q477	206	36	26	6	5
Q178	209	35	26	6	5
Q278	211	35	26	6	5
Q378	213	36	26	6	5
Q478	215	37	20	6	5
Q179	213	40	20	6	5
Q279	212	43	21	6	5
Q379	212	44	21	6	5
Q479	211	44	23	6	5
Q180	211	46	23	5	6
Q280	212	50	24	5	6
Q380	218	51	26	5	6
Q480	233	56	35	5	6
Q180	244	60	36	5	6
Q281	244	59	39	5	6
Q381	250	61	40	4	6
Q481	265	71	46	4	7
Q182	267	82	46	4	7
Q282	269	85	46	4	7
Q382	268	86	46	4	6
Q482	267	82	45	4	6
Q183	265	80	44	4	5
Q283	259	79	44	4	5
Q383	254	78	42	3	5

*The number of residential and hotel-motel properties constitute subsamples which are too small to be meaningful.

TABLE TWO
Number of Properties in the 20-Quarter Sample

TOTAL	EAST	MIDWEST	WEST	SOUTH
220	12	75	97	36

IND*	OFFICE	RETAIL	RES*	HOT/MOT*
176	23	15	3	5

SIZE 1	SIZE 2	SIZE 3	SIZE 4	SIZE 5	SIZE 6
76	73	35	20	12	4

FAST-GROWTH SMSA	SLOW-GROWTH SMSA
145	75

Note: There are 220 properties in each quarter, therefore one quarter is representative of all. Property size is the only exception, as market values increase from quarter to quarter.

*Industrial, Residential and Hotel/Motel

REFERENCES

[1] Bernard, Victor V. and T. Frecka. Evidence on the Existence of Common Stock Inflation Hedges. *Journal of Financial Research* 6(4): 301-312, 1983.

[2] Z. Bodie. Common Stocks as a Hedge Against Inflation. *Journal of Finance* 31(2): 459-470, 1976.

[3] G.E.P. Box and G.M. Jenkins. *Time Series Analysis, Forecasting and Control.* Holden-Day, 1970.

[4] B. Branch. Common Stock Performance and Inflation: An International Comparison. *Journal of Business* 47(1): 48-52, 1974.

[5] W. B. Brueggeman, A. H. Chen and T. G. Thibodeau. Real Estate Investment Funds: Performance and Portfolio Considerations. *AREUEA Journal* 12(3): 333-354, 1984.

[6] E. F. Fama. Short-Term Interest Rates as Predictors of Inflation. *American Economic Review* 65(3): 269-282, 1975.

[7] E. Fama and M. Gibbons. Inflation, Real Returns and Capital Investment. *Journal of Monetary Economics* 9(3): 297-324, 1982.

[8] _____. A Comparison of Inflation Forecasts. Working Paper, 1983.

[9] E. Fama and G.W. Schwert. Asset Returns and Inflation. *Journal of Financial Economics* 5(2): 115-146, 1977.

[10] R.H. Fogler. A Mean-Variance Analysis of Real Estate. *Journal of Portfolio Management*, Winter 1983.

[11] H.C. Friedman. Real Estate Investment and Portfolio Theory. *Journal of Financial and Quantitative Analysis*, April 1970.

[12] J.W. Hoag. Towards Indices of Real Estate Value and Return. *Journal of Finance* 35(2): 569-580, 1980.

[13] R.G. Ibbotson and C.L. Fall. The United States Market Wealth Portfolio. *Journal of Portfolio Management* 7(1): 82-92. 1979.

[14] R.G. Ibbotson and L.B. Siegel. The World Wealth Portfolio. *Journal of Portfolio Management* 9(2): 5-17, 1983.

[15] R.G. Ibbotson and R.A. Sinquefield. Stocks, Bonds, Bills and Inflation: The Past and the Future. Financial Analysis Research Foundation, 1982.

[16] M. Miles and T. McCue. Commercial Real Estate Returns. *AREUEA Journal* 12(3): 355-377, 1984.

[17] _____. Historic Returns and Institutional Real Estate Portfolios. *AREUEA Journal* 10(2): 184-199, 1982.

[18] J. Peek and J.A. Wilcox. The Postwar Stability of the Fisher Effect. *Journal of Finance* 38(4): 1111-1124, 1983.

[19] *Pension and Investment Age*, January 1984

[20] G.W. Schwert. The Adjustment of Stock Prices to Information About Inflation. *The Journal of Finance* 36(1): 15-30, 1981.

[21] P. Wendt and S. Wong. Investment Performance: Common Stocks vs. Apartment Houses. *Journal of Finance* 20(4): 633-646, 1965.

Real Estate Risk and Return Expectations: Recent Survey Results

*David J. Hartzell**
*James R. Webb***

Abstract. Investment and portfolio studies generally use ex post risk and return data, although expected risk and return data is what should be used. This is probably due to the dearth of such data or the difficulty and/or cost of obtaining it on a current basis. This study reports the results of a survey of major real estate investors and researchers, i.e., large life insurance companies, real estate advisors, large pension funds and selected academics. The survey examined investment horizon, expectations about inflation, total returns on real estate, distribution between income and appreciation returns, the volatility of real estate returns, and the correlation of real estate returns with stocks returns, bond returns, and inflation. In addition, the study contains results for the above before and after the October 19, 1987 stock market crash.

Introduction

For investment and portfolio studies, the expected risks, returns, etc., not the historical risks and returns, are the most appropriate data according to financial theory. However, such data is rarely available, due to the difficulty and/or costs to gather it. This is especially true for real estate.

This study is an attempt to partially alleviate this problem. A survey was conducted using major real estate investors and researchers. Included in the survey subjects were large life insurance companies, real estate advisors, large pension funds and academics active in real estate investment research. The survey examined expectations about inflation, total returns from real estate, the volatility of real estate returns and the correlation of real estate returns with stock returns, bond returns and inflation.

Section two contains the methodology and results while section three discusses the conclusions.

Methodology and Results

The methodology used in this study is a questionnaire. The survey was designed by the Salomon Brothers, Inc. Real Estate Research Group and reviewed by the Institute for Research

*Department of Finance, School of Business, University of North Carolina, Chapel Hill, North Carolina 27514.
**Department of Finance, College of Business Administration, University of Akron, Akron, Ohio 44325.

Date Revised — September 1988; Accepted — October 1988.

in the Social Sciences at the University of North Carolina at Chapel Hill. Copies of the questionnaire are available from the first author upon request.

Of the 240 surveys sent out, 110 were returned by mid-December, 1987. The first mailing of the survey was made on October 1, 1987 and a follow-up letter was mailed on October 26, 1987. A further follow-up and a new survey was sent to all respondents on November 15, 1987. The results of the responses show interesting differences about expected performance among insurance companies, pension funds, and academics. Interestingly, of the 100 pension funds to whom the survey was sent (largest by asset size), some indicated that either they a) did not respond to surveys, b) did not manage any of the real estate decisions in the portfolio (that is, the actual allocation to the asset class was made by one advisor, and the actual investment was made by another advisor), or c) did not feel that they had enough expertise to respond to the survey. Given the fact that pension funds have begun to play a major role in the real estate markets, these types of responses were quite unexpected.

Of the 110 surveys which were returned, 23 of 45 sent were from insurance companies, 42 of 56 sent were from real estate consultants and advisors, 18 of 35 sent were from academics, and 19 of 100 sent were from pension funds. The remainder of the responses were either from Canadian life insurance companies or from other groups which were not easily classified into the above categories.

An obvious consideration of the survey, given its timing, is the effect that the collapse of the stock market on October 19, 1987 had on the respondents' attitudes toward real estate performance. Since each survey respondent was asked the date on which the survey was completed, an analysis of these changes was performed. While not a matched sample of the same respondents before and after the collapse the differences among before- and after-collapse respondents do supply some useful information. Of the 110 respondents, 51 indicated that the survey was completed prior to October 19, while the remainder (59) responded after the collapse of the stock market.

Investment Horizon

The first part of the survey asked the time interval that should be used for short–term and long–term strategic decisions in real estate investment. Virtually all of the respondents agreed that about a three–year perspective was correct for analyzing short-term real estate investment performance. Furthermore, all respondents think that about a ten–year horizon is correct for long–term performance evaluation.

Inflation Expectations

Since inflation has been shown to be important for real estate returns [2], the subjects were asked their three–year and ten–year average annual inflation expectations. Exhibit 1 contains the results for this question by type of respondent and pre- or post-collapse response.

Overall, the respondents generally believe that the average inflation level will increase over the next ten years relative to the next three-year period. For example, of the 100 who answered the inflation questions, the mean response for average annual inflation over the next three years was 4.9%, while the average expectation for inflation over the next ten-year period was 5.5% (see Exhibit 1). Therefore, while inflation is expected to be somewhat moderate, the rate is expected to increase, on average, by .6%. These levels are indicated by pre-collapse and post-collapse respondents.

Exhibit 1
Inflation Expectations

	All Respondents	Pre-Collapse	Post-Collapse
No. of responses	100	45	55
3–year Horizon	4.9%	4.9%	4.8%
10–year Horizon	5.5%	5.5%	5.4%
Life Insurance Cos.			
N	23	13	10
3–year	5.1%	5.1%	5.0%
10–year	5.5%	5.7%	5.3%
Real Estate Advs.			
N	41	17	24
3–year	4.7%	4.9%	4.5%
10–year	5.5%	5.5%	5.5%
Academics			
N	18	8	10
3–year	5.1%	4.9%	5.3%
10–year	5.7%	5.8%	5.7%
Pension Funds			
N	18	8	11
3-year	4.9%	4.8%	5.0%
10–year	5.1%	4.8%	5.3%

When the respondents are sorted by their affiliation, the results are quite similar. The average expectation, both pre- and post-collapse for the next three years is close to 5% for respondents from life insurance companies, real estate advisors and consultants, academics, and pension funds. Over the next ten years, the expectations increase along the same lines as indicated above, with all respondents, except for the pension funds, expecting somewhat higher inflation for the longer period. Real estate advisors and consultants responding after October 19 expect average inflation to increase by a full percentage point over the ten-year relative to the three–year horizon. However, the pre-collapse pension fund respondents do not expect inflation to increase as much as the post-collapse respondents and their expectations change little over the two horizons.

Of the 23 life insurance company respondents to the survey, seven, or 30%, expected average inflation to decrease over the ten-year, as opposed to the three-year horizon. Similarly, only seven of forty-one (17%) real estate advisors, four of eighteen (22%) academics, and six of eighteen (33%) pension funds expected average inflation to fall. Taking these responses out of the sample, the average inflation expectation for those expecting inflation to increase, on average, over the two horizons is 4.7% over three years and 5.9% over ten years.

Total Return Expectations

Next, subjects were asked about their total return expectations (income and appreciation) over a three–year and a ten–year horizon and what factors they thought would affect the returns. A summary of the responses is shown in Exhibit 2 by type of respondent and pre- or post-collapse response.

Although the pre-collapse and post-collapse respondents are different, it is instructive to compare the expectations for total return from the two perspectives. On average, the expectations

Exhibit 2
Expectations of Total Return

	All Respondents	Pre-Collapse	Post-Collapse
No. of responses	100	45	55
3–year Horizon	9.2%	9.1%	9.2%
10–year	11.3%	11.6%	11.0%
Horizon			
Life Insurance Cos.			
N	23	13	10
3–year	9.7%	10.2%	9.1%
10–year	11.8%	12.4%	11.1%
Real Estate Advs.			
N	41	17	24
3–year	8.9%	9.0%	8.9%
10–year	11.2%	11.6%	11.0%
Academics			
N	18	8	10
3–year	9.6%	8.6%	10.5%
10–year	11.4%	11.3%	11.4%
Pension Funds			
N	18	7	11
3–Year	8.6%	8.2%	8.8%
10–Year	10.5%	10.2%	10.7%

*partially adapted from [3]

differ little. Short–term expectations are for a 9.1% return in both the pre-collapse and post-collapse cases, and the long–term expectations in both cases are similar (11.0% vs 11.6%). While, on average, there is similarity, the responses show some differences by affiliation.

Life insurance company respondents were far more bullish on the prospects for real estate before the collapse, than after the collapse, in the short term. Prior to October 19, representatives from life insurance companies expected average returns over the next three years to be 10.2%, but after October 19 their expectations were for a 9.1% total return. A similar drop in return expectation (130 basis points) exists for the ten-year horizon. On the contrary, academics exhibited a marked increase in expectations after the collapse, as their expected returns increased to 10.5% from 8.6%. However, ten-year expectations are similar at 11.3 and 11.4% respectively. It appears that while there are some differences in opinion over the short term, all respondents expect similar returns over the longer run.

Consultants and academics were most bullish in responses dated prior to October 19, with expected returns increasing by 260 and 270 basis points respectively over the two horizons. However, after the collapse, academics only expected a 90–basis-point increase in total return from three to ten years. Otherwise, after the collapse, the responses generally indicate a 200–basis-point increase in expectations for the three-year relative to the ten-year horizon.

Distribution between Income and Appreciation Returns

The expectation of the proportion of total return for the next three years which is composed of the appreciation component is, on average, 21%. This, combined with the 9.2% expectation of total return, implies a 1.93% expected appreciation in value. For the ten–year horizon, this proportion is expected to increase to 36% for all respondents, signifying an expectation of

Exhibit 3
The Historical Performance of Real Estate and Financial Assets, Annualized Returns, 4Q77–1Q87

	Real Estate (FRC Index)	Bonds (Sal. Bros. Bond Index)	Stocks (S&P 500)
Mean Return	13.3%	11.9%	20.2%
Volatility	2.7	15.7	15.1

more rapidly increasing values for real estate. Indeed, given the 11.6% expected return for post-collapse respondents, this implies an expected appreciation rate of over 4% per year, on average.

Among the respondent types, there was very little divergence among expectations regarding the relative income and appreciation components of total return. The only significant exceptions are pre-crash pension fund respondents, who expect only a 10% appreciation component over the next three years, relative to the 21% average reported above.

Volatility for Real Estate Versus Stocks and Bonds

The results for this part of the study are discussed extensively by Hartzell and Shulman elsewhere [3] and so, for the most part, will not be repeated here. However, Exhibit 3 displays the ex post mean returns and volatility (standard deviation) of commercial real estate (as estimated by the Frank Russell Company Index), bonds (as estimated by the Salomon Brothers Bond Index) and common stocks (as estimated by the S&P 500). Real estate volatility is about one-sixth of that for stocks and bonds. Only 18% of the respondents (18/102) said they believed that the FRC, Frank Russell Company Index approximated the actual volatility of real estate! Respondents generally believed real estate risk to be between 65% of stock risk (pre-collapse) to 54% of stock risk (post-collapse).

Real Estate Return Correlations

Correlations of returns for various assets classes play a key role in asset allocation decisions. The degree to which movements in asset returns offset each other, along with expectations of returns and volatility, serve as the inputs to techniques which have been developed to determine optimal portfolios. Previous studies have shown that real estate returns, which include appreciation returns measured by appraisals to estimate market values, have experienced high positive correlations with inflation, insignificant correlations with stocks and marginally negative correlations with bonds [2]. These studies have used data that typically included the late 1970s and early 1980s, periods in which real estate markets were generally in supply and demand balance.

Since 1982 however, the nation has experienced an unprecedented construction boom, which has increased national vacancy rates to 16% in downtown areas, and 23% in suburban markets. Given relatively weak market fundamentals, rents and values are not expected to increase as closely with rates of inflation, and therefore future behavior of real estate returns, stock returns, and bond returns is difficult to estimate.

Exhibit 4
Average Correlations of Real Estate with Inflation, Stocks, and Bonds

| | Horizon | Correlation Coefficients | | |
		Inflation	Stocks	Bonds
All Respondents	3–Years	0.36	−0.13	0.00
	10–Years	0.59	−0.02	−0.04
Pre-Collapse	3–Years	0.28	−0.06	−0.04
	10–Years	0.58	0.06	−0.08
Post-Collapse	3–Years	0.42	−0.19	0.04
	10–Years	0.60	−0.09	−0.01
Life Insurance Cos.				
All Respondents	3–Years	0.39	−0.16	0.01
	10–Years	0.60	0.02	0.05
Pre-Collapse	3–Years	0.51	−0.09	−0.03
	10–Years	0.69	0.19	0.01
Post-Collapse	3–Years	0.22	−0.26	0.07
	10–Years	0.48	−0.21	0.11
Consults/Advs.				
All Respondents	3–Years	0.33	−0.21	−0.06
	10–Years	0.59	−0.15	−0.10
Pre-Collapse	3–Years	0.17	−0.08	−0.12
	10–Years	0.61	0.16	−0.12
Post Collapse	3–Years	0.44	−0.31	−0.02
	10–Years	0.60	−0.23	−0.02
Academics				
All Respondents	3–Years	0.38	0.06	0.11
	10–Years	0.62	0.16	0.00
Pre-Collapse	3–Years	0.32	0.07	−0.03
	10–Years	0.61	0.16	−0.12
Post-Collapse	3–Years	0.43	0.05	0.22
	10–Years	0.63	0.16	0.10
Pension Funds				
All Respondents	3–Years	0.36	−0.11	0.01
	10–Years	0.55	0.04	−0.07
Pre-Collapse	3–Years	0.13	−0.13	0.10
	10–Years	0.39	0.00	0.09
Post-Collapse	3–Years	0.52	−0.09	−0.15
	10–Years	0.66	0.08	−0.18

Since the cross-correlation of real estate with other assets is important for portfolio allocations and diversification benefits [4,5,6], it was allocated a major portion of the survey. Subjects were asked their cross-correlation expectations for real estate in relation to stocks, bonds and inflation for three–year and ten–year horizons. The responses are contained in Exhibit 4 by type of respondent and pre– or post–collapse response.

On average, respondents believe that real estate will not provide the same amount of inflation protection that it has in the past. Overall, respondents estimate real estate and inflation correlations of .36 and .59 for horizons of three and ten years respectively. Thus, in the short term, it appears that weak fundamentals will reduce the ability of the asset class to keep pace with inflation, but over the longer term a reduction in the supply and demand imbalance will allow rents and values to rise with inflation. The results do not differ substantially for before- and after-collapse respondents or by affiliation.

With regard to the correlation with stock returns, real estate returns are expected to exhibit a correlation coefficient of −.13 over the next three years, and −0.2 over the next ten years.

For bonds and real estate, the correlations are roughly zero. As with the inflation correlations, little difference is reported between pre- and post-collapse respondents, or between affiliations.

These findings are consistent with those reported in previous studies. For example, since diversification benefits increase as correlation coefficients get further from one, responses of correlation coefficients that are zero and marginally negative indicate that the addition of real estate to portfolios of stocks and bonds is expected to reduce total portfolio risk.

The sample for this study was not randomly chosen and a good argument could be made that the responses are not totally independent. Some "group think" may be involved. This is a survey of experts selectively chosen. Therefore, any statistical tests of the differences between pre– and post–collapse results would not meet the appropriate conditions. However, all pre– and post–collapse results appear to be very close, except for academics' three–year expectation of total return.

Conclusions

While very few categorical conclusions are possible from a survey such as this, it allows a glimpse into the expectations of real estate market participants and observers at a specific point in time. However, many findings of other studies or just general attitudes believed to exist have been empirically confirmed. For example, a ten–year investment horizon for long-term real estate investment decisions is the virtual consensus. Also, few people believe the volatility of the FRC (Frank Russell Company) Index as an indication of real estate risk. Furthermore, the cross-correlations of stock returns and bond returns with real estate returns are believed to be significantly different from one and/or not significantly different from zero in most cases. This indicates that real estate is expected to continue to provide diversification benefits for investors.

The advent of the October 19, 1987 stock market collapse further complicates all the results. As the results of the collapse are more fully known, the perceptions of real estate investors will change and the results of this survey will become less representative. Nevertheless, these results are extremely unique in the sense that this survey was ongoing at the time of the stock market collapse. Therefore, due to luck, this survey supplies us with a view of real estate investors' changes in expectations during the early phases of the stock market collapse aftermath.

References

[1] David D. Hartzell, John S. Hekman and Mike E. Miles. Diversification Categories in Investment Real Estate. *AREUEA Journal* 14 (Summer 1986), 230–54.
[2] _____. Real Estate Returns and Inflation. *AREUEA Journal* 15 (Spring 1987), 617–37.
[3] David J. Hartzell and David G. Shulman. Real Estate Returns and Risks: A Survey. Salomon Brothers, Inc., February 12, 1988 (6 pgs).
[4] David J. Hartzell and James R. Webb. The Allocation of Equity Real Estate Investments in Real Estate Portfolios. Unpublished working paper, 1988 (28 pages).
[5] James R. Webb, Richard J. Curcio and Jack J. Rubens. Diversification Gains from Including Real Estate in Mixed-Asset Portfolios. *Decision Sciences* 19 (Spring 1988), 434–52.
[6] James R. Webb and Jack H. Rubens. Effects of Alternative Return Estimates on Restricted Mixed-Asset Portfolios. *AREUEA Journal* 16 (Summer 1988), 123–37.

Current value reporting by real estate fiduciary managers

Performance measurement through comparison of rates of return is one of the principal ways investors make investment decisions. Fiduciary managers of real estate investments, however, do not necessarily prepare consistently the financial reporting information upon which investors base their decisions.

by The National Council of Real Estate Investment Fiduciaries

Historical cost is the generally accepted method of accounting promulgated by the Financial Accounting Standards Board (FASB) and required for public entities by the Securities and Exchange Commission and for reporting on financial statements by CPAs who are members of the American Institute of Certified Public Accountants (AICPA). Accounting literature on current value reporting has been somewhat limited.

The focus of this article is on the current value accounting policies and procedures used in the fiduciary management of real estate investment vehicles for tax-exempt entities. By examining the results of a survey conducted by The National Council of Real Estate Investment Fiduciaries (NCREIF), the article provides an understanding of various current value accounting policies and procedures utilized by fiduciary managers in their reporting to investors and analyzes the effects of such policies on current rates of return.[1] Although there are many accounting policies and procedures utilized in preparing current value financial statements, this ar-

ticle concentrates on selected policies that directly affect real estate market values.

---

[1] For purposes of this article, current rates of return are calculated using an annual time-weighted return formula as follows:

$$\frac{\text{Net income} + \text{Capital appreciation}}{\text{Weighted average equity}} = \text{Total return}$$

Where:

Net income is the difference between revenues and expenses per the income statement (statement of operations).

Capital appreciation is the difference between (1) beginning market value plus capital improvements (less amortization, if any) less capital retirements (sales) and (2) ending market value.

Weighted average equity is the sum of beginning market value increased by "weighted contributions" and reduced by "weighted distributions." Weighted contributions are calculated as the product of contributions multiplied by a fraction, of which the numerator is the number of days in the period that the contribution was in the fund, and the denominator is the number of days in the period. Weighted distributions are calculated as the product of distributions multiplied by a fraction, of which the numerator is the number of days in the period remaining after the distribution was made and the denominator of which is the total number of days in the period. For purposes of this article, returns shown assume that all cash flow is distributed in the period.

A copy of the survey is shown in Appendix 1. The tabulation of the results of the survey is shown in Appendix 2. Also included in this article are figures illustrating the effects on current rates of return when different accounting policies are utilized.

Reporting Items examined

During October 1986, the NCREIF conducted a survey of thirty-two member firms to determine the differences among them with respect to their accounting policies for tenant improvements (both standard and above-standard), tenant allowances, leasing commissions, building improvements, and free rent. These terms are defined as follows:

☐ *Tenant improvements.* Tenant improvements are the costs associated with preparing a space for tenant occupancy. Generally, a building has a standard allowance package that is available to a tenant, which may include (but need not be limited to) floor, walls, window, and ceiling treatments. Above-standard tenant improvements are those above the normal allowance that are paid for by the landlord, such as a higher grade of carpeting.

☐ *Tenant allowances.* Tenant allowances are cash inducements paid to a tenant. These allowances can take many forms, including moving allowances, payments on existing leases, lump-sum cash payments, etc. Allowances can, but do not always, replace tenant improvements. Allowances may also be additional amounts over and above the amount of tenant improvements.

☐ *Leasing commissions.* Leasing commissions are fees paid to brokers to lease space.

☐ *Building improvements.* Building improvements are costs that add to the market value or benefit the real estate asset in the future. Generally, building improvements have a useful life in excess of one year.

☐ *Free rent.* Free rent is an abatement of base rent at any point during the term of the lease. Free rent may be a full or partial abatement. A lease containing fixed increases in rent over the term of the lease is also a form of rental abatement (i.e., stepped rent). Rental abatements exist when the average annual payment over the lease term is different from the current payment required under the lease.

Recording market value

The portfolios established by NCREIF members serve as investment vehicles for tax-exempt institutions. Many of these funds are subject to the reporting requirements of the Employee Retirement Income Security Act of 1974 (ERISA). Preparers of the books and records of these plans are required to follow the "AICPA Audit and Accounting Guide for Audits of Investment Companies," which requires the reporting of investments at current market value. Many current value accounting techniques have been adopted to properly report investments in real estate at market value. The preferred accounting treatment for state and local government pension plans is also current value. As a result, most fiduciary managers have adopted current value reporting as a standard for investor reporting.

The survey conducted revealed that many members have adopted accounting policies for recording tenant improvements, tenant allowances, leasing commissions, building improvements, and free rent that differ from the historical cost method of accounting. These differences result from two divergent schools of thought concerning the preparation of current financial statements:

1. Financial statements are prepared using a strict application of GAAP for the calculation of net investment income, but market values for real estate assets (and the corresponding increases/decreases in market value) are calculated through the appraisal process; and

2. Financial statements are prepared in a manner consistent with the valuation process whereby net income is calculated in a manner similar to cash flow.

Market values of real estate assets are determined by appraisal. Three different valuation techniques are used: (1) replacement cost adjusted for depreciation; (2) comparable market values (based on recent sales with similar demographics); and (3) the income approach. The income approach is generally calculated by capitalizing a stabilized net operating income or by discounted cash flows. Inasmuch as the majority of the assets managed by NCREIF member firms are income-producing, the preferred and predominant valuation technique is the discounted cash flow method whereby income and expense are recognized when there exists a contractual obligation for receipt or payment of cash. The discounted cash flow method of appraisal projects future cash inflows and outflows and presumes a sales price generally at the end of the presumed ten-year holding period. Such amounts are discounted at an appropriate rate of return that a prudent buyer would currently require to purchase the real estate asset.

Capitalized costs

Tenant improvements, allowances, leasing commissions, and building improvements are the significant costs that were studied.

More than 50 percent of all respondents believe that amortizing such costs is not consistent with the appraisal process upon which market values are calculated.

GAAP reporting. Generally accepted accounting principles (GAAP) for financial statements prepared using the historical cost basis of accounting require the capitalization of tenant improvements, allowances, leasing commissions, and building improvements. Such costs are capitalized because their useful life extends beyond one year. Since there is a finite useful life for each of these costs, amortization (or depreciation) is also recognized in the historical cost basis financial statements. Useful lives for these costs can be determined in several ways; for building improvements, the useful life is frequently determined by the tax basis useful life; for the tenant concessions, useful lives are generally tied to the length of the lease.

Survey findings. According to the survey, at least 75 percent of all respondents capitalize tenant improvements, allowances, leasing commissions, and building improvements. The remaining survey respondents expense these items. Under the capitalization theory, tenant improvements, allowances, and leasing commissions are costs that represent an additional investment that is being made to generate an income stream from the lease. Just as the acquisition investment was capitalized to attain a given

income stream, additional investments may be required as tenant leases expire to attain additional income streams. The objective of any leasing program is to maximize cash flows and to maintain or increase the market value of the real estate asset. Therefore, the associated costs that are expected to benefit future periods should be added to the existing carrying value. Capitalizing such costs as tenant improvements, leasing commissions, and building improvements is justified because these costs have utility that extends beyond one year. In certain cases, tenant improvements have some value beyond the lease term, particularly when an existing tenant remains in tenancy. Tenant allowances are in some cases given to tenants in lieu of other concessions, which justifies the capitalization of such items to the extent that such concessions would be capitalized. Finally, proponents of this policy indicate that expenditures for tenant improvements, allowances, leasing commissions, and building improvements are capital investment activities and are nonperiodic and, as such, should be capitalized.

Amortization of costs. There are some differences in opinion from the respondents as to whether such costs should be amortized (depreciated). Seventy-two percent of the respondents that capitalize tenant improvements, 67 percent of those that capitalize allowances, 59 percent of those that capitalize leasing commissions, and 87 percent of those that capitalize building improvements do not amortize these items. Respondents that do amortize generally do so over the term of the lease, except for building improvements, which are generally amortized over the useful life of the improvement.

Inconsistencies of amortization. More than 50 percent of all respondents believe that amortizing such costs is not consistent with the appraisal process upon which market values are calculated. The appraisal process does not recognize the accounting convention of amortization, and it only distinguishes between capital items and expense items generally when calculating reversionary values (i.e., presumed sales price at the end of the valuation period). Thus, by capitalizing these costs as incurred, net income is calculated on the same basis as the discounted cash flow appraisal. In addition, such costs are not amortized under the theory that the relative success of the fiduciary manager will be realized when the property is sold, and gains (or losses) should be calculated as the difference between all the costs associated with the investment and the realized gains or losses, using an assumed sales price rather than a known sales price. In summary, proponents of not amortizing such costs would argue that the amortization process is arbitrary, has no relevance in the current value reporting environment, and is inconsistent with appraisal methodology.

In support of amortization. In contrast, the justification for amortizing such items is that such treatment is consistent with GAAP for historical cost basis financial statements. There are several arguments supporting the use of GAAP when calculating net investment income for current value financial statements. Primarily, proponents of this method would argue that the two components of total return — net investment income and realized and unrealized gain/loss — are significant in making investment decisions; therefore, consistent determination of net investment income in accordance with GAAP is appropriate. This method calls for the unamortized balance of tenant improvements, tenant allowances, leasing commissions, and building improvements to be included as part of the total cost of the real estate asset in the calculation of the unrealized gain or loss.

This method views tenant-related items (i.e., tenant improvements, allowances, and leasing commissions) as special purpose items that provide value over the lease term generally only to the tenant for whom they are incurred. For building improvements, the useful life is frequently determined by tax laws. There is a gradual "wearing" of the worth of these items, and that expense is reflected in the amortization. GAAP dictates that expenses should be matched with total revenues throughout the lease term. Net income includes both a return of and a return on tenant improvements, tenant allowances, leasing commissions, and building improvements. Using this analysis, a return of "cost" should not be a component of net investment income and therefore, the proponents of this accounting policy would argue that expensing such items is improper. Finally, supporters of this theory would argue that net income is the more concrete measure of total return whereas the market value

and the corresponding unrealized gain/loss are more susceptible to discretionary judgment. Therefore, these proponents would argue that net income should be calculated utilizing a strict application of GAAP.

Rate of return. Provided that market values are determined in the same period, the current *total* return is the same using the expense method and capitalization method (and either amortizing or not amortizing) provided that the capitalized amounts are included in the carrying value of the asset when calculating the appreciation adjustment. Figure 1 illustrates these differences.

When such costs are not amortized, they will be offset against the gain realized upon the sale of the asset

Twelve percent of the survey respondents did not include the capitalized amount of leasing commissions in the carrying value of the asset when calculating changes in market value. It is interesting to note that none of the respondents surveyed adopted accounting policies whereby tenant improvements, tenant allowances, and building improvements were not a component of the rate of return. Proponents of the accounting theory that elect not to include the amount of the commissions in the carrying value of the asset (and also not as a component of net income) would argue that such costs, although nonperiodic in nature and having a useful life longer than one year, are intangible and should not be included in the market value of the tangible real estate asset. For these reasons, leasing commissions are properly classified as an other asset.

Adopting this accounting policy will yield different returns than any of the previously discussed methods. Additionally, differences will result depending on whether such costs are amortized or not amortized. Figure 1 illustrates these differences. It is important to note that when such costs are not amortized, the costs will be offset against the gain realized upon the sale of the asset. Therefore, the expenditure ultimately affects the appreciation component of return.

FIG. 1. Current Returns Using Various Accounting Policies for Tenant Improvements, Allowances and Leasing Commissions

Assumptions:

Property is acquired January 1, 1987 for $6,000,000 cash.

Net income before tenant improvements, etc. is eight percent of the acquisition cost in years 1–5.

Tenant improvements of $30,000 are paid January 1, 1987 to secure a five-year lease.

The property is appraised at the end of each of the five years at $6,100,000, $6,100,000, $6,400,000, $6,300,000 and $6,400,000.

Cash flow is equal to net income after tenant improvements and all cash flow is distributed at the end of each year.

	Year 1	Year 2	Year 3	Year 4	Year 5	Average Return Over Holding Period
Net income before tenant improvements	$ 480,000	$ 480,000	$ 480,000	$ 480,000	$ 480,000	
Tenant improvements	30,000	—	—	—	—	
Ending market value	6,100,000	6,100,000	6,400,000	6,300,000	6,400,000	
Beginning market value	6,000,000	6,100,000	6,100,000	6,400,000	6,300,000	
Amortization per year	6,000	6,000	6,000	6,000	6,000	
Returns: expense						
Net income	7.50%	7.87%	7.87%	7.50%	7.62%	
Appreciation	1.67	—	4.92	(1.56)	1.59	
Total	9.17%	7.87%	12.79%	5.94%	9.21%	9.00%

Returns: capitalize and do not amortize and include unamortized amount in carrying value of asset when recording appreciation adjustments

	Year 1	Year 2	Year 3	Year 4	Year 5	
Net income	8.00%	7.87%	7.87%	7.50%	7.62%	
Appreciation	1.17	—	4.92	(1.56)	1.59	
Total	9.17%	7.87%	12.79%	5.94%	9.21%	9.00%

Returns: capitalize and amortize and include unamortized amount in carrying value of asset when recording appreciation adjustments

	Year 1	Year 2	Year 3	Year 4	Year 5	
Net income	7.90%	7.77%	7.77%	7.41%	7.53%	
Appreciation	1.27	.10	5.02	(1.47)	1.68	
Total	9.17%	7.87%	12.79%	5.94%	9.21%	9.00%

Returns: capitalize and amortize and do not include unamortized amount in carrying value of asset when recording appreciation adjustments

	Year 1	Year 2	Year 3	Year 4	Year 5	
Net income	7.90%	7.77%	7.77%	7.41%	7.52%	
Appreciation	1.67	—	4.92	(1.56)	1.59	
Total	9.57%	7.77%	12.69%	5.85%	9.11%	9.00%

Returns: capitalize and do not amortize and do not include unamortized amount in carrying value of asset when recording appreciation adjustments

	Year 1	Year 2	Year 3	Year 4	Year 5	
Net income	8.00%	7.87%	7.87%	7.50%	7.62%	
Appreciation	1.67	—	4.92	(1.56)	1.59	
Total	9.67%	7.87%	12.79%	5.94%	9.21%	9.09%

Expensing costs.

At least 16 percent of all survey respondents expense tenant improvements, allowances, and leasing commissions. These respondents indicated that items are capitalized (i.e., reflected as an increase in the current carrying value of the real estate asset) only if they add value to the asset. It is the opinion of these respondents that all other things being equal, a buyer would not pay more for a building because an allowance was paid to secure one tenant as opposed to another, or because a leasing commission was paid for one tenant and not the other. Leasing commissions and tenant allowances have no value once a tenant has vacated its space. The justification for expensing tenant improvements is that such items have specific value to the tenant that utilized them. All of these items represent period costs that are an ongoing routine cost of real estate investment activities.

> **All other things being equal, a buyer would not pay more for a building because an allowance was paid to secure one tenant as opposed to another.**

For these reasons, 9 percent of the member firms expense tenant improvements, tenant allowances, and leasing commissions. Provided that real estate market values are calculated during the same period that the expense is recorded, the current *total* return is the same as if these items were capitalized, provided that the capitalized amount is included in the carrying value of the asset when recording the appreciation adjustment. As shown in the example in Figure 1, however, the *components* of the total return are different.

Rental Income

The survey also revealed different methods of accounting for rental income.

GAAP reporting. GAAP for financial statements prepared using the historical cost basis of accounting require the recognition of effective rent ratably over the lease term in accordance with Statement of Financial Accounting Standards (SFAS) 13:

"Rent shall be reported as income over the lease term as it becomes receivable according to the provisions of the lease. However, if rentals vary from a straight-line basis, the income shall be recognized on a straight-line basis, unless another systematic and rational basis is more representative of the time pattern in which use benefit from the leased property is diminished, in which case that basis shall be used.[2]"

This method is also reiterated in Financial Accounting Standards Technical Bulletin 85-3, which concluded that the accounting standards promulgated by SFAS 13 are appropriate for current value basis financial statements.

Survey findings

There are two methods utilized by survey respondents for accounting for contract rent (the face rental rate stipulated in the lease): the billable method and the as-earned method. If there is free rent or any rental abatement included in a lease, the billable method recognizes rental income on the books and records only when a tenant is obligated to pay. Except for the question of collectibility, the billable method is more consistent with recording income on a cash basis. The earned method of recording contract rents recognizes a steady stream of income over the lease term even though the provisions of the lease may grant rental abatement at differing periods. This method recognizes as current income the effective rental rate inherent in the lease. The differences in the two methods are illustrated in Figure 1.

Survey respondents were asked to assume that rental abatement was significant to the amount of total rental income reported in the income statement. At least 69 percent of the respondents agreed that contract rents should be accounted for on a billable basis.

Billable basis. There are several arguments for using the billable basis for current value reporting. The predominant method utilized in appraising properties today is the discounted cash flow method in

---

[2]As noted in Accounting Standards Current Text, General Standards as of June 1, 1986, published by the FASB.

FIG. 2 Six-Year Lease Term[a]

	Year						Total
	1	2	3	4	5	6	
One year free rent — first year:							
Billable	$ —	$60,000	$60,000	$60,000	$60,000	$60,000	$300,000
As earned	50,000	50,000	50,000	50,000	50,000	50,000	300,000
Months free in each of first four years:							
Billable	45,000	45,000	45,000	45,000	60,000	60,000	300,000
As earned	50,000	50,000	50,000	50,000	50,000	50,000	300,000
Lease-specified stepped rent beginning at $25,000 and increasing $10,000 each year over term:							
Billable	25,000	35,000	45,000	55,000	65,000	75,000	300,000
As earned	50,000	50,000	50,000	50,000	50,000	50,000	300,000

(a) $60,000 rent per year; one year of free rent.

which all rights to receive cash under contractual agreements (such as leases) are included in the estimate of market value. For example, assume a real estate asset is purchased in the beginning of 1987 with a lease in place having a ten-year term starting in 1985 with free rent for the first two years. The purchaser will pay a price based (in part) on the present value of the anticipated cash flows from 1987 forward and an anticipated sales price at the end of a presumed holding period, which for purposes of this example is ten years, or 1997. Therefore, the contract rent received in years 1987-1995 in this example is included in the market value (i.e., sales price of the asset). Were this same lease entered into in 1986 rather than 1985, the purchase price paid would be less than in the first example (because there is still one year during which the lease would not produce rental income). Assuming no other changes in market conditions, appreciation would first be recorded in 1988 and thereafter during each appraisal as the free rent period expires and the stream of cash flows approaches its end. Therefore, if accounting for the operations of the real estate asset included the recording of contract rents on an earned (effective rent) basis, there would be some overstatement of the total return during the free rent period.

Effective rent is the value of the average contract rent receivable from the tenant per year over the term of the lease. When current value is utilized, it is the annuity whose present value equates to the present value of the stipulated rent. A discussion of the effect of discounting is beyond the scope of this article.

Accordingly, proponents of the billable basis of recording contract rents maintain that using an effective rent formula, as required by the earned basis, is inconsistent with the appraisal process and current value accounting theory. Additionally, proponents of the billable basis would argue that the billable method is more consistent with the calculation of the amount of distributable cash, which is more meaningful to investors.

Finally, proponents of recording contract rents on a billable basis question using the earned basis method with respect to the collectibility of the amount recorded as rental income. Rental abatements are more common in real estate markets where supply exceeds demand. In these soft markets, leasing is both competitive and risky. Unfortunately, some solvent companies today may face financial difficulties in the future. The amount of an appropriate bad debt reserve may be even more difficult to determine when effective rents are recorded as opposed to billable rents.

Although billable rents are not always collectible, the status of the tenant is known currently rather than speculating what will happen in the future. Accordingly, specific reserves for collectible billable rents are

FIG. 3. Current Returns Comparing Free Rent Accounted for as Billable Versus As-Earned ($000's omitted)

Assumptions:

Property is acquired January 1, 1987 for $50,000 cash.

Lease term January 1, 1987 to December 31, 1996:

    One year free rent

    Rent $6,000 per year

    No other allowances given

Cash flow is equal to received net income and all cash flow is distributed at the end of each year.

Property is valued at end of each year through December 31, 1996 based on the present value of the cash flows discounted at 11 percent through 1996.

	1987	1988	1989	1990	1991	1992	1993	1994	1995	1996
Earned net income	$ 5,400	$ 5,400	$ 5,400	$ 5,400	$ 5,400	$ 5,400	$ 5,400	$ 5,400	$ 5,400	$ 5,400
Received net income	0	6,000	6,000	6,000	6,000	6,000	6,000	6,000	6,000	6,000
Accounts receivable balance at end of year for earned net income	5,400	4,800	4,200	3,600	3,000	2,400	1,800	1,200	600	0
Market value at end of year	53,409	59,284	59,805	60,384	61,026	61,739	62,530	63,408	64,383	65,466
Returns: as earned with accounts receivable balance included in carrying value of asset when recording appreciation adjustments										
Net income	10.80%	10.11%	9.11%	9.03%	8.94%	8.85%	8.75%	8.64%	8.52%	8.39%
Appreciation (depreciation)	(3.98)	12.12	1.89	1.97	2.06	2.15	2.25	2.36	2.48	2.61
Total return	6.82%	22.23%	11.00%	11.00%	11.00%	11.00%	11.00%	11.00%	11.00%	11.00%
Returns: as billable										
Net income	0.00%	11.23%	10.12%	10.03%	9.94%	9.83%	9.72%	9.60%	9.46%	9.32%
Appreciation	6.82	11.00	0.88	0.97	1.06	1.17	1.28	1.40	1.54	1.68
Total return	6.82%	22.23%	11.00%	11.00%	11.00%	11.00%	11.00%	11.00%	11.00%	11.00%
Returns: as earned with accounts receivable balance excluded from carrying value of asset when recording appreciation adjustment										
Net income	10.80%	9.18%	8.43%	8.44%	8.44%	8.43%	8.42%	8.39%	8.36%	8.31%
Appreciation	6.82	9.99	.81	.90	1.00	1.11	1.23	1.36	1.51	1.67
Total return	17.62%	19.17%	9.24%	9.34%	9.44%	9.54%	9.65%	9.75%	9.87%	9.98%

more easy to identify. Figure 3 illustrates the effect on rates of return of accounting for contract rents as billed versus as earned.

In summary, proponents of recording contract rents on a billable basis would argue that doing so reflects the terms of the lease, the right to receive cash, a proper matching of net income with the valuation process, and is more meaningful and understandable by investors and should, therefore, be used when preparing current value financial statements. As a result, the GAAP method of recording contract rents on an effective rent basis should not apply.

Earned income method. In contrast, 31 percent of the survey respondents are proponents of the earned method of accounting for free rent. All of these respondents calculated the rental amount in the financial statements as the total rental consideration payable over the lease term divided by the number of years in the lease. Approximately 70 percent of these respondents used the as-earned theory for all forms of rental abatement. The remaining respondents used this theory on all forms of rental abatement with the exception of stepped rents. Respondents argue that the earned method conforms with GAAP (specifically, the matching concept and SFAS). The matching principle applies in that rental income should be matched with the related use of the property. Proponents of this theory first account on a GAAP basis and then apply the provisions of current value reporting.

Recording contract rents as earned provides for a steady income stream that translates into a relatively constant income return. Component returns for any holding period would differ based on whether contract rents are recorded as billed rather than as earned. If there is free rent in the initial term of the lease, the net income return would be higher under the as-earned method in the period when there is free rent and lower than the billable basis in the later periods. However, when the abatement receivable is included in the carrying value of the asset for purposes of calculating the appreciation adjustment, the total return under the as-billable and as-earned methods are the same for each year. Figure 3 illustrates these differences.

The decision-making process

As this article indicates, there are many divergent accounting policies utilized by the NCREIF's member firms in accounting for tenant improvements, allowances, leasing commissions, building improvements, and free rent. Although there are some areas in which nearly all the members have adopted the same accounting policies, in other areas policies are quite different. Performance measurement through comparison of rates of return is one of the principal ways investors make investment decisions. Therefore, it is important for such investors to understand the underlying accounting policies that form the basis for calculating the data to which the return formula is applied. ∎

APPENDIX 1 — NCREIF Accounting Subcommittee
Current Value Subcommittee Questionnaire — October 22, 1986

Please check the policy currently in effect for Current Value Financial Statement Reporting purposes (*assume materiality*):

	Type of Expenditure				
	Tenant Improvements				
Method	**Standard**(b)	**Above Standard**	**Tenant Allowances**(c)	**Lease Commissions**	**Improvements**(d)
Expensed					
Capitalize and do not amortize; include capitalized amount(s) in the carrying value of the asset when calculating the appreciation adjustment(a)					
Capitalize and do not amortize; do not include capitalized amount(s) in the carrying value of the asset when calculating the appreciation adjustment(a)					
Capitalize and amortize; include unamortized amount(s) in the carrying value of the asset when calculating the appreciation adjustment(a)					
Capitalize and amortize; do not include unamortized amount(s) in the carrying value when calculating the appreciation adjustment(a)					
If amortized, select method:					
Over specific lease terms:					
Over average lease terms:					
Other (describe):					

"Free rent" is defined as a concession given to a tenant in the form of a payment abatement (full or partial) of contract rents at any time during the lease. Partial abatements may take the form of reduced payments or stepped increases in contract rent over the life of the lease. *Assume materiality* in answering these questions.

1. How do you recognize contract rents in reporting operating income (check one):
_____ (a) As received, that is, when the tenant is obligated to pay.
_____ (b) As earned in accordance with some "effective rent" formula.

2. If you responded to 1(b), select effective rent amortization method:
_____ (a) Straight line
_____ (b) Present value
_____ (c) Other (describe)

3. If you responded to 1(b), when computing the effective rent amortization, do you recognize the effects of:
_____ (a) Full payment abatement only
_____ (b) Full and reduced payments (excluding stepped increases)
_____ (c) All abatements

(a) Appreciation adjustment is defined as the entry that affects the unrealized appreciation component reported to investors.

(b) "Standard" is that which is typically given to a tenant in that marketplace.

(c) E.g., cash, moving allowances, lease layout payments.

(d) Improvements not directly associated with leasing that extend the economic life of the asset, improve its quality, or increase its value.

APPENDIX 2 — NCREIF Accounting Subcommittee Results on the Current Value Subcommittee Questionnaire Dated October 22, 1986 (Updated: February 29, 1988)

| | Tenant Improvements | | | | | | | | | |
| | Standard | | Above Standard | | Tenant Allowances | | Leasing Commissions | | Improvements | |
	Number	%	Number	%	Number	%	Number	%	Number	%
Expensed	3	9	3	9	8	25	5	16	0	0
Capitalize and do not amortize; include capitalized amount(s) in carrying value of asset when calculating appreciated adjustment	21	66	21	66	16	50	14	44	28	87
Capitalize and do not amortize; do not include capitalized amount(s) in carrying value of asset when calculating appreciated adjustment	—	0	—	0	—	0	2	6	—	0
Capitalize and amortize; include unamortized amount(s) in carrying value of asset when calculating appreciated adjustment	8	25	8	25	8	25	9	28	4	13
Capitalize and amortize; do not include unamortized amount(s) in carrying value of asset when calculating appreciated adjustment	—	0	—	0	—	0	2	6	—	0
Totals	32	100	32	100	32	100	32	100	32	100

If amortized, select method:

| | Standard | | Above Standard | | Tenant Allowances | | Leasing Commissions | | Improvements | |
	Number	%	Number	%	Number	%	Number	%	Number	%
Over specific lease term	8	100	8	100	8	100	11	100	3	75
Other	—	0	—	0	—	0	—	0	1	25
Totals	8	100	8	100	8	100	11	100	4	100

Recognition of contract rents in reporting operating income:

	Response	%
As received (billable)	22	69
As earned	10	31
Totals	32	100

If earned, select effective rent amortization method:

	Response	%
Straight line	10	100
Totals	10	100

If earned, when computing effective rent amortization what is recognized?

	Response	%
Full payment abatement only	2	20
Full & reduced payments	1	10
All abatements	7	70
Totals	10	100

If earned, when revaluing asset what policy is employed?

	Response	%
Include unamortized amount of free rent in appreciated adjustment	6	60
Do not include unamortized amount of free rent in appreciated adjustment	4	40
Totals	10	100

171

Real Estate versus Financial Assets — An Updated Comparison of Returns in the United States and the United Kingdom

Summary

● Real estate returns in the United States and the United Kingdom are not highly correlated, which suggests that international diversification of real estate portfolios merits consideration.

● Real estate was an inflation hedge in both countries when inflation was high, but its effectiveness as such has declined in the United States since 1983 and has varied considerably in the United Kingdom since then.

● Previous similarities in nominal real estate returns were largely inflation driven. However, with low inflation rates in the mid-1980s and the booming U.K. property market in 1987 and 1988, the returns diverged. This highlights the danger of relying exclusively on historical data to make asset allocation decisions.

In a previous report, we documented parallel trends in U.S. and U.K. real estate returns from 1980 through 1986.[1] We also noted that market conditions in the two countries were diverging, with generally rising vacancies in the United States and tighter U.K. markets. An updated analysis shows that recent returns have reflected these altered conditions: There has been virtually no correspondence between U.S. and U.K. real estate returns during 1987 and 1988. We also find that returns on real estate, derived from appraisal-based data, are uncorrelated with returns on financial assets.

Real Estate Performance Measures

The Frank Russell Company (FRC) tracks the performance of a diversified portfolio of high-quality U.S. commercial real estate. The properties in the portfolio are the unleveraged holdings of a group of institutional equity real estate managers. As of September 30, 1988, the FRC Property Index was based on a sample of 1,048 properties having a total market value exceeding $13.5 billion. The index measures total return for the quarter, consisting of each property's actual net operating income plus the change in the property's appraised value during the quarter. The infrequent trading of the assets in the sample portfolio dictates the use of appraisals to capture the appreciation component of total return.

Weatherall Green and Smith (WGS), a U.K.-chartered surveyor (equivalent to an appraisal firm), produces a similarly constructed index of investment-grade real estate in the United Kingdom. The WGS Index is derived from a portfolio containing nearly £612 million ($1.03 billion) of U.K. property. The WGS Index tracks the more broadly based annual U.K. Investment Property Databank Index and is available quarterly.[2]

---

[1] See *Real Estate Market Review*, Salomon Brothers Inc, April 1987.

[2] The analysis was also performed using the Jones Lang Wootton Index. Results based on this smaller (£400-million) portfolio were quite similar to those reported here.

The author would like to thank Ann Pegg for her editorial guidance; David Shulman for his comments; Sharon Anne Meyers and Jill Krutick for their research assistance; and Carmela Nardi and Joanna Steves-Kennedy for their diligent preparation of this report.

Real Estate versus Financial Assets

From 1980 through the third quarter of 1988, U.S. real estate returns exhibited considerably less volatility than stocks and bonds, although some of this is undoubtedly caused by appraisal "smoothing" (see Figure 1).[3] The diversified real estate portfolio's returns have declined over time, reflecting a decrease in inflation and the write-down of some property values in oil-dependent regional economies.

Figure 1. Total Returns — U.S. Real Estate, Stocks and Bonds, 1980-3Q 88
(Quarterly Data)

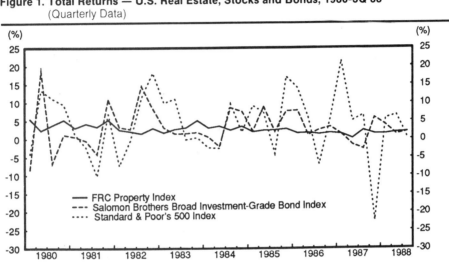

Sources: Frank Russell Company and Salomon Brothers Inc.

A comparison of U.K. real estate to financial assets shows that U.K. real estate was also less volatile than financial assets over the period (see Figure 2). Moreover, stock and bond markets in both countries continued to move in tandem during 1987 and 1988. The relatively flat performance of U.S. real estate in recent years contrasts sharply with the major upswing in U.K. returns during 1987 and 1988.

Figure 2. Total Returns — U.K. Real Estate, Stocks and Bonds, 1980-3Q 88
(Quarterly Data)

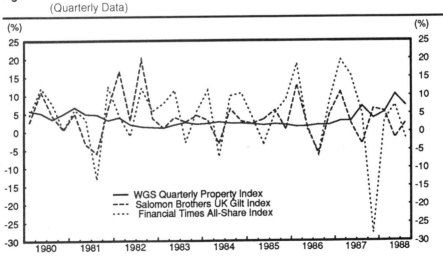

Sources: Weatherall Green and Smith, *Financial Times* and Salomon Brothers Inc.

---

[3] For a discussion of potential problems resulting from the use of appraisals to compute returns, see *The Relative Risk of Equity Real Estate and Common Stock: A New View*, David Shulman, Salomon Brothers Inc, June 1986, and "A Note on the Use of Appraisal Data in Indexes of Performance Measurement," Michael Giliberto, *Journal of the American Real Estate and Urban Economics Association*, Spring 1988.

Stocks were the riskiest assets over the period, followed by bonds and real estate. Figure 3 shows average returns and volatility for each asset category. The October 1987 market collapse clearly increased historical stock market volatility in both countries. Real estate had the lowest return, not surprising given its lower apparent risk. Furthermore, average returns for all assets except U.K. real estate declined in recent years.

Figure 3. U.S. and U.K. Total Returns — Real Estate, Stocks and Bonds, 1980-3Q 88
(Quarterly)

	Real Estate	Stocks	Bonds
United States (Dollars)			
Mean Return	3.0%[a]	4.2%[b]	3.1%[c]
Volatility[d]	1.2	8.9	5.5
United Kingdom (Sterling)			
Mean Return	3.4%[e]	4.6%[f]	3.8%[g]
Volatility	2.1	9.1	5.6

[a] Returns calculated from the FRC Property Index. [b] Total returns earned by the S&P 500. [c] Returns calculated from the Salomon Brothers Broad Investment-Grade Bond Index. [d] Measured by standard deviation. [e] Returns calculated from the WGS Quarterly Property Index. [f] Returns calculated from the Financial Times All-Share Index. [g] Returns calculated from the Salomon Brothers UK Gilt Index.
Sources: Frank Russell Company, Weatherall Green and Smith, *Financial Times*, and Salomon Brothers Inc.

Ignoring exchange rates, a U.S. investor would have obtained a higher total return from holding U.K. real estate for the entire holding period (see Figure 4). However, when exchange rates are considered, the picture changes because sterling declined relative to the dollar in the early 1980s. If a U.S. investor recognized gains and losses from currency translation each quarter, the cumulative total return on U.K. properties would have been lower than that on U.S. properties. This "reversal" occurs because of the choice of starting point, holding period and the assumed marking to market each quarter. Altering these would lead to different measured returns and relative performance. For example, had a U.S. investor purchased U.K. real estate in 1985 when the pound was at its low relative to the U.S. dollar, the investor's return would have benefited from the rise in both the pound and the U.K. property market.

Figure 4. U.S. versus U.K. Cumulative Total Returns, 1980-3Q 88

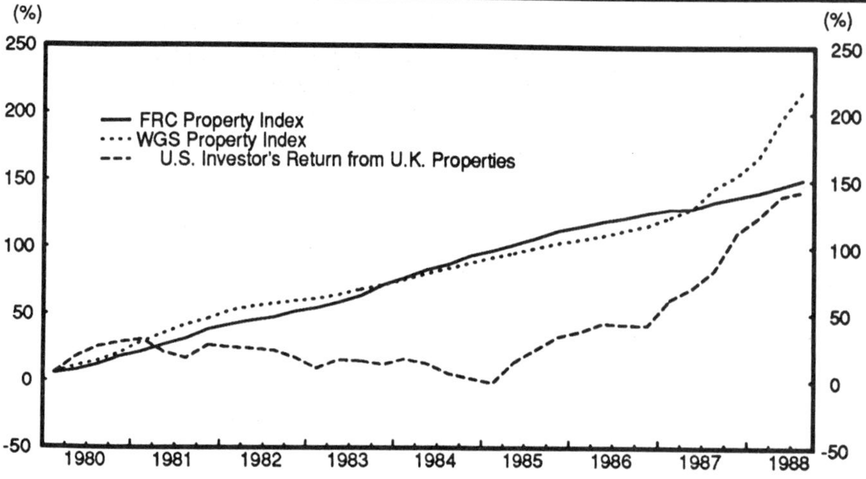

Correlations Between Real Estate Returns, Financial Asset Returns and Inflation

U.S. real estate shows slightly negative correlations with U.S. stocks and bonds (see Figure 5). Most of the numerical values are small, and it is quite reasonable to regard the actual correlations as zero. Similarly, correlations between stock returns and inflation and bond returns and inflation are essentially zero. The positive correlation between U.S. real estate returns and U.S. inflation is significant, suggesting that real estate can be a useful inflation hedge.

Figure 5. Correlations between U.S. Real Estate, Financial Assets and Inflation, 1980-3Q 88

	Real Estate	Stocks	Bonds	Inflation
Real Estate	1.00	-0.10	-0.22	0.58
Stocks		1.00	0.34	-0.08
Bonds			1.00	-0.15
Inflation				1.00

Sources: Frank Russell Company and Salomon Brothers Inc.

Correlations between U.K real estate, financial assets and inflation resemble those in the United States (see Figure 6). U.K. investors too could regard real estate as an inflation hedge. Again, stocks and bonds are negatively correlated with inflation and real estate, and the values are not significantly different from zero.

Figure 6. Correlations between U.K. Real Estate and Financial Assets, 1980-3Q 88

	Real Estate	Stocks	Bonds	Inflation
Real Estate	1.00	-0.13	-0.23	0.40
Stocks		1.00	0.41	0.06
Bonds			1.00	-0.05
Inflation				1.00

Sources: Weatherall Green and Smith, *Financial Times* and Salomon Brothers Inc.

Overall, return patterns and correlations between different assets are strikingly similar, except for the recent divergence in real estate returns between the two countries. Investors in either the United Kingdom or the United States would have obtained substantial benefits from portfolios that contained real estate, assuming that the appraisal-based indexes yield valid returns. Low correlations with other assets carried diversification benefits, and high positive correlation with inflation implied usefulness as an inflation hedge. But the divergence in returns during 1987 and 1988 commands attention.

Performance of Real Estate in Real Terms

Periods occurred when real returns in the two countries tracked one another, as seen in Figure 7, a graph of the inflation-adjusted performance of real estate in both countries. However, the correlation between U.S. and U.K. real returns is actually -0.22. This low value indicates the lack of a consistently predictable relationship between real returns in the two countries.

Average real returns in the two countries have been comparable, with real returns being somewhat more volatile in the United Kingdom (see Figure 8). However, much of the higher U.K. volatility arises from the United Kingdom's strong results during 1987 and 1988, which pushed up measured volatility. Figure 8 also provides some information on real risk-return trade-offs. The coefficient of variation (ratio of standard deviation to the mean return) is 1.18 in the United Kingdom and only 0.70 in the United States. Therefore, on a real basis over nearly nine years, U.S. real estate investors have achieved a slightly better average risk-reward trade-off.[4]

Figure 7. U.S. and U.K. Real Estate Inflation-Adjusted Returns, 1980-88[a]

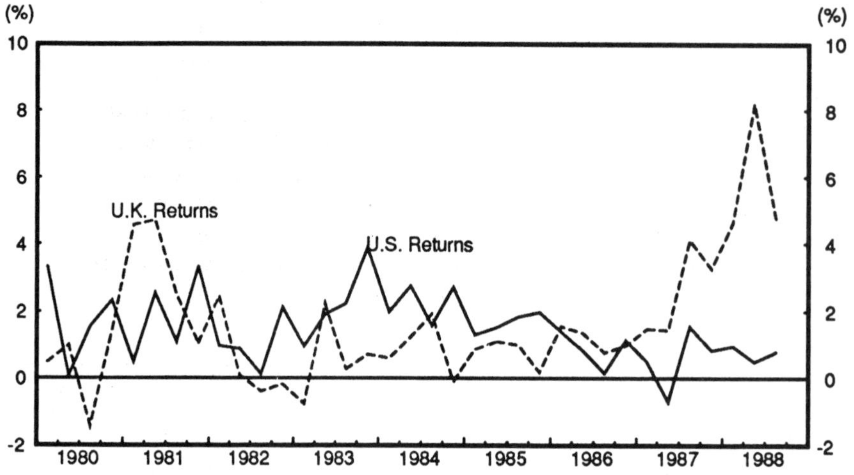

[a] Gross national product deflators are used for both countries to convert nominal returns to real returns.
Sources: Weatherall Green and Smith, Frank Russell Company and Salomon Brothers Inc.

Figure 8. U.S. and U.K. Real Estate Inflation-Adjusted Returns (Quarterly)

	United States	United Kingdom
Mean Real Return	1.46%	1.66%
Volatility	1.02	1.95

Sources: Weatherall Green and Smith, Frank Russell Company and Salomon Brothers Inc.

Examining the correlation between nominal returns in the two countries provides useful information, as well (see Figure 9). Early values are relatively large and indicate that real estate performed similarly in the United States and the United Kingdom from 1980 through 1986. Over time, the correlations decrease; in recent years, returns have moved independently. Indeed, the relationship between returns appears to be turning negative, albeit only to a slight degree.

Figure 9. Correlation Between U.S. and U.K. Nominal Returns

Period	Correlation
1980-3Q 88	0.14
1980-84	0.43
1981-85	0.35
1982-86	0.34
1983-87	-0.03
1984-3Q 88	-0.11

Sources: Weatherall Green and Smith, Frank Russell Company and Salomon Brothers Inc.

The explanation for the correlation pattern depicted in Figure 9 is that nominal returns are correlated as a result of similar inflation experiences in the United States and the United Kingdom during the decade. The correlation of inflation in the two countries is high — (0.70). During the early part of the decade, nominal property returns were largely driven by

---

[4] High recent returns in the United Kingdom are not entirely causing this: From 1980 to 1986, the coefficient of variation for the FRC Index was 0.59 and for the WGS Index 1.27.

inflation: Rents and values increased sharply in response to high inflation rates. This meant that market differences in the two countries were obscured by the inflation veil. As inflation abated (and nominal returns declined), differences in supply and demand in each country played a more prominent role in determining nominal returns on real estate.

This has implications for real estate as a hedge against inflation. Most of the observed correlation between U.S. nominal real estate returns and inflation comes from the 1980-82 period. When this period is excluded, there is no relationship between the FRC Index and inflation. The United Kingdom's experience is similar: The correlation between inflation and real estate returns declined substantially when the 1980-82 period was removed, although the relationship remained marginally positive. However, if U.K. returns continue to be high while inflation remains modest, the correlation will tend toward zero. Thus, the blanket statement "real estate is an inflation hedge" is not warranted. Real estate was an effective hedge against *high* inflation but will not necessarily hedge *all* inflation.

Implications for Investors

What does this mean to investors? First, it says that the recent divergence of returns results from country-specific market conditions, not differential inflation. Second, it highlights a need to consider whether a correlation between returns in different markets results from fundamental similarities in market conditions or simply from correlated inflation. Last, these results confirm the pitfalls of relying exclusively on historical data to make asset allocation decisions. Based on statistical data from 1980 to 1986, investors might have deemed U.S. and U.K. real estate to be "substitutes" for one another, with little benefit accruing from international diversification. However, the lack of correlation in real returns would have suggested diversification. Coupled with a reasonable forecast of future returns based on expected market conditions, an investor would have recognized benefits from holding a portfolio containing both U.S. and U.K real estate.

*　*　*　*　*

Real estate as an investment is misunderstood by both
critics and true believers.

Toward the Discipline of Real Estate Portfolio Management

BY RANDALL C. ZISLER

Investors have only recently begun to think of their real estate investments as a portfolio. Individual investments are typically evaluated on a stand-alone basis. Moreover, an investment's contribution to overall portfolio risk and return is seldom evaluated by the buy side, much less the sell side, with respect to portfolio impact. However, without a proper evaluation of assets in their portfolio context, it is difficult to construct meaningful and explicit strategies for achieving portfolio goals, either within real estate or among the major asset classes.

Who Should Care?

Who should be concerned with real estate portfolio management? Any significant real estate portfolio investor should adopt a portfolio approach to real estate acquisitions, dispositions and ongoing management. Corporations, in particular, need to adopt a portfolio approach to real estate.

There are two valid reasons why: One, real estate is often a significant but poorly managed, undervalued and underutilized component of total corporate assets and liabilities (e.g., leases); and two, many corporate pension funds contain real estate.

Public funds are also major real estate portfolio investors, often retaining full or partial in-house discretion over real estate portfolio and asset management decisions. And, of course, real estate has often been the bulk — and the springboard — of large privately held fortunes.

No matter who the investor, both the portfolio benefits and the limitations of real estate are seldom appreciated. Real estate portfolio management discipline is either weak or nonexistent. The following discussion is an attempt to understand the uniqueness of real estate and its place in an investment portfolio.

Real Estate Is a Complex Hybrid Investment

There is no such thing as "pure" real estate. For example, a 100 percent fee ownership investment in a property can be thought of as a portfolio of bond equivalents, called leases, and an equity residual. Thus, real estate, even if it is not leveraged in the traditional sense, has both fixed-income and equity characteristics. It is possible to create different debtlike cash flows and durations by adjusting lease terms. Leases, as well as the financial structure applied to net operating income, can be designed to incorporate complex put and call features, inflation hedges and other financial technology.

Real estate returns, real and nominal, are shaped by the combination of: the interaction of lease structure, leasing market disequilibrium (or the supply and demand cycle), financial structure, replacement cost and product obsolescence and enhancement.

As a consequence of real estate's heterogeneity, "real estate," the asset class, is too broad to be meaningful for purposes of managing a real estate portfolio. Moreover, even the term "office building," given the multitude of factors differentiating one office building from another, is too vague for purposes of devising a portfolio strategy.

Understanding a property's basic financial building blocks is critical when evaluating a portfolio's performance under alternative economic scenarios. For example, it is not widely appreciated that the impact of inflation on real estate valuation is theoretically ambiguous (although the statistical record indicates that real estate is an effective inflation hedge).

The ambiguity arises from the complex interaction among lease structure, nominal interest rates, nominal rents and operating expenses. Specifically, nominal interest rates typically increase with inflation. However, the demand for space may increase or decrease depending on the macroeconomic factors generating inflation. Even if demand increases, vacancy rates may be high enough and rise quickly enough, due to excess construction, that real and nominal effective rents actually fall.

The present value of leases written during a period of excess supply and weak rental growth, without full pass-through of expenses to rent, will decline as nominal interest rates rise. If vacancy rates are excessive, nominal rents will stagnate or fall. However, despite weak property markets, inflation-driven operating expenses will undoubtedly rise. Thus, owners will be faced with the double risks of falling net operating income discounted by higher nominal interest rates.

Leases with longer durations will experience greater interest rate sensitivity but less re-leasing exposure. Similarly, leases with short durations will permit more rapid rental increases as long as the leasing market is not weak. Short duration, therefore, is associated with greater re-leasing risk. Generally, a building with high-credit, long-term leases and 100 percent occupancy will perform very differently than a similar building, in the same location, with short-term leases. Lease structure management is an important but frequently neglected facet of real estate portfolio management.

Most of the recent practical applications of real estate portfolio diversification take a macro or top-down approach. We believe that the top-down analysis, while essential, must be combined with a lease-by-lease or bottom-up approach if enduring, practical benefits are to be realized. By itself, a macro approach primarily produces important educational, and even marketing, benefits. Combined with a bottom-up analysis, the macro analysis leads to a portfolio strategy from which practical management guidelines can flow.

A Major Asset Class with Minor Pension Interest

Commercial real estate is a major asset class. Table 1 shows the 1987 third-quarter estimate of commercial real estate value, $3.1 trillion, compared to common stock, Treasuries, mortgages and bonds. The value of commercial real estate, including office, retail, warehouse and hotel buildings, is comparable in size to common stock and is now more than twice the value of domestic and foreign bonds.

However, real estate's pension asset allocation is still small. Equity real estate — that is, real estate with little or no leverage — still receives a small weighting in most pension portfolios. According to *Pensions and Investment Age*, real estate comprises only 3.6 percent of the portfolios of the top 200 private and public plans.

Real estate's relatively minor pension asset allocation is in dramatic contrast to its share of national wealth and its role in aggregate capital formation. High transaction costs, the lack of a deep public market for real estate, and real estate's lack of liquidity compared to stocks and bonds are important factors. However, the general lack of a real estate portfolio discipline, compared to that of stocks and bonds, may be a reason why institutional investors have not adopted higher real estate allocations.

The size and diversity of U.S. real estate offers the real estate investor a wide range of diversification strategies. The U.S. commercial real estate inventory, when compared globally, is unique not only for its absolute and relative size, but also for its distribution across cities. In most countries, the largest city accounts for a significant fraction, if not most, of the total national investment real estate value.

We estimate that the value of all London office property, for example, is approximately 50 percent of the total valuation of the U.K. office inventory. By contrast, the New York metropolitan area, which includes parts of New Jersey and Connecticut, contains less than 5 percent of all U.S. office property value.

Thinking Strategically

Geographic diversification is an effective way to reduce overall portfolio risk without sacrificing return. Unfortunately, most attempts by managers to diversify by location have been naive at best because the covariance of returns by region is either ignored or analyzed superficially. The traditional four-region diversification, for example, is a misleading way to define geographical opportunities for purposes of diversification, for the following reasons.

First, four-region diversification is too coarse. Within each of the four regions, there remain substantial opportunities for risk reduction without sacrificing return. Second, regions should be defined on the basis of economic similarity. Third, cities with similar economic bases, and presumably similar systematic risk, may not necessarily be contiguous. For example, San Francisco, Boston and New

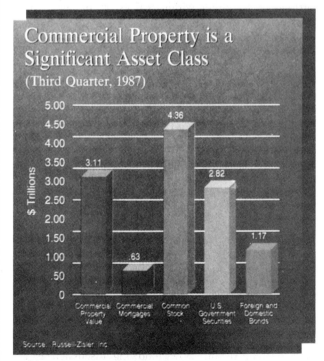

Table 1: *The value of commercial real estate is comparable in size to that of common stock and more than twice the value of domestic and foreign bonds.*

York each have above-average concentrations of finance, insurance and real estate workers.

Real estate returns for unleveraged property, based on the Frank Russell Co. (FRC) property index, are less volatile than either stock or bond returns.

True real estate volatility, after correcting for the sluggishness of appraisal data, is between 9 and 13 percent, a bit less than that of common stocks. Even after correcting for appraisal-based sluggishness in the return data, the return, volatility and covariance characteristics of real estate make this asset class very attractive.

Measured real estate volatility may understate true volatility of property, particularly leveraged property. However, the low correlation between real estate and other asset classes makes real estate a particularly attractive component of a well-diversified portfolio.

Property returns are mildly correlated with inflation, indicating that real estate has provided some inflation protection. However, when excessive vacancies persist, as they do in many property markets today, a general economy-wide inflation will not translate immediately into higher property prices.

The negative correlations between property and stocks and bonds indicate that real estate, when included in sufficient amounts in institutional portfolios, can significantly reduce overall portfolio volatility.

Real Estate Is Misunderstood

Individual property management is often disguised as portfolio management. Management decisions that seem optimal at the property level may be suboptimal for the entire portfolio. Similarly, properties that appear lackluster on a stand-alone basis may significantly reduce overall portfolio risk without sacrificing return.

Recent studies suggest that "the selection of sectors in which to invest is likely to have more impact on results than . . . a few good individual property investments and traditional property asset management." (P.A. Firstenberg, S.A. Ross and R. Zisler, "Real Estate: The Whole Story." *Journal of Portfolio Management*, Spring 1988.)

The operating, renovating, and particularly the leasing of properties are critical elements in effective portfolio management. Leasing terms are dictated by market forces. Escalation provisions, options to renew, base rents and the like are important elements that determine effective rents. Similar effective rents can usually be attained through a variety of lease-term combinations. While the leasing agent may be indifferent to the tradeoffs, the portfolio manager should carefully weigh the portfolio implications of alternative lease clauses with respect to duration, re-leasing risk and other factors.

Selling, or not selling, a property should be an explicit decision that is consistent with the investor's overall market philosophy and portfolio strategy. Often properties are sold on the basis of poor historical performance. However, such a strategy would have incorrectly dictated the sale in 1983 of many large office properties and shopping centers in the Northeast. Office, and particularly retail, properties in the Northeast outperformed most other real estate sectors following the last recession.

On the other hand, pressure to invest excess cash may encourage unrealistic and inconsistent acquisition assumptions that conveniently justify so-called "opportunistic" investments.

There are two kinds of risk in real estate investment: systematic and unsystematic risk. Systematic risk is inherent in the overall market and cannot be avoided. Unsystematic risk can be reduced to a negligible level in a well-diversified portfolio without sacrificing return, by investing in assets that have non-covariant returns.

The market does not reward investors for risk that can be eliminated through diversification. By contrast, above-market returns are achievable by accepting greater systematic risk. To the extent that real estate portfolios are poorly diversified, investors are assuming needless and uncompensated risk, or, conversely, sacrificing return.

How to Measure the Risk?

Portfolio strategies are either undefined, ill-defined or too narrowly defined. Plan sponsors and their real estate consultants have generally done a poor job of designing meaningful guidelines for their money managers. Existing guidelines, e.g., "office property shall constitute no more than 50 percent of the total real estate portfolio," typically fail to respond to the diversity of real estate financial structures, underlying leases and geographic markets that affect portfolio performance.

Asset allocation is the most important factor affecting real estate portfolio performance, and yet, its execution is often naive. The use of multiple money managers and the trend toward separate account investing places a premium on the management of the managers by plan sponsors, the design of portfolio strategies and the elaboration of guide-

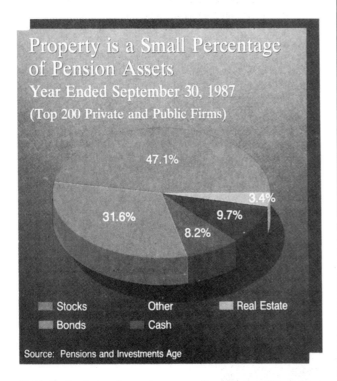

Table 2: Real estate's pension asset allocation is still small.

Pension Fund Asset Mix

Asset type	1983 $ Billions	1983 Percent	1984 $ Billions	1984 Percent	1985 $ Billions	1985 Percent	1986 $ Billions	1986 Percent
Stocks	267.7	44.2	264.3	41.2	338.0	41.6	441.1	43.6
Bonds	211.4	34.9	214.2	33.4	270.5	33.3	346.0	34.2
Cash	49.7	8.2	66.7	10.4	69.1	8.5	78.9	7.8
Real estate equity	20.0	3.3	21.2	3.3	34.1	4.2	36.4	3.6
Mortgages	21.2	3.5	14.1	2.2	17.9	2.2	15.2	1.5
Mortgage-backed securities	0.0	0.0	18.6	2.9	25.2	3.1	39.5	3.9
GICs	14.5	2.4	19.2	3.0	30.1	3.7	25.3	2.5
Other	21.2	3.5	23.1	3.6	27.6	3.4	29.3	2.9
Total	605.6	100.0	641.4	100.0	812.4	100.0	1,011.8	100.0

SOURCE: Reprinted with permission, *Pensions & Investment Age*. Copyright, Crain Communications, Inc. 1987.

lines that money managers can implement and against which they can be properly evaluated.

The control of risk is an essential element of portfolio management. In real estate, however, risk is too often treated anecdotally or, worse, simply ignored. It is not unusual to hear talk of "risk-adjusted real estate returns," when in fact there is great controversy regarding how risk should be measured and just how returns ought to be adjusted.

Investors typically do not understand their risk exposure, whether it relates to tenant default, interest rate risk, leasing risk, inflation or even natural and environmental hazards. Effective risk control requires quantitative indices specially designed for real estate portfolio management. The careless borrowing of risk measures from other asset classes creates false expectations and has not convinced skeptical real estate professionals.

Another way in which the management of real estate portfolios lags behind other asset classes is that managers provide plan sponsors with too much information — irrelevant, overly technical or just incorrect information — for purposes of making intelligent portfolio decisions. The sponsors, who in many cases are learning real estate's basic principles, typically do not demand consistent, timely and meaningful reporting from their managers.

On the other hand, manager reporting systems tend to ignore information that is critical for effective portfolio management. Plan sponsors generally know less about their real estate than they do about their equity and bond portfolios. Many managers do not perceive the benefits associated with a properly educated client. In fact, some managers actively pursue a policy of disinformation and nondisclosure (e.g., "It's our data, not the client's").

Lastly, there is a lack of standardized performance measurement. Managers simply do not report using standardized performance calculations. Much effort is expended by consultants and the plan sponsor's staff in deciphering manager-supplied performance data.

Not only is it difficult to attribute manager performance, but it is equally hard to assess a portfolio's current performance status on a risk-adjusted basis. For example, commingled fund managers generally do not report the kinds of statistics necessary to permit an understanding of the financial characteristics (e.g., risk, duration and so on) of a "unit investment" in the fund. And each commingled fund reports differently.

What the Future Holds for Portfolio Management

Real estate portfolio management, even at its most sophisticated, is not a substitute for, but a complement to, traditional asset management skills.

Under pressure from plan sponsors, real estate managers will attempt to incorporate quantitative portfolio management technologies with varying success. The best efforts will be undermined by the fact that the manager is only one of several managers, each lacking the mandate, the perspective and, at times, the objectivity to manage the entire portfolio.

Plan sponsors will assume greater portfolio management responsibilities. Specific decisions will remain in the hands of the real estate money manager, where they belong, but a set of properly defined guidelines will shape the acquisition and asset management of property.

The art of real estate portfolio management will evolve, albeit slowly. Greater institutional involvement in real estate, the growth of new financial technologies for managing portfolios, an expanding array of real estate vehicles, heightened concern about risk, regulatory and accounting changes and the growing need to evaluate real estate in the context of other asset classes should all stimulate the development of real estate portfolio management.

Randall C. Zisler is president of Russell-Zisler, a Princeton, NJ–based subsidiary of Frank Russell Co. Previously, he was vice president and director of real estate research at Goldman, Sachs & Co., senior vice president at Landauer Associates and a partner of Jones Lang Wootton. Mr. Zisler was also an assistant professor at Princeton University, where he received his Ph.D.

A Practical View of Real Estate and Modern Portfolio Theory

This is the first of two articles dealing with the impact of portfolio theory on real estate decision-making. In this issue, a layman's view of the basic logic is developed. A description of how various institutional players use this logic follows in the next issue.

by Bob Conroy, Mike Miles and Charles Wurtzebach

Fifteen years ago few real estate practitioners thought much about portfolio theory. It was generally acknowledged that diversification was a good thing, but most deals were done on a project-by-project basis, with little formal analysis of the benefits of diversification. In the early 1970s, pension funds first began to invest in real estate equities[1]. They have become the major new investment player in many real estate markets, and they have brought with them a portfolio-conciousness in decision-making.

As a new player, the pension funds came from a world of stocks and bonds, where portfolio theory was already an established part of the decision-making. As the pension funds diversified into real estate, they sought to explain their decisions with the same logic they had heretofore used in diversifying their portfolio across the broad array of stocks and bonds. But real estate investment counselors, developers and other players often found the pension funds' logic alien to their own ways of thinking. Yet the sheer size of the pension funds has forced real estate people to cater to the funds — to change traditional ways of doing business to adapt to the funds' ways. Furthermore, the huge pools of money in the funds have swamped some markets — i.e., the big new player joining traditional lenders has pumped too much funding into several markets. In areas where excess supply met con-

---

[1] For many years, insurance companies, through their general accounts (their own funds invested to pay off future policy claims), had been investing in real estate. However, the entrance of the pension funds, which typically used outside investment managers rather than manage their own real estate investments, made institutional real estate equity investment "public" for the first time.

Bob Conroy *is an Assistant Professor of Finance at the University of North Carolina at Chapel Hill. He has done extensive research and teaching in the area of investment management.*

Mike Miles *is Foundation Professor of Urban Development at the University of North Carolina at Chapel Hill. The author of over 50 articles, books and cases on various aspects of real estate, his recent work has concentrated on pension fund real estate investment.*

Charles H. Wurtzebach *is Associate Professor and Real Estate Program Director at the University of Texas at Austin. He has published numerous articles in several leading real estate journals. He is the co-author, with Mike Miles, of the textbook entitled* Modern Real Estate.

tracting demand (e.g., oil towns such as Denver and Houston) the result was an absolute glut of constructed space.

Notwithstanding these problems, the authors believe that modern portfolio theory is consistent with traditional real estate analysis. The bundle of rights was always both separable and divisible, and there were always many creative ways to structure a transaction to best benefit the various claimants of the cash flow. The better one knows a client, the better one can use all the creative possibilities inherent in real estate rights to structure a transaction to suit everyone in the deal. In fact, knowing modern portfolio theory is no more than knowing the mind and the needs of an important new client, the pension funds. Even if you do not deal directly with pension funds yourself, you must understand their logic, or you will fail to understand the marketplace. If you do deal directly with them and you fail to acknowledge the importance to them of modern portfolio theory, you are very likely to pay too much, sell too cheap or finance at too high a cost.

> *"... Knowing modern portfolio theory is no more than knowing the mind and the needs of an important new client, the pension funds. Even if you do not deal directly with pension funds yourself, you must understand their logic, or you will fail to understand the marketplace."*

We begin with a short description of the evolution of institutional real estate investment. We will look quickly at how modern portfolio theory has developed over the last 30 years and at how this theory "fits" in the real estate marketplace. We will then look at where the institutional player is used to finding "investment numbers," i.e., the historical numbers that describe the performance of various assets. "Investment numbers" include the New York Stock Exchange Index, the Dow-Jones averages and various other return series. The historical data on real estate returns are far less reliable than those on stocks, though still very useful. After having looked at the historical record, we will look at academic research using these data and see what the real estate claim offers to the institutional investor. Finally, and most important, we will move from past research explaining historical returns to a consideration of future directions. This is the hardest yet certainly the most important part of analyzing portfolio theory. We study its history not because we believe

the future will be an exact replica of the past, but because we seek to learn whatever the past can teach us about being better players in the future.

Background: Six Essential Lessons

Table 1 lists six essential lessons as a prelude to our study of real estate in portfolio theory. First, portfolio theory is new to most real estate people, but it is old hat to the stock and bond people who manage pension fund investments. This means 1) that they have a tremendous amount of human capital invested in the theory and its applications, and therefore will seek to apply it as they move into real estate markets, and, 2) possibly less obviously, they understand that portfolio theory is qualitative as well as quantitative. In other words, they understand that the theory does not fit the marketplace perfectly and that there are many problems in using the theory to structure an investment portfolio. As an example, a commonly used market risk measure of a stock, its "beta," changes over time depending on which historical interval analysts use to track the stock's performance in relation to the market. In other words, numbers vary over time; measurements taken at one point in time are not valid for all time. Consequently, as stock and bond people move into real estate portfolio analysis, they will not be intolerant of difficulties; yet they do wish to understand the limits that arise from weakness in the data.

TABLE 1
Essential Background Lessons

1. Portfolio theory is old hat to stock and bond people.
2. It didn't become important in real estate because of some college professor.
3. Since it is the logic behind most capital allocation models, it drives the thinking of the major source of savings in the U.S. economy.
4. The theory is both simple and logical.
5. Historical empirical studies are fraught with problems.
6. Moving from empirical ex-post studies to real world applications is a perilous journey.

Second, we must always remember that portfolio theory did not become important in real estate because a professor fit a theory to last year's reality. Portfolio theory became important and has remained important because it helps people make money. Making money is, of course, the bottom line on Wall Street as well as Main Street. So as we go through the theoretical derivations later, we need to remember that the theory is useful. If it wasn't, it would not have survived so long.

Third, portfolio theory is the logic driving the capital allocation models used by the pension funds. In other words, it helps them decide how much to put in real estate, in stocks, in bonds, in venture capital and in other investment vehicles. Why should we care about pension funds' capital allocations? Well, let's take a look at their size and significance. Pension funds are a major new source of savings in the economy. In early 1986, pension funds have total assets of around $1.3 trillion. By 1995, the Dept. of Labor estimates that their total assets will be approximately $3 trillion.

Since $3 trillion is a lot of money to most people, let's break it down and see what it means in the real estate game. If approximately 15 percent of the total were invested in real estate (the figure recently cited by Goldman Sachs & Co. as typical of the diversified institutional portfolio), that would mean $450 billion by 1995. Today, pension funds have about $40 billion invested in real estate. So over the next nine years they would need to acquire over $400 billion worth of real estate.

Now look at the real estate investment manager, who recommends and executes investments for the pension funds. Managers typically receive about one percent of assets under management as their fee. (That's investment management, not property management). One percent of $450 billion is $4.5 billion in fees a year. Today, Prudential Insurance is the market leader in real estate investment management with a nearly 20 percent share. If Prudential held that market share for the next nine years, it would eventually receive approximately $900 million a year in management fees (assuming the fee structure remains the same). Clearly this is a big incentive to serious players. Furthermore, beyond management fees there are development profits, brokerage profits, appraisal fees and all the other money-making parts of the real estate industry.

Fourth in our list of essential items, portfolio theory is both simple and logical. (Much more so in theory than in practice, we admit. But it *is* widely practiced, despite all difficulties). It behooves those of us who want to be players to make the effort to understand the theory and its practical applications to real estate. In 1970 real estate was a nontraditional investment on Wall Street. But as of 1985, after two position papers by Goldman Sachs & Co. advocating real estate for the institutional investment portfolio, real estate is no longer outside the mainstream. Wall Street people are in the game, and understanding how they play is important to all players. Wall Streeters are smart, and they play hard. If you want to play against them, you have to be good.

Fifth, as we will see later, a variety of empirical studies have attempted to apply portfolio logic in various real estate markets. These studies have been flawed in many very important ways. And yet, in a world where information is expensive and comparative advantage is possible, the studies are still relevant for what good information they do contain. Furthermore, as Aetna, Trust Co. of the West, Prudential, Goldman Sachs, Salomon Brothers, Equitable, Wells Fargo, First Chicago and others enhance their research staffs, empirical studies will improve.

Sixth, and last, we repeat that we study the past to prepare for the future. The problem with using the past, i.e., using historic numbers (ex-post), is that conditions change and the same numbers may not apply in the future. Yet we estimate future numbers (ex-ante) based on past experiences along with our best guesses of what changes will occur. To the extent that we project future risks and returns, our models are only as good as our underlying assumptions. Moral: study the past and apply its lessons thoughtfully.

This article should prepare you for the next issue where we will use portfolio logic to understand the players of the game. Modern portfolio theory affords us even more creativity in structuring real estate investment vehicles. And as we have seen from a couple of examples above, it can be a very lucrative business.

Modern Portfolio Theory — What is It?

Modern portfolio theory is still evolving; it is not dogma. Its basic principles are debated, yet still used by practitioners. To understand the theory, we might look at its evolution. Table 2 lists the major stages.

TABLE 2
Major Stages in the Evolution of Modern Portfolio Theory

		Source
A	*Expected* return and the risk associated with that expected return determine value.	Ancient Greek thinker
B	In a portfolio, develop the *efficient frontier.*	Markowitz, 1952
C	The Capital Asset Pricing Model	Sharpe, 1964
D	Arbitrage Pricing Theory	Ross, 1976
E	Options pricing	Black and Scholes, 1973 Cox, Ross, Rubinstein (binomial), 1979* Rendleman and Bartter (binomial), 1979*

* *Only when the more intuitive binomial approach was introduced did options pricing theory become widespread in practice.*

For as long as anyone can remember, value of any single project has been defined as a function of expected return and the risk associated with that return. This is clearly traditional real estate analysis; it is the heart of the income approach to value used in appraisal practice. On Wall Street, the technical definition of risk is the variance of the distributions of expected returns.

The expected return and variance of return can be calculated from historical data using the formulas:

Average Return:
$$\bar{X} = \sum_{t=1}^{N} X_t / N$$

Variance of Return:
$$Var(X) = \sum_{t=1}^{N} (X_t - \bar{X})^2 / N$$

Standard Deviation of Return:
$$SD(X) = \sqrt{Var(X)}$$

where X_t is the observed percentage return over some holding period, typically one year for stocks and bonds, $\bar{X}$ is the mean (average) of the observed returns, $Var(X)$ is the variance of the observed returns, $SD(X)$ is the standard deviation of observed returns and N is the number of observed returns.

In the average return formula, the sigma notation "Σ" simply means take the sum of X_t (X in period t) over N periods (t=1,2,...N). Dividing this sum by N gives the average of X. The variance formula says take the sum of the difference each time period between X_t and the average of X (which is $\bar{X}$) (square the difference because X_t will be less than $\bar{X}$ for many periods, and hence the difference will be negative) and divide by the number of time periods (N) to get the "average deviation" from the norm. A large variance of X indicates that X is volatile, i.e., it changes a lot from period to period (high risk). The standard deviation is simply the square root of the variance.

Figure 1 shows the expected returns and variances for holding various types of stocks and bonds. As can be seen, the higher the expected or mean return, the higher the variance. This is the well known tradeoff between risk and return. The key issue in terms of portfolio theory is whether the variability or the variance of the return on a single stock or, for real estate the return on a single property, is the risk we should be concerned about.

FIGURE 1
Basic Series — Total Annual
Returns (1926-1981)

SERIES	GEO-METRIC MEAN	ARITH-METIC MEAN	STANDARD DEVIATION
Common Stocks[A]	9.1%	11.4%	21.8%
Small Stocks[B]	12.1%	18.1%	37.3%
Long-Term Corporate Bonds[C]	3.6%	3.7%	5.6%
Long-Term Government Bonds[D]	3.0%	3.1%	5.7%
U.S. Treasury Bills[E]	3.0%	3.1%	3.1%
Inflation[F]	3.0%	3.1%	5.1%

Source: Ibbotson and Sinquefeld, 1982

[A] S&P 500
[B] S&P 500 — smallest quintile, ranked by capitalization
[C] Salomon Brothers High-Grade Long-Term Corporate Bond Index, yield basis
[D] 20-year term bond portfolio
[E] Short-term T-Bills, one-month holding period returns
[F] Consumer Price Index

The general approach is to calculate from historical data an expected return and variance of return for every security. From this, decisions would be made as to what assets should be chosen on the basis of risk as compared to expected return. The basic point of portfolio theory is that this is not enough. It is not enough to consider the risk-return tradeoff of a specific investment. In order to fully understand the risk of an individual asset, we must consider how it interacts with the return on other assets.

In order to see this, let us consider two individual investments, A and B. The expected return on A is $\overline{X}_A = 12$ percent, and the expected return on B is also 12 percent. In addition, assume that they both have the same standard deviation $SD_A = SD_B = 25$ percent. It would seem that they have the same risk-return tradeoff. But what about a portfolio of the two? What is the expected return and standard deviation of such a portfolio? Suppose we invested 50 percent of our wealth in A and 50 percent in B. The expected return and standard deviation would be:

$$\overline{X}_p = (50\% \cdot \overline{X}_A) + (50\% \cdot \overline{X}_B)$$

$$SD_p = \sqrt{(50\% \cdot SD_A)^2 + (50\% \cdot SD_B)^2 + 2(50\% \cdot SD_A \cdot 50\% \cdot SD_B \cdot r_{AB})}$$

Note that the expected return of the portfolio is simply a weighted average of the expected returns, but the stand-

ard deviation has a rather different form. In particular, there is the term, r_{AB}, which is the correlation coefficient between A and B. This is a statistical measure of how two things move relative to each other. It can take on values of 1, -1, or any value in between. Positive values indicate that they move in the same direction, while negative values indicate that they move in opposite directions. Table 3 gives the values of the expected return and standard deviation of the portfolio for different values of r_{AB}. As can be seen, the portfolio of A and B has a better risk-return tradeoff than either A or B alone as long as the correlation coefficient is less than 1. In addition, the benefit from diversification increases as correlation between the two assets decreases.

TABLE 3
Expected Returns and Standard Deviations
for a Portfolio of A and B

r_{AB}	$\overline{X}_p$	SD_p
+1.0	12%	25%
.5	12%	22%
.1	12%	19%
0.0	12%	18%
- .1	12%	17%
- .5	12%	13%
-1.0	12%	0%

This is a key point. In a portfolio, the total return is simply a weighted average of the return on all the assets in the portfolio. However, portfolio risk is *not* simply a weighted average of the risk of the individual projects in the portfolio. In a portfolio, high returns on one project may offset low returns during the same period on another project, so that overall portfolio risk is lowered.

To the traditional stock and bond analyst this means that a hotel isn't necessarily more risky than a warehouse leased for 20 years to IBM. Certainly the hotel individually would be expected to exhibit more variance in its future returns. However, if those returns are *not* highly correlated with the stocks and bonds already held by the institutional investor, the hotel, when included in the institutional investment portfolio, may contribute less to portfolio risk than the warehouse that, when leased on a long-term basis to a triple-credit, looks a great deal like a bond.

This example points out a unique aspect of real estate with respect to diversification. It is clear that diversification can be achieved by having different types of properties in a portfolio but this can be very expensive and in some sense difficult to manage. Another way of achieving diversification with real estate is to focus on a real estate portfolio as a collection of leases. By using a mix of different types of leases even within the same property type, a significant amount of diversification can be obtained. This can be a cheaper way of getting diversification with real estate and is actually more in keeping with the traditional view of real estate, which tends to emphasize specialization.

What this implies is that risk must be measured in a portfolio context. This was the point made by Harry Markowitz in his pioneering work on portfolio theory begun in 1952. He showed in clear mathematical language how to look at risk in a portfolio context. Risk and return collectively still determine value; however, since most

Portfolio Risk According to Markowitz

Value of a single project is a function of the mean and variance of the expected return.

$$\text{Variance (V)} = \frac{\sum\limits_{i=1}^{N}(X_i - \overline{X})^2}{N}$$

where V = variance

X_i = total return percentage

$\overline{X}$ = average total return percentage

N = number of periods

Standard Deviation

$$\text{SD} = \sqrt{\text{Variance}}$$

Covariance =

$\text{SD}_X \bullet \text{SD}_Y \bullet \text{Correlation of X and Y}$

Using historical data on the returns of the various possible investment opportunities, the analyst estimates the mean and covariances of the expected future returns. The covariance includes both the standard deviation of the individual securities' returns and the correlation of returns among the different securities.

Points on the efficient frontier are the particular portfolios that offer the highest expected return for any given level of risk, or, conversely, the lowest level of risk for any given level of expected return. Once the analyst has developed the efficient frontier, the investor can select any point on that frontier based on the amount of risk he wishes to assume.

The Efficient Frontier

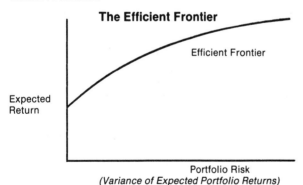

Efficient Frontier

Expected Return

Portfolio Risk
(Variance of Expected Portfolio Returns)

The more risk-adverse investor moves logically toward the left on the curve, the less risk-adverse toward the right. No investor can do better with any other portfolio than the efficient frontier.

In developing the frontier, remember that the expected return for the portfolio as a whole is simply the weighted average of the return of each of the securities held in the portfolio. Portfolio risk, however, is not an additive function. A formula for the standard deviation of portfolio return is shown in the next column.

$$\sigma_p = \sqrt{\sum_{i=1}^{N} X_i^2 \sigma_i^2 + \sum_{i=1}^{N}\sum_{j=1}^{N} X_i X_j \sigma_i \sigma_j r_{ij}}$$
$$(i \neq j)$$

$$= \sqrt{\underbrace{\sum_{i=1}^{N} X_i^2 \sigma_i^2}_{\substack{\text{Weighted}\\\text{security risk}} } + \underbrace{\sum_{i=1}^{N}\sum_{j=1}^{N} X_i X_j \sigma_{ij}}_{\substack{\text{Effect of correlation}\\\text{between securities}}}}$$

X_i is the % of the portfolio invested in asset i

σ_i is the standard deviation of the expected return of asset i

r_{ij} is the correlation of returns between assets i and j

σ_{ij} is the covariance of i and j

As you can see, the standard deviation can be broken into two different parts — the unique security risk and the effect of the correlation between securities.[2] In a widely diversified portfolio, the first component approaches zero, thus leaving the second component as the primary measure of risk. In this measure the covariance includes the standard deviation of each security as well as the correlation between the securities. Thus it is the correlation of returns that becomes the most important item.

Since the correlation coefficient is such an important item, it behooves us to look more closely at this measure. Shown below are both the ex-ante and ex-post calculations of the correlation coefficient. The analyst develops the ex-post measure from historical securities' returns, and then uses this along with other information, to develop ex-ante expectations for the correlation coefficient.

---

[2] For those of you familiar with the capital asset pricing model, you will quickly recognize the first as the unsystematic component, and the second as the systematic component.

The Correlation Coefficient

Ex-ante:

$$r_{ij} = \frac{\sum\limits_{s=1}^{S} P_s (R_{is} - E(R_i))(R_{js} - E(R_j))}{\sigma_i \, \sigma_j}$$

P_s = Probability of outcome s

$E(R_i)$ = Expected (average) return on asset i

R_{is} = Return on asset i given outcome s

σ_i, σ_j = The standard deviations of the expected returns from assets i and j

Ex-post:

$$r_{ij} = \frac{\sum\limits_{t=1}^{N} (R_{it} - \overline{R}_i)(R_{jt} - \overline{R}_j) / N}{\sigma_i \, \sigma_j}$$

Where R_{it} and R_{jt} refer to the return on securities i and j during period t, R_i and R_j are average rates of return earned during the past N periods, and σ_i and σ_j are ex-post standard deviations.

major investors are diversified, what they care about is not the unique risk of any one project, but, rather, the risk that a project contributes to their portfolio. It is this perspective that the new players are bringing to their investment in real estate. An important element to all of this is not only the correlation between real estate projects themselves, but also the correlation between real estate and the more traditional assets such as stocks and bonds. To the extent that these new players view *risk in a portfolio context*, they are bringing a whole new definition of risk to the real estate markets. This can and will have a profound impact on the way real estate assets are valued.

"Another way of achieving diversification with real estate is to focus on a real estate portfolio as a collection of leases. By using a mix of different types of leases even within the same property type, a significant amount of diversification can be obtained. This can be a cheaper way of getting diversification with real estate and is actually more in keeping with the traditional view of real estate, which tends to emphasize specialization."

Academics applauded Markowitz's idea, but practitioners found the concept difficult to use since it required the estimation of the correlation between every pair of assets. For 50 to 100 assets, doing the math is practical. Above that number, even with computers the calculations are cumbersome and the number of correlation coefficients to be estimated becomes unreasonably large. Remember that institutional portfolios are huge, and managers are faced with an enormous number of potential acquisitions, be they stocks, bonds, other securities or individual real estate projects. Therefore, while intuitively pleasing and mathematically correct, Markowitz's definition of portfolio risk proved all but impossible to apply on an asset-by-asset basis to large institutional portfolios.

In 1964, William Sharpe made a major advance with

what has come to be known as the capital asset pricing model. The capital asset pricing model is a simplification of Markowitz's idea. Sharpe argues that the only variance that matters to the truly diversified portfolio is the covariance of the individual asset's return with the return of the overall market total. This represented a single measure of portfolio risk which is referred to as the "beta" of the asset. Portfolio risk in the capital asset pricing model is the weighted average of the individual assets' betas. Beta is estimated using the statistical technique of linear regression to correlate an asset's historical return with the historical returns of the market (usually applied to stocks). The mechanics of the theory are described on the next page.

"To the traditional stock and bond analyst (portfolio theory can mean) that a hotel isn't necessarily more risky than a warehouse leased for 20 years to IBM."

Since the capital asset pricing model was intuitively pleasing and at first appeared to be a reasonable approximation of the marketplace, it became the darling of both professors and Wall Street analysts. For the next 14 years, both groups tried to force empirical reality to fit the theory. As forcing a fit became increasingly difficult, more doubts about the theory arose. Then in 1978, Richard Roll delivered the final blow when he demonstrated mathematically that the theory was at best untestable.

Unfortunately, there was no ready replacement for what had become the major capital market paradigm, widely used in practice by Wall Street. Lack of a better model, coupled with the reluctance of many people to discard a heavy investment in human capital, has led to a lingering death for the capital asset pricing model. Many people still refer to it, and it is conceptually useful; however, it is not the model of the future for applied institutional real estate investment.

Also during the 1970s, in search of an alternative capital market paradigm, Steven Ross offered an even more intuitively appealing model known as arbitrage pricing theory (APT). First developed by Ross in 1976 and elaborated by Ross and Roll over the next few years, this theory assumes investors hold well-diversified portfolios and argues that there is not one market risk factor only, but several systematic (common to the market) risk factors and that investors are paid for bearing risks in each area. Arbitrage pricing theory is particularly appealing when applied to real estate because it says that investors should receive a higher return for greater exposure to risks like unexpected inflation, unexpected changes in the term structure of interest rates, changes in the market risk premium and unexpected changes in gross national prod-

The Capital Asset Pricing Model

Capital asset pricing theory involves a simple mean-variance approach to investment analysis. All assets are priced based on their expected return (the mean of that return) and the riskiness associated with that return (defined as the variance associated with incorporating the given expected return in the portfolio).

Overall variance in any asset's expected return can be divided into a systematic and an unsystematic component. The systematic component is the amount of the asset's variance that can be explained by the variance of the overall market. The unsystematic component is the variance in the individual asset's return that is unique to the particular asset. That is, the security's variance is broken down into two parts: one is a function of the general market and the other is unique to the particular asset. In a fully diversified portfolio, unique (unsystematic) variances will cancel out in the aggregate. Consequently, it is only systematic (market-related) risk that is important in pricing assets in the capital markets.

A measure of systematic risk can be determined by regressing the historical return of any particular asset on the historical returns of the market as a whole. The regression coefficient for that asset is termed its beta. A beta of 1.0 is equal to the market overall (i.e., an investment with a beta of 1.0 moves up or down in value 1 for 1 with the market). A beta of more than one, say 1.6, represents an aggressive investment that moves up or down in value faster than the market. A beta of less than 1, say 0.8, represents a somewhat defensive investment that moves up more slowly than the market but also declines more slowly.

The higher this beta, the greater the systematic risk associated with the security's return. That is, the higher the beta the more a particular asset will contribute to the variance of the overall portfolio. (Remember, the investor is concerned with the variance of the total portfolio.)

Figure 2 illustrates the typical relationship between return and risk according to the capital asset pricing model. Again, risk and expected return are positively correlated. The higher a particular investment's beta, the greater the investor's required return (see Figure 3).

The investor would be particularly attracted to any investment whose returns are negatively correlated with the market. Such negative correlation would be indicated by a negative beta (signifying an investment whose returns generally move in the opposite direction from the market). By combining assets that are negatively correlated with the market, the overall return on the portfolio becomes more stable (i.e., the variance is reduced) without necessarily sacrificing returns.

FIGURE 3
Calculating Beta

The beta is calculated using historical data and estimating the following figures using regression analysis:

$$R_s = a + \beta_s(MRP)$$

where

R_s = Return on investment s (Both periodic cash flow and appreciation in value)

a = Risk-free rate

β_s = Investment s beta

MRP = Average market risk premium (historical average market return less the corresponding historical risk-free return)

R_s and MRP are known for each month over a substantial period, say 20 years; a and β are then produced through regression analysis

---

Once a particular security's beta is known, in theory the calculation of an appropriate risk premium for use in discounted cash flow analysis is straightforward. The appropriate risk premium (now in a portfolio context) is the market risk premium (MRP) times beta. (MRP is simply the average market return less the risk-free return.) This product is then added to the risk-free rate appropriate for the anticipated holding period to obtain the appropriate required rate of return (discount rate).

Example: Assume that the stock of a hypothetical company, the U.S. Homebuilders, Inc., has a beta of 1.4. Historically the average market risk premium has been about five percent. (Note that the market risk premium varies and the most current figure should be used for investment calculations.)

The discount rate to be applied to U.S. Homebuilders' return (dividends plus appreciation) is the risk-free rate (say, T-bills at nine percent), plus risk premium (five percent MRP X 1.4 = seven percent) = 16 percent. The discount rate here is calculated as 16 percent.

(Theoretically, this application is only the tip of the iceberg. The issues include what returns to measure, how to measure them and what historic time period to use. However, an example like this one does help in understanding the model, regardless of theoretical uncertainties.)

FIGURE 2
Capital Asset Pricing Model

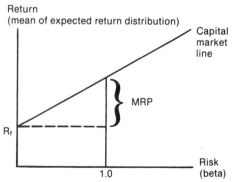

MRP= Mean of expected return distribution — Risk-free rate

Discount Rate= (MRP•B$_s$)+Risk-free rate

R$_f$= Risk-free rate

uct. The theory is logical, but practical use requires factor analysis, a fairly loose form of multivariate statistics. Unfortunately, factor analysis is so flexible that analysts can come up with almost any number as a risk premium for each of the factors. In short, even through arbitrage pricing theory is intuitively appealing, its empirical relevance is limited by the fact that everyone seems to arrive at a different set of numbers.

The final item shown in Table 2 is options pricing theory. While options pricing is not a complete capital market model, it is probably the theory that will have the greatest impact on real estate investment over the next decade. The option is quite common in real estate investment, and pricing an option can serve as a model for pricing other interests in real estate.

"Corporate real estate executives, whether concerned only with managing their firm's current portfolio of fixed assets or negotiating a joint venture arrangement, should understand the implications of portfolio theory for real estate valuation."

The question has always been, "How do you price the option? What is the option worth?" Black and Scholes developed an options pricing formula; several authors have subsequently contributed to its development. Let's use the simple example of a vacant lot in an industrial park, Lot 15. According to the Black-Scholes formulation, the price of an option on Lot 15 is a function of 1) the current market price of the asset (Lot 15), 2) the exercise price of the asset when sold (as stated in the option contract), 3) the length of the option period, 4) the risk-free interest rate (measured by T-bills of comparable maturity) and, most importantly, 5) the variance of the price of the asset over the option period (e.g., the day-to-day estimated variation in the market price of Lot 15 over a 90-day option period). It is this last item which is very difficult to measure in real estate. The math underlying this model is well beyond our scope here, but the authors believe that in the future, as more data become available, options pricing will become much more important in real estate decision making.[3]

The Basic Paradigm

Now that we have looked at the evolution of portfolio theory, what have we got that we can use? Well, with the capital asset pricing model fallen from grace, and arbitrage pricing theory failing to provide a ready substitute,

we are left with basic Markowitz, i.e., portfolios can reduce risk. Although his portfolio theory cannot be applied to make decisions among hundreds of potential acquisitions, it can be, and is, applied to groups of assets: for example, returns on gold, collective returns on stocks from an industry, and collective returns on real estate projects categorized by size, type or geographic area. So while investment managers today use many tools, most do use some version of the Markowitz model to make basic allocation decisions among the S&P 500, small capitalization stocks, venture capital, corporate bonds, government bonds, treasury bills, real estate, commodities, foreign securities and the other investment alternatives available. However, the key to making these allocation decisions is information on the relationship between the returns on these different assets. While this information is readily available for a large number of assets, in the next section we will see that this is not the case with real estate.

Sources of Investment Returns Data

Before we look further at portfolio theory in real estate, we need to see where institutional investors are used to obtaining data on investment returns. Table 4 shows the three ways to calculate the performance returns. As you can see, the Dow-Jones industrial average is certainly the best known price-weighted series. A price-weighted series is one in which the weight that any particular security carries in the overall index varies with its price. Thus, the Dow-Jones Industrial Average changes every time there is a stock split. This is really quite illogical; however, it is the oldest and best known overall performance measure.

TABLE 4
Performance/Return Indices
(Beware the ex-post to ex-ante extrapolation.)

A Price-Weighted — Dow-Jones Industrials (It changes and it's illogical, but it's still the best known)

B Value-Weighted — S&P, NYSE, NASDAQ, American, Wilshire 5000, (FRC)

C Unweighted Price Indicators — Fisher, Indicator Digest

The most accepted way to calculate an index is the value-weighted series. Here we have the Standard & Poor's 500, the New York Stock Exchange Index, the American Stock Exchange Index, the NASDAQ Index, the Wilshire Index and, in real estate, the FRC Index. FRC stands for the Frank Russell Company, which produces, along with the National Council of Real Estate Investment Fiduciaries, a quarterly return index for income-producing real estate. It is the standard of the real estate industry, and is the closest real estate index to the stock indices most frequently used by the Wall Street banks.

---

[3] For an example of the application of the Black-Scholes pricing formula to real estate options pricing, see *California Real Estate Indicators,* Summer/Fall 1985, published by Housing Real Estate and Urban Studies, Graduate School of Management, University of California, Los Angeles, pp. 4 & 5.

There are also unweighted price indices, such as the Fisher Index, but these are used mainly for academic purposes and need not concern us here. They are being presented only for completeness.

Most indices are developed from extensive data bases which the New York Securities analysts use on a regular basis. Securities analysts have on computer tape or disk the daily, weekly, monthly and annual returns of a host of securities going back many, many years, along with extensive supplementary information such as earnings per share, dividends per share and so forth. As securities analysts move into real estate, they look for similar information. Although the FRC Index is now available, the data underlying the FRC Index are not yet public. As a result, traditional securities analysts are left wondering how different real estate is from stocks and bonds and whether they can trust what information they do get.

Real Estate Return Data Bases and Indices

As Wall Streeters have moved to real estate over the last 15 years, they have searched for historical information on real estate returns. The table of suggested reading at the end of this article summarizes the various studies which have been done. While the list looks extensive, it is trivial compared to the number of studies done on stocks and bonds, and after careful analysis, most of the studies are found wanting. Still, while the information is not all the Wall Street analyst seeks, nor all the traditional real estate analyst would like, there is significant information contained in these studies. In a world where information is costly and comparative management possible, such information remains important.

Research Results to Date

Many studies (refer to suggested reading), working from different data bases, have come to some general conclusions regarding real estate as a portfolio asset. These results are summarized in Table 5. (A more extensive overview of 20 years of research is presented empirically by Zerbst and theoretically by Miles in the references cited in the suggested reading).

TABLE 5
Research Results to Date

A Real estate has offered higher returns and lower project risk (standard deviation of project returns) than stocks or bonds.

B Real estate has offered an attractive diversification opportunity for those invested in stocks and bonds (a low correlation of real estate returns with stock and bond returns).

C Real estate has offered an attractive inflation hedge while stocks and bonds have not.

Looking at Table 5, real estate seems too good to be true; in fact, that is exactly the conclusion of most stock and bond people looking at real estate research. Real estate has offered higher returns and lower project risks (forgetting for the moment about portfolios) than have either stocks or bonds. This result appears largely because most of the real estate data bases were constructed during the 1970s, when many real estate markets experienced substantial appreciation. No one expects that much rela-

tive appreciation to be sustained over the long run. Two other explanations of anomalous returns to real estate in comparison with stocks and bonds are that 1) we have failed to measure risk correctly in the past (as discussed earlier in connection with arbitrage pricing theory) and, 2) we have underestimated costs, thereby overestimating returns (Roger Ibbotson's New Equilibrium Theory, discussed briefly in the next issue).

"Real estate appears to offer attractive diversification opportunities. . . . And real estate has also offered attractive inflation protection, while stocks and bonds have not. If these two findings hold in the future, we will witness a great deal of institutional investment in various real estate markets."

The other two findings are more interesting and possibly of longer-term significance. Real estate appears to offer attractive diversification opportunities, i.e., there is a low correlation between real estate returns and stock and bond returns. And real estate has also offered attractive inflation protection, whereas stocks and bonds have not. If these two findings hold in the future, we will witness a great deal of institutional investment in various real estate markets. Recall that moving just 15 percent of the aggregate U.S. pension funds portfolio to real estate would result in investment of over $400 billion by 1995.

Criticisms of Real Estate Investment Research

Table 6 lists the three primary criticisms of the real estate research described in the previous sections. The first two criticisms (A & B) come from traditional stock and bond people. They argue that the research is based on data from only one manager or on data from government-compiled data, such as the price of an agricultural acre of land in Iowa or the average price of a residential house, neither of which is a relevant measure to the pension fund investor buying shopping centers and office buildings. The stock and bond people also complain that the return series are based on appraised values, not market prices, and therefore are far less reliable.

Another criticism (C) comes from traditional real estate analysts. They argue that in trying to accommodate the new institutional investors we have lost much of great value. They argue that traditional real estate analysis (location, location, location), construction type, lease-term, etc., are all relevant and that in attempting to accommodate the new pension fund investor, we have homogenized an asset heterogeneous by definition.

TABLE 6
Primary Criticism of Research to Date

A It's idiosyncratic, i.e., from only one or a few managers, or it's non-property-specific, i.e., it is an average which smoothes returns. (An average always reduces the variance.)

B It's based not on actual sales from the market, but on appraised value.

C It's all finance; it's lost the "real estate."

Where Are We and Where Are We Going?

Institutional real estate investment is here to stay and will be a growing influence in most major real estate markets. The people making these investment decisions have a tremendous amount of human capital invested in modern portfolio theory, and this theory will help shape their decisions over the next several years. If a major player is using this logic, all serious real estate players must understand it.

When we apply the logic to real estate, our data leaves much to be desired. Stock and bond analysts are used to extensive information available at relatively low cost on computer tape and disk. In real estate, a variety of return indices have been constructed, none of which is truly comparable to stock indices such as the S&P 500. The best of the real estate data bases is the FRC Index, which will be the source of considerable research in the future.

Research results to date (derived from admittedly inferior data) suggest that real estate is an attractive investment in and of itself. Research further suggests real estate is an excellent diversifier for the stock and bond investor and an excellent inflation hedge. While these results would portend a tremendous shift of wealth into real estate, we must emphasize that no one completely believes the research done in the past. The main criticisms are that idiosyncratic data has been used and that appraisals rather than market prices establish the total return series. Further, traditional real estate analysts have argued that the new demand for "institutional-type analysis" has caused us to lose sight of traditional factors in real estate value.

All of this implies some new directions for institutional investment in real estate. Originally, diversification meant constructing a portfolio with different property types and locations. This contradicted the more traditional view of real estate, which emphasized specialization in property type or location. The evidence now indicates that a better marriage of the institutions and real estate is made if the diversification is considered not just within real estate, but obtained by combining real estate with stocks and bonds. This means that we may not have to worry about the lack of diversification that we get when we specialize in one type of property or location, since we get the diversification we need when the "ideal" real estate portfolio is combined with stocks and bonds to form a truly

mixed asset portfolio.

In the future, we believe you will see heightened activity in real estate investment research. The major institutional players need it, and are now doing a good bit of it themselves. As you will see in the next issue, there are tremendous rewards for the person who develops an interesting strategic niche in institutional real estate investment. Corporate real estate executives, whether concerned only with managing their firm's current portfolio of fixed assets or negotiating a joint venture arrangement, should understand the implications of portfolio theory for real estate valuation.

SUGGESTED READING

1 Black, F. and Scholes, M. "The Valuation of Options Contracts and a Test of Market Efficiency." *The Journal of Finance,* May 1972.

2 Cox, J., Ross, S., and Rubinstein, M. "Options Pricing: A Simplified Approach." *Journal of Financial Economics,* September 1979.

3 Ibbotson, R., Siegel, L. and Love, K. "World Wealth: Market Values and Returns". *Journal of Portfolio Management,* Fall 1985.

4 FRC Property Index — The NCREIF Report, Quarterly. Available from the Urban Land Institute, 1090 Vermont Avenue, N.W. Washington, DC 20005.

5 Markowitz, H. *Portfolio Selection: Efficient Diversification of Investments,* John Wiley, 1959.

6 Miles, M. Special Editor. *American Real Estate and Urban Economics Association Journal,* Fall 1984.

7 Rendleman, R., Jr. and Bartter, B. "Two-State Options Pricing." *Journal of Finance,* December 1979.

8 Roll, R. "A Critique of the Asset Pricing Theory's Tests." *Journal of Financial Economics,* May 1977.

9 Ross, S. "The Arbitrage Theory of Capital Asset Pricing." *Journal of Economic Theory,* December 1976.

10 Sharpe, W.F. "Capital Asset Prices: A Theory of Market Equilibrium Under Condition of Risk." *Journal of Finance,* September 1964.

11 Zerbst, R.H. and Cambon, B.R. "Historical Returns on Real Estate Investment." *Journal of Portfolio Management,* Spring 1984.

12 Zister, R. "The Real Estate Report." Goldman Sachs, April 1985.

ID INDEX
CORPORATE MANAGEMENT
CONROY, BOB, MILES, MIKE
and WURTZEBACH, CHARLES
"A Practical View of Real Estate and Modern Portfolio Theory,"
May/June 1986, Vol. 155, No. 3
1. Portfolio Theory
2. Investments
3. Real Estate — Corporate

Real estate:
The whole story

We allocate too little to it and pay too little heed to real estate diversification.

Paul M. Firstenberg, Stephen A. Ross, and Randall C. Zisler

Investors traditionally have thought of equity real estate as an inefficient market in which the key to success is in the skill with which an individual investment is selected and negotiated. The general approach seems to be to buy properties when they become available if they look like "good deals," with little regard for the equally important issue of how the acquisition fits with the other holdings in the portfolio and what effect, if any, it will have on the overall risk and return objectives of the portfolio. Only recently have some investors begun to think of the aggregate of their real estate investments as a *portfolio*, with its own overall risk and return characteristics, and to adopt explicit strategies for achieving portfolio goals.

This article takes the view that investors should examine equity real estate investments not only on their individual merits but also for their impact on the investor's overall real estate portfolio. In addition, investors need to assess how the real estate segment fits into their entire portfolio. In turn, this means:

- setting risk and return objectives for the equity real estate portfolio as a whole that are compatible with the goals for the investor's entire portfolio,
- devising a strategy for achieving these objectives, and
- evaluating the extent to which individual transactions conform to the strategy and are likely to further portfolio objectives.

These processes are, of course, familiar to anyone in the business of managing security portfolios. By contrast, there has been a nearly complete neglect of such theory and techniques in the management of real estate portfolios and in their integration into institutional portfolios. This, in turn, has deprived managers of the modern tools that they now employ when considering other financial decisions. Often, for example, the pension fund asset allocation process that results in a decision to "put 10% of the portfolio into real estate" seems governed at least as much by hunch as by any rational mechanism.

Again by way of contrast, probably there is not a single major institutional portfolio in the common stock area that does not make serious use of modern portfolio techniques to continually monitor overall portfolio risk and to assess portfolio performance. These techniques are often the central mechanism for determining management strategy and selecting managers.

While some funds rely much more heavily on quantitative techniques than others do, the implementation of these procedures clearly has moved well beyond the cosmetic and lip service stage. Furthermore, a good general rule is that the larger the portfolio, the greater the reliance on such techniques. This is no doubt a consequence of the realization that even a few good stock picks will have less of an influence on the performance of a $5 billion portfolio than over-

PAUL M. FIRSTENBERG is Executive Vice President of the Prudential Realty Group in Newark (NJ 07101). STEPHEN A. ROSS is Sterling Professor of Economics and Finance at the Yale School of Management in New Haven (CT 06520) and consultant to the Real Estate Research Group at Goldman Sachs & Co. RANDALL ZISLER is Vice President of Goldman Sachs & Co. and director of their Real Estate Research Group in New York (NY 10004). The authors are grateful to William N. Goetzmann of the Yale School of Management for his fine assistance.

all structuring decisions will. These decisions include how much to put into different categories of assets or stocks and the overall risk level of the portfolio.

Moreover, within an asset category, the selection of sectors in which to invest is likely to have more impact on results than the choice of individual investments. These types of decisions for real estate are likely to be as critical for performance as a few good individual property "investments" and individual property asset management will be.

Our intention is to show how pension funds and other large investors can use modern portfolio techniques both to construct real estate portfolios and to allocate funds to asset categories including real estate. Our concern, however, is not with a cookbook application of some handy formulas to the real estate market.

Because the real estate market is not an auction market offering divisible shares in every property, and information flows in the market are complex, these features place a premium on investment judgment. Managers who want to own some of IBM simply buy some shares. Managers who want to participate in the returns on, say, a $300 million office building must take a significant position in the property. One alternative is to purchase a share of a large commingled real estate fund, but that does not relieve the fund's managers from the problems of constructing their portfolio.

Our aim is not to eliminate the analysis of each individual property acquisition, but rather to supplement it with a thorough consideration of its contribution to overall portfolio performance. Modern portfolio analysis provides the tool for examining the risk and return characteristics of the overall portfolio and the contribution of the individual elements. The result of its application is a method for selecting properties whose inclusion in the portfolio is of overall benefit.

Before we consider this point in more detail, we examine how real estate performance results compare with those for stocks and bonds. In this analysis, the absence of the large and continuous data record available in the securitized markets presents some special problems.

TOTAL RETURN AND REAL ESTATE DATA

In all modern investment work, the focus of interest is on the total rate of return on assets, that is, the return inclusive of both income and capital gain or loss. The logic underlying this is the basic philosophy of "cash is cash." An investment with a total return of 10%, all from capital gains, is equivalent to one with a total return of 10%, all from income, be-

cause the sale of 9% of the shares in the investment that has risen in value will realize for the holder the same cash as the all-income investment provides. This basic truth, though, does not deny the possibility that, for some holders, there may be an advantage to receiving the return in one form or another.[1]

A real estate fund might rationally have an income as well as a total return objective, yet the transaction cost of selling appreciated property to realize income is particularly severe for real estate. While we recognize that this is an important issue, space considerations do not permit us to deal with it explicitly. Fortunately, too, this is not a serious limitation to our analysis, because the income component of large real estate funds is relatively insensitive to the decision as to how to allocate the funds across different types of real estate.

To determine the total return on real estate or any other asset, we just add the income component and the capital gain or loss. The income component of an asset's return is relatively straightforward to determine, as it is just a cash flow, and good data generally are available for the computation.

The price appreciation component, however, is much more difficult to assess. If an asset is traded in a continuous auction market, like the common stock of a major company, price quotes in the market provide a good method for valuing the asset. Most real estate assets trade infrequently, however, and valuation is more problematic. For some of the commingled funds, appraisals are the only source of property valuations.

The appraisal process merits a paper of its own, but a few points are sufficient for our purposes. Appraisals usually are conducted annually and are based on one of two methods or a combination of the two. If comparable properties have recently been bought or sold, then the appraisal can use their prices as benchmarks for estimating the value of properties that have not been traded. Comparability is increasingly difficult to achieve as the number and complexity of leases increases. Alternatively, the property can be valued by the discounted cash flow (DCF) method of discounting the projected net cash flows at some discount rate determined by prevailing market conditions. Neither of these methods can be as accurate as an actual market price, but there is also no reason to think that they will be biased in the long run. Furthermore, even if appraisals are biased, the appreciation computed from appraisals will not be biased as long as the bias is constant over time.

Although appraisals are not necessarily biased, there is evidence of considerable sluggishness or inertia in appraised values. By any of the common measures of the volatility of returns, real estate returns from appraisals appear to vary far less over time than other asset return series. Standard deviation is a measure of the spread or volatility of investment returns, and we will use the standard deviation also as a measure of the riskiness of real estate returns.[2]

The data below reveal that the standard deviation of stock returns, for example, is over five times greater than that of real estate returns. The extent to which this difference is a consequence of real estate returns actually being far less volatile than stock returns or a consequence of the use of appraisal values is not really known. In the data that follow, we make a correction that raises the volatility of the real estate returns to a level that seems more reasonable to us.

The major sources of data on real estate returns come from commingled funds. We have made use of three series of aggregate real estate returns and a separate series of the returns on different subcategories of real estate. For comparison purposes, we also use returns on other assets such as stocks and bonds. The data and the sources appear in the Appendix.

Table 1 describes how real estate returns have compared with the returns on stocks and bonds and with inflation. As the Frank Russell (FRC) and Evaluation Associates (EAFPI) series are based on appraisals, they might move more sluggishly than a true market value series — if one were available. The two adjusted series under the FRC heading report the result of alterations in the FRC data designed to recognize this weakness. The "cap-rate adjusted" series estimates the change in value from a DCF model, and the "appraisal adjusted" series adjusts the standard deviation of the series upward.[3]

Even when the standard deviation of real estate returns is adjusted upward, both the return and the standard deviation make real estate an attractive asset category in comparison with stocks and bonds. Its lower risk and its comparable return partially offset the lack of liquidity inherent in real estate investments.[4]

We turn now to the issues involved in managing an equity real estate portfolio and the implications of modern portfolio analysis for real estate.

REAL ESTATE PORTFOLIOS: THE BASIC PRINCIPLES

In an imperfect real estate market, the skill with which individual assets are acquired, managed, and disposed of will be a major determinant of total return. Portfolio management is not a substitute for, nor should it divert attention from, property-specific management. Nevertheless, the composition of the portfolio as a whole will impact both the level and the variability of returns.

The twin considerations of individual property-specific management and portfolio analysis require different human skills and make use of different information. This leads naturally to a two-tiered approach to management:

- A macro analysis that employs portfolio management concepts and focuses on the composition and investment characteristics of the portfolio as a whole, identifying major strategic investment options and their long-run implications. Each property that is a candidate for acquisition or disposition should be analyzed for its impact on overall portfolio objectives.

- A micro analysis that employs traditional real estate project analysis, and focuses on the selection of the individual properties that make up the portfolio, evaluating a property's specific risk–reward potential against the investor's performance targets.

We will not have much to say here about the micro analysis; it is the traditional focus of real estate analysis. We make suggestions for it, but we do not propose changing it. Our interest is in the macro analysis.

Macro analysis derives the characteristics of risk and return for the portfolio as a whole from different combinations of individual property types and

TABLE 1

Real Estate Series and Other Assets

Index	Total Return (%)	Annualized Standard Deviation (%)	Series Begins (*)
Real Estate			
FRC	13.87	2.55	6/78
FRC (cap-rate est.)	13.04	11.28	6/78
FRC (appraisal adj.)	13.87	4.37	6/78
EAFPI	10.78	2.80	3/69
EREIT	22.26	19.71	3/74
Other Assets			
S&P 500	9.71	15.35	3/69
Small Stocks	14.51	23.90	3/69
Corporate Bonds	8.38	11.29	3/69
Government Bonds	7.91	11.50	3/69
T-Bills	7.51	0.82	3/69
Inflation	6.64	1.19	3/69
Risk Premium (spread over T-Bills)			
EAFPI	3.27	2.43	
FRC	4.36	1.29	
S&P 500	1.48	17.54	
Small Stocks	7.38	18.04	

* All series end in December 1985. For details and full titles of each series, see the Appendix.

geographic locations. It establishes the trade-off between the given level of return and the volatility of return that result from different mixes of assets. Selecting the particular risk–return trade-off that best meets an investor's requirements is the most crucial policy decision one can make and is one of our major concerns.

The macro policy is implemented only through the individual selection of properties at the micro level. A thorough analysis of a property should involve an analysis of its marginal contribution to overall portfolio return, volatility, and risk exposure. The difficulty in conducting such an analysis at the individual property level is what gives rise to the separation between the micro and macro analyses. In general, the macro goals are implemented at the micro level by choosing categories of properties to examine with the micro tools, rather than by examining each individual property's marginal effect on the portfolio.

We will employ some familiar principles from modern portfolio theory as guides in portfolio construction:

- To achieve higher-than-average levels of return, an investor must construct a portfolio involving greater-than-average risk. An investor whose risk tolerance is lower than that of the average investor in the market must expect relatively lower returns. Risk may be defined as the variability or dispersion from the mean of future returns or, simply put, the chance of achieving less-than-expected returns. The variability of returns usually is measured by the standard deviation.

- It is possible and useful to measure risk and return and to develop, in an approximate manner, a portfolio strategy that balances the trade-off between these two performance criteria. Because of the difficulty and costs of transacting in the real estate market, and because of the resulting lack of precise "marked-to-market" prices for real estate, it is unrealistic to attempt to fine-tune actual investment decisions in response to risk–return estimates. Even if an investor specifies a preference for a mean return of 15% with a standard deviation of 3%, to a 14% mean return with a standard deviation of 2.5%, translating that preference into a precise strategy is probably not feasible. Broader relationships between risk and return must guide real estate investment strategy.

- The total risk on any investment can be decomposed into a systematic and an unsystematic component. Unsystematic risk will largely disappear as an influence on the return of a well-diversified portfolio. To the extent that the return on an individual property is influenced by purely local events, it is unsystematic and washes out in a large diversified portfolio.[5] A regional shopping center, for example, might find its sales adversely affected by a plant closing. A chain of shopping centers spread across the country, however, would find total revenues unaffected by such local influences. Its revenues would depend on the overall economic conditions that affect costs and consumer demand. An investor who owned many such centers would not be subjected to the ups and downs of individual industries and markets and would be affected only by the general economic conditions that influence all retail businesses simultaneously.

- The risk from changes in economic conditions throughout the country is systematic and will influence any portfolio, no matter how large and well-diversified, because it influences each of the parts. For example, a downturn in consumer demand and a rise in wages will probably adversely affect all business, which means that even a conglomerate would suffer a decline in profits. Systematic risk can be lowered only by lowering long-run average returns. A conglomerate might attempt to lower such risks by implementing a strategic decision to sell some businesses and invest the proceeds in cash securities. The resulting revenues will have less sensitivity to the business cycle but also will have a lower average return. An investor could do the same.

In the sections that follow we will illustrate how investors can apply these principles in portfolio construction by examining how different combinations of property types and economic regions affect the risk and return characteristics of a portfolio.

Investors can reduce the unsystematic and, therefore, the overall risk level of the portfolio without sacrificing return by diversifying real estate investments among property types that have non-covariant returns and across geographic areas or leaseholds that are not subject to the same macroeconomic variables. Diversification also protects the investor from overemphasizing a particular asset class or area of the country that then falls victim to unforeseen, or more often unforeseeable, negative developments.

Spreading assets geographically has been a commonly used rough proxy for selecting areas that are economically non-covariant. A more detailed analysis, however, is required to determine whether geographically separate areas are actually subject to the same macroeconomic variables. The economic base of a particular geographic area may be broad-based, with multiple and widely diversified sources of revenues, or its economy may be largely dependent on a single economic activity. The latter is obviously a riskier area in which to invest, but much of its risk is unsystematic.

As a consequence, a diversified portfolio of areas, each of which is influenced by a different industry-specific risk, can avoid such risk at no cost in returns. For instance, the economies of Houston, Denver, and New Orleans were all highly vulnerable to one variable — oil prices; San Jose, California, Austin, Texas, and Lexington, Massachusetts, are all vulnerable, to a lesser degree, to the fortunes of the high-tech industries. A portfolio made up of properties in these cities is diversified geographically, but subject to significant systematic risks. By contrast, a portfolio made up of properties in Lexington, New Orleans, and, say, New York and Reno would have less overall risk.

This line of reasoning explains the power of diversification across geographic areas whose economies are independent. Within a given city, the same economic forces that influence the business demand for industrial and office space also affect the demand of workers for residential space, the demand of customers for hotel room nights, and the demand of retailers who sell to the workers. Too often, casual real estate market research leads to a claim of urban or regional diversification without an adequate analysis of the inter-industry and inter-occupational linkages affecting returns. Diversifying across different areas lowers risk to the extent to which the economies of the areas are independent of each other. Ultimately, the goal of diversifying a real estate portfolio should be to diversify across leaseholds.

Intuition also suggests that international diversification would be a powerful tool for accomplishing this goal. The question of whether a portfolio with London and New York properties is more economically diverse than a portfolio of Boston and New York is really the question of whether the underlying economy of Boston will move more or less with that of New York than will London.

REGIONAL DIVERSIFICATION

Figure 1 illustrates the trade-off between risk and return that is available when we break real estate investment into different regions and examine various portfolio possibilities for diversifying holdings across the regions. The four regions are the East, the Midwest, the South, and the West.[7] Figure 1 displays all the possible combinations of return and risk available from the different combinations of holdings across these four regions.

The expected return is graphed on the horizontal scale in Figure 1, and the vertical scale gives the standard deviation. The data are all historical.

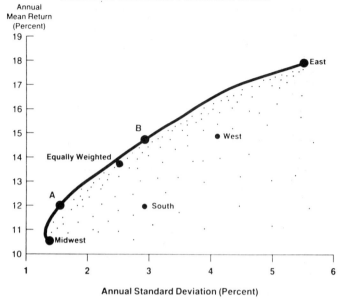

FIGURE 1

EFFICIENT REGIONAL PORTFOLIO MIXES

History is a guide to the future, but this is not to say that the next ten years will mimic the last ten. Rather, we are asking how different portfolios would have performed in the past. We contend that an intelligent look at past risk and return patterns is necessary for an understanding of the future. This, of course, is a weakness of all analysis, whether quantitative or not, but what else can we use to study the future if not the past?

By choosing different combinations of the four regions, all the points in the shaded part of Figure 1 are available. The labeled points describe the four pure regional portfolios. The East alone, for instance, shows a return of 17.9% and a standard deviation of 5.6%. The equally weighted portfolio in Figure 1 gives the return and the risk of a portfolio that puts one-quarter of its investment in each of the four regions.

Table 2 gives the background data underlying Figure 1. Here we have listed the return and standard deviation for each of the regions as well as the correlations in the returns across the four regions. Correlations are interpreted in the usual fashion. A positive correlation between two regions indicates that the returns tend to rise and fall together, and, as the table shows, all the regional correlations are positive. A zero correlation means that the returns tend to move independently of each other. All the correlations are low, and the correlation between the Midwest and the South is nearly zero. Combining asset categories that are only weakly correlated with each other greatly lowers overall portfolio risk. Figure 1 certainly reveals that this is the case for regional diversification.[8]

TABLE 2

Returns by Region, 1978-1985

| | Annualized | |
Region	Mean Return (%)	Standard Deviation (%)
East	17.91	5.58
Midwest	10.49	1.44
South	11.96	2.92
West	14.83	4.11

| | Regional Correlation Matrix | | | |
Region	East	Midwest	South	West
East	1.00	0.16	0.25	0.32
Midwest	0.16	1.00	0.04	0.14
South	0.25	0.04	1.00	0.46
West	0.32	0.14	0.46	1.00

TABLE 3

Efficient Portfolio Mixes by Region
(Proportions, %)

East	Midwest	South	West	Mean (%)	Portfolio Standard Deviation (%)
	99		1	10.50	1.43
0%	81	18%	1	10.80	1.31
5	74	17	5	11.30	1.36
9	66	15	9	11.80	1.49
14	59	13	13	12.30	1.67
19	52	12	18	12.80	1.89
23	45	10	22	13.30	2.14
28	38	8	26	13.80	2.41
32	31	7	30	14.30	2.70
37	23	5	35	14.80	2.99
41	16	3	39	15.30	3.30
46	9	2	43	15.80	3.60
51	2	0	47	16.30	3.91
64			36	16.80	4.28
80		20		17.30	4.80
96		4		17.80	5.43

Using Figure 1, we can show that investing the entire portfolio in any single region is unnecessarily risky. For three of the regions, there is a superior alternative that involves combining the regions. The only exception is the all-East portfolio. As it had the highest return in the period used to construct Figure 1 (see Table 2), putting the entire portfolio into the East would have been the best choice, but, of course, we have no basis for assuming that the next ten years would still put the East on top.

As for the other three choices, take, for example, the South. The South had a mean return of 11.96% and a standard deviation of 2.92%. Compare these results with those of Point A, directly above the South on the curve that bounds the possible combinations of return and risk. This point has the same standard deviation of 2.92% as that of the all-South portfolio, yet its return is nearly 15%, or 300 basis points, greater than that of the all-South portfolio. Similarly, Point B, just to the left of the South, is also superior to the all-South portfolio. It has the same return of 11.96% as the all-South portfolio, but its risk level is about 1.5%, or nearly half that of the all-South portfolio. The points on the curve of Figure 1 are called efficient portfolios, because they give the best possible returns for their levels of risk. The points between A and B are efficient portfolios that dominate the all-South portfolio.

Table 3 lists the efficient regional portfolios for each level of return and shows their risk level. These portfolios are the ones that give the returns and standard deviations on the curve in Figure 1. Table 3 provides a great deal of valuable information on the optimal regional diversification of a real estate portfolio.

As we move from low returns to high returns — and higher risk — we see that in the range from an 11.3% return with a 1.4% standard deviation to a 15.8% return with a 3.6% standard deviation, the efficient portfolios diversify to include all the regions. In other words, as we avoid the extremes of the highest returns and risks and the lowest returns and risks, a characteristic of the efficient portfolios is that they are fully diversified. Indeed, as Figure 1 shows, the equally weighted portfolio that puts exactly the same investment into each region is essentially an efficient portfolio with its return of 14% and its standard deviation of 2.3%.

This is as far as this quantitative analysis can take us. At this point judgment takes over. The quantitative analysis can weed out the inferior choices, but, in the end, it cannot make the final choice for the manager. The manager is left with the central question: What combination of risk and return should be chosen and, therefore, which efficient portfolio?[9] Each investor will have particular requirements for establishing the trade-off between risk and return.

We offer here only some broad considerations. For a publicly-held fund, the basic issue is one of marketing; the combination of return and risk and, therefore, the regional diversification should be chosen according to an evaluation of the clients' demands. For a pension fund, the decision should be based on how the real estate portfolio is expected to contribute to the overall objectives of the fund. We will look at this matter more closely when we consider allocating funds across asset classes, including real estate. When regional diversification and property type diversification are combined, the resulting reduction in risk is considerable.

PROPERTY TYPE DIVERSIFICATION

Figure 2 illustrates the trade-off between risk and return that is available from forming portfolios of the five different property types, and Table 4 gives the data underlying Figure 2. The properties are classified into five major property types: apartments, hotels, office buildings, retail properties including shopping centers, and industrial properties such as warehouses. This classification corresponds both to the available data and to an a priori sensible breakdown into non-covariant business groupings. As we would expect, the efficient portfolios are diversified by property type, but here the results are different from those obtained when we consider regional diversification.

As Table 5 reveals, the efficient portfolios can have as few as two asset types in them. For returns above 16.3%, the efficient portfolios are dominated by hotels and office properties. For the low-risk alternatives, apartments, industrial properties, and retail dominate. At all levels of risk and return, though, some diversification is appropriate.

It is difficult to say to what extent these results predict future patterns and to what extent they are the consequence of the relatively short statistical history. There is reason to believe, though, that we should depend less on the property diversification results than on the regional analysis. For one thing, the numbers themselves are less reliable. The hotel category, for example, is based on a relatively small number of properties, and they are unduly concentrated in New York City. For another, it may well be

TABLE 4

Returns by Property Type, 1978-1985

	Annualized Mean Return (%)	Standard Deviation (%)
Apartments	15.29	3.97
Hotels	18.25	12.08
Industrial	13.63	2.27
Office	15.38	4.72
Retail	11.56	2.19

Property Type Correlation Matrix					
	Apartments	Hotels	Industrial	Office	Retail
Apartments	1.00	0.56	0.41	0.21	0.13
Hotels	0.56	1.00	0.17	0.11	−0.01
Industrial	0.41	0.17	1.00	0.65	0.59
Office	0.21	0.11	0.65	1.00	0.21
Retail	0.13	−0.01	0.59	0.21	1.00

TABLE 5

Efficient Portfolio Mixes by Property Type
(Proportions, %)

Apartments	Hotels	Industrial	Office	Retail	Mean (%)	Portfolio Standard Deviation (%)
4		4		92	11.80	2.10
9		20		71	12.30	1.97
13		36		51	12.80	1.94
18		50	1	31	13.30	2.01
23		61	3	13	13.80	2.18
30		61	9		14.30	2.43
41	2	34	24		14.80	2.81
53	3	7	38		15.30	3.29
38	16		46		15.80	4.03
15	33		53		16.30	5.23
	49		51		16.80	6.67
	67		33		17.30	8.40
	84		16		17.80	10.29
	98		2		18.20	11.88

that some of these returns reflect the economics of relatively tight leasing markets in the late 1970s and early 1980s. Furthermore, fundamental changes in the tax laws since 1986 probably will affect these property types differently.

For these reasons, we would advocate using Table 5 as a rough guide and tend to give greater weight to the middle region where all property types are represented. The final choice of a risk and return trade-off, as with regional diversification, rests with the manager and is governed by the same considerations as affect the regional choice.[10]

IMPLICATIONS FOR PORTFOLIO MANAGEMENT

We conclude from the foregoing analysis of the risk–return characteristics of portfolios constructed with different mixes of property types and geographic regions that:

FIGURE 2

EFFICIENT PROPERTY TYPE MIXES

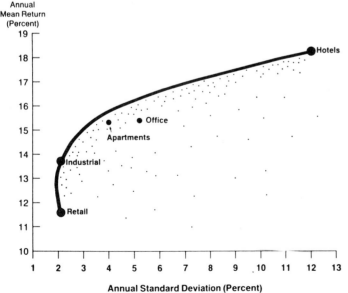

- There is a trade-off between the riskiness (as measured by standard deviation) of a real estate portfolio and the total expected return it generates. Consistent with experience with financial assets, the degree of risk an investor is willing to assume will be the single most important factor in determining return.

- Diversifying the composition of a portfolio among geographic locations and property types can increase the investor's return for a given level of risk. Diversification among holdings with non-covariant returns will reduce risk without sacrificing return. To construct such a portfolio, each investment category identified as offering diversification potential should be represented; the goal should be to have a substantial minimum threshold investment across property types and geographic regions (e.g., no property type or region should be below, say, 15% of the total portfolio).

- There are at least two alternative strategic approaches to diversifying a real estate portfolio. One approach calls for all investments to be made in strict accordance with diversification criteria, even though the assets allocated to different categories may exceed the minimums necessary to gain significant benefits. Under such a strict policy, an investor would not shift allocations because of perceived future changes in the payoffs from different allocations. The investor would modify the initial diversification slowly and generally only in response to some sort of significant long-term change in the marketplace. The assumption underlying this approach is that such modifications always create additional risk and that the investor lacks the forecasting ability to earn sufficient additional return to compensate for the risk.

  The second approach allows for strategic deviations from the strict plan, provided that the threshold minimum allocations are met. Such an approach could reflect an investor's confidence in the ability to project changes in the risk–return differential of various geographic areas or property types. Or it could stem from pursuing a high risk–return strategy of, say, investing in development projects or in less than fully leased properties in currently out of favor markets in the hope of producing results outside of the efficient frontier of Figures 1 and 2. In such cases, the portfolio will reflect the strategic investment selections that deviate from a strict diversification policy, with the expectation that the added risk will be compensated for by additional return. One way to implement such a strategy is to divide the portfolio into a strictly diversified component (a core portfolio) and a higher risk/higher return portion (an opportunity portfolio), with the blend between the two reflecting an overall risk–return target.

  In sum, an investor can target a real estate portfolio to lie at any point along the risk–return continuum; the crucial step is to articulate and explicitly adopt an investment strategy that fits this goal and that both the investor and the investment manager fully understand and agree upon. The strategies to be pursued in managing a real estate portfolio should be explicit, not unspoken.

- We need to learn a good deal more about the factors that, in fact, produce genuine diversification (i.e., non-covariant returns). Present categories of broad geographic regions or property types provide only crude guidelines for achieving efficient mixes. This lack of the proper economic classifications and the accompanying data are the most serious weaknesses of our analysis.

ASSET ALLOCATION: STOCKS, BONDS, AND REAL ESTATE

In principle, the same considerations that govern the construction of the all-real estate portfolio apply to the asset allocation decision. Table 1 gives the basic return and risk information, while Table 6 gives the correlations between real estate and other asset categories.

TABLE 6

Correlations Among Asset Classes*

	FRC	EAFPI	EREIT	S&P 500	Government Bonds	T-Bills	Inflation
FRC	1.00	0.71	−0.14	−0.26	−0.38	0.30	0.38
EAFPI	0.71	1.00	−0.20	−0.28	−0.10	0.54	0.48
EREIT	−0.14	−0.20	1.00	0.78	0.36	−0.23	0.03
S&P 500	−0.26	−0.28	0.78	1.00	0.49	−0.43	−0.15
Government Bonds	−0.38	−0.10	0.36	0.49	1.00	−0.09	−0.35
T-Bills	0.30	0.54	−0.23	−0.43	−0.09	1.00	0.41
Inflation	0.38	0.48	0.03	−0.15	−0.35	0.41	1.00

* For details and full titles of each series, see Appendix.

In constructing Table 6, we have treated real estate as a single category, even though different regions or property types will have different relations with other assets. Whenever we aggregate asset classes and consider their relationship with each other as classes, we always lose some of the fine detail. This is true of stocks as well as real estate. As these asset categories are managed as individual classes, however, the separation of management forces the separation of our analysis.[11]

From a portfolio perspective, the great attractive feature of real estate is its lack of correlation with other assets. Even if real estate risk is understated, the lack of correlation makes real estate a particularly attractive feature of a well-diversified portfolio.

Look first at the correlations among the three real estate indexes FRC, EAFPI, and EREIT. The two appraisal-based indexes, FRC and EAFPI, are highly correlated with each other, and both are negatively correlated with the stock market-traded REIT index, EREIT. This striking difference points up the difficulty with the real estate data. Indeed, both FRC and EAFPI are negatively correlated with the stock market as well, while EREIT with a 0.78 correlation with the S&P 500 actually looks like a stock index rather than the other two real estate indexes. (A closer look reveals that individual REITs can behave like the other real estate indexes; it all depends on the particular REIT.) Presumably, the truth lies somewhere between these two, and we can conclude that real estate returns, if not negatively correlated with those on stocks, are at least far from perfectly correlated with them.

One point with which all of the real estate indexes agree, however, is that real estate hedges against increases in inflation. All three indexes are positively correlated with changes in inflation. By contrast, the S&P 500 index has responded negatively to inflation.

Our argument for including real estate as a substantial portion of an overall investment portfolio is, thus, based on its significant diversification value in reducing risk, whatever the goal for returns.

Using the correlation data from Table 6 and the return data from Table 1, we created the efficient frontier of real estate, stocks, and bonds displayed in Figure 3 and tabulated in Table 7. We used the upward adjustment in the standard deviation of real estate in constructing Table 7 so as to avoid any possible underemphasis of its risk. The efficient portfolios in Table 7 display the same characteristics as the efficient portfolios of the real estate categories. In the middle ranges of return and risk, the portfolio is evenly diversified among the three categories, although real

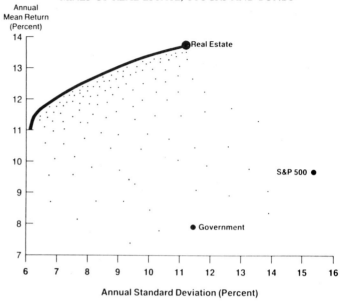

FIGURE 3

MIXES OF REAL ESTATE, STOCKS AND BONDS

TABLE 7

Efficient Portfolio Mixes of Real Estate, Stocks, and Bonds.
Real Estate Standard Deviation 'Cap-Adjusted' = 11.28%
(Proportions, %)

Real Estate (FRC Index)	Stocks (S&P 500)	Government Bonds	Mean (%)	Portfolio Standard Deviation (%)
49	11	40	11.00	6.16
52	12	36	11.20	6.20
55	13	32	11.40	6.29
58	14	28	11.60	6.44
61	15	24	11.80	6.65
65	16	19	12.00	6.91
68	17	15	12.20	7.22
71	18	11	12.40	7.56
74	19	7	12.60	7.94
77	20	3	12.80	8.35
80	20		13.00	8.79
85	15		13.20	9.30
90	10		13.40	9.89
95	5		13.60	10.56
100	0		13.80	11.28

estate has the major share. Insofar as the risk of real estate is still understated by the 11.3% standard deviation, these numbers will overstate real estate's role in an efficient asset allocation.

To examine this matter further, we raised real estate's standard deviation to be the same as that for the S&P 500, 15.4%. The resulting efficient portfolios are given in Table 8. Although the increase in the risk level of real estate lowers its contribution to the efficient portfolios and raises the proportion of bonds, the amount of the change is surprisingly small. For example, the efficient portfolio with a 12% mean return has a 61% holding in real estate when real estate

TABLE 8

Efficient Portfolio Mixes of Real Estate, Stocks, and Bonds.
Real Estate Standard Deviation = Stock Standard Deviation = 15.35%
(Proportions, %)

Real Estate (FRC Index)	Stocks (S&P 500)	Government Bonds	Mean (%)	Portfolio Standard Deviation (%)
38	13	49	10.40	7.05
41	15	44	10.60	7.09
44	17	39	10.80	7.19
47	18	35	11.00	7.37
50	20	30	11.20	7.61
53	21	26	11.40	7.91
56	23	21	11.60	8.26
58	25	17	11.80	8.66
61	26	12	12.00	9.10
64	28	8	12.20	9.57
67	30	3	12.40	10.80
71	29		12.60	10.61
76	24		12.80	11.22
80	20		13.00	11.92
85	15		13.20	12.70
90	10		13.40	13.54
95	5		13.60	14.42
100	0		13.80	15.35

is assumed to be as risky as stocks and a 65% holding when real estate is assumed to have a risk level below that of stocks but above its measured level. Of course, this result is dependent upon the limitations of the data and our model.

The important conclusion to draw from this analysis is that, even with an upward risk adjustment, real estate belongs in efficient portfolios at significantly higher levels than the 3.6% allocation for the top 200 public and private funds in 1986. Taking a pragmatic perspective, we feel that pension funds should seek initial real estate asset allocations of between 15 to 20%.

A second level of consideration in choosing among these possible asset allocations makes use of the additional data presented in Table 6, the correlations between asset returns and inflation and interest rates. Similar data can be collected for other major economic variables that influence asset returns, such as real productivity and investor confidence (see Chen, Roll, and Ross, 1986). We can see from Table 6 that real estate is positively correlated with inflation and, at least for the FRC and the EAFPI indexes, it is also positively correlated with interest rates. This is in marked contrast to stock returns, which are negatively correlated with the inflation variable and with interest rates.

This means that real estate returns have been a superior hedge against an increase in inflation or in interest rates as compared with the experience of the stock market. As inflation or interest rates have risen, the stock market historically has tended to fall, and

real estate returns have tended to rise. Of course, this will depend on the source of the increase in inflation and interest rates. The Monday, October 19, 1987, crash in the stock market produced the opposite result, where sellers of stock ran to the bond market, pushing these prices up. Rather, we are primarily concerned here with a change in stock prices accompanied by a change in inflationary expectations. This differs from a once-and-for-all shift in prices, such as a jump in commodity prices because of formation of a cartel.

A corporate pension fund that is funded ultimately by the earnings of the company would find real estate a relatively attractive asset category if its earnings tend to be negatively related to inflation. For example, suppose that a manufacturing company believes that an increase in inflation brings about a more rapid rise in its wage and material costs than in the prices of its products. A fund with a tilt toward real estate would tend to offset this profit squeeze by rising when corporate earnings fell off.

This does not mean that companies whose earnings rise and fall with inflation should shun real estate. For example, a natural resource company with relatively fixed costs would find its earnings down in a period of low inflation. But the analysis of Tables 7 and 8 is still relevant, and the pension fund of such a company should still hold a significant proportion of its assets in real estate, simply to take advantage of the return and risk diversification characteristics. The proper conclusion to draw is that such a company should hold relatively less real estate than the manufacturing company.

In the end, the allocation decision among the three categories we have studied involves a judgment that is associated with the particular needs of the fund being considered. If, in addition to the considerations of risk and return on which we have focused, there is also a concern for liquidity, this will tend to push the fund toward marketed assets such as stocks and bonds and out of real estate.[12] There is no single answer that is best for all portfolios, only a range of desirable choices. Modern portfolio analysis limits this range to the manageable alternatives presented in Tables 7 and 8.

CONCLUSION

We have shown how modern portfolio analysis can be used both to optimally diversify a real estate portfolio and to allocate overall fund assets among real estate, stocks, and bonds. Real estate is an enormous percentage of world assets, and, as our final tables show, even with an upward risk adjustment, it may belong in efficient portfolios at significantly higher levels, such as 15 to 20%, compared to the 3.6% allocation in 1986 for the top 200 public and private pension funds.

REFERENCES

The two modern portfolio techniques used in the paper are the Capital Asset Pricing Model (CAPM) and the Arbitrage Pricing Theory (APT). Expositions of these approaches can be found in most textbooks on corporate finance. Two references are:

Brealey, Richard, and Stewart Myers. *Principles of Corporate Finance,* 2nd ed. New York: McGraw-Hill Book Company, 1984.

Copeland, Thomas, and J. Fred Weston. *Financial Theory and Corporate Policy,* 2nd ed. Reading, Mass.: Addison-Wesley Publishing Company, 1983.

The following article outlines the APT approach to strategic planning:

Roll, Richard, and Stephen A. Ross. "The Arbitrage Pricing Theory Approach to Strategic Portfolio Planning." *Financial Analysts Journal,* May/June 1984.

Other articles of interest include the following:

Chen, Nai fu, Richard Roll, and Stephen Ross. "Economic Forces and the Stock Market." *Journal of Business,* July 1986.

Hoag, J. "Toward Indices of Real Estate Value and Return." *Journal of Finance,* May 1980.

Miles, M., and T. McCue. "Commercial Real Estate Returns." *Journal of the American Real Estate and Urban Economics Associations,* Fall 1984.

Zerbst, R. H., and B. R. Cambon. "Historical Returns on Real Estate Investments." *Journal of Portfolio Management,* Spring 1984.

[1] Regulatory and accounting conventions may lead to a preference for income over capital gains. Tax issues also influence this preference. Furthermore, some funds may be precluded from realizing income through sales, and, even if they can sell appreciated assets to generate income, the transaction costs of doing so will detract from the return. On the other side, some investors actually may prefer capital gains to income (ignoring tax effects) to avoid being faced with the need to reinvest the cash.

[2] A rule of thumb is that two-thirds of the returns tend to fall within one standard deviation of the mean return and 95% of the returns fall within two standard deviations. The higher the standard deviation, the greater the range of the effective returns, and the greater the probability or likelihood of loss.

[3] The first correction uses a "cap-rate" proxy in place of appraisal returns. Net operating income is a commonly used yardstick for the valuation of real estate. By treating changes in the current income stream as indications of changes in the market value of the asset, we can estimate an appreciation return. Although this approach has a number of problems, at least it allows us to base the estimate of appreciation on known data. The result is an FRC series with an annual standard deviation of 11%.

We generated a series of appreciation returns on the change of an estimated value of the real estate index, where the value is given by the present value of a perpetual stream of income flows. The income flows are taken to be the current period income, and the discount rate can be

modeled either as a spread over T-bills, or simply as a fixed rate.

$$Cr_t = \frac{(Ve_{t-1} - Ve_t)}{(Ve_{t-1})},$$

$$Ve_t = D_t/r_t,$$

where:

Cr = cap-rate return

Ve = cap-rate value

D = income per invested dollar

r = discount rate

Y = income return

I = appreciation index value

This simplifies to:

$$Cr_t = \left[\frac{I_t}{I_{t-1}} \cdot \frac{Y_t}{Y_{t-1}} \cdot \frac{r_{t-1}}{r_t} \right] - 1.$$

This method may have some validity, insofar as a similar procedure on the stock market produces estimates near the true value for volatility.

The appraisal-adjusted series is derived from an analysis of the appraisal process and estimates a volatility of returns based on the reported data. This method is an attempt to correct returns by removing any inertia or sluggishness inherent in the appraisal process. True rates of return should be uncorrelated with each other across time. Insofar as there is excessive correlation in the FRC returns, they will not accurately reveal the true return on real estate.

To model the appraisal process, we assumed that a property's appraised value is a mixture of the series of previous appraised values and the appraiser's estimate of the current market price the property would bring if sold. In other words, the appraiser incorporates past appraisals into the current appraisal.

The basis of this estimation is as follows. An estimated mean return can be expressed as the true mean, M_t, and some random error term, e_t:

$$M_t = R_t + e_t,$$

where the standard deviation of e_t is the true standard deviation of returns.

The appraiser can be thought of as combining the true mean return with a lagged return to make the following estimation:

$$E[R_t] = (1 - A)M_t + AR_{t-1}.$$

More generally, the process might use a whole year's worth of past returns in combination with the true mean to produce the current estimation:

$$E[R_t] = (1 - A)M_t + a_1R_{t-1} + a_2R_{t-2} + a_3R_{t-3} + a_4R_{t-4},$$

where

$$A = a_1 + a_2 + a_3 + a_4.$$

A linear regression based on this model yields the following information:

$$R_t = b_0 + b_1R_{t-1} + \ldots + b_4R_{t-4} + z_t,$$

where z_t is the residual error term.

Combining these two equations, we can solve for the true mean and standard deviation from the estimates of b_1, b_2, b_3, and b_4 as follows:

$$b_1 = a_1, b_2 = a_2, b_3 = a_3, \text{ and } b_4 = a_4,$$

and, therefore, the true mean:

$$M = b_0/(1 - A), b_0/(1 - A),$$

where

$$A = b_1 + b_2 + b_3 + b_4,$$

and the true standard deviation of returns is given by:

$$\sigma = \sigma(z_t)/(1 - A),$$

where $\sigma(z_t)$ is the standard deviation of the regression residual, z_t.

[4] We know very little about the effect of illiquidity on investment returns beyond the intuition that liquidity is certainly no worse than illiquidity. As we do not know much more than this, we will adopt the sensible policy of not saying much more.

[5] In practice, real estate managers spend most of their resources investigating local market conditions and negotiating terms of sale. Little if any attention is directed toward the role of a property in the overall portfolio. This is not as misdirected as it might seem. While diversification removes individual and unsystematic property risk, it does not help portfolio returns if misunderstanding the local markets results in overpaying for every property. Nevertheless, without understanding the marginal contribution that properties make to overall portfolio goals, the whole can be less than the sum of the parts.

[6] It is important that property returns be noncovariant, that is, that they not move together, or the risk will be systematic and the advantages of diversification will be lost. For example, a $100-million stock portfolio with 100 holdings of $1 million each will not be terribly well diversified if all of the stocks are utilities.

[7] Data are reported by the Frank Russell Company on a quarterly basis.

[8] We have used the appraisal based returns and have not adjusted the resulting standard deviations in Table 2 and Figure 1, but the possible low volatility of appraisal returns has no effect whatsoever on our analysis. If we were to increase all of the standard deviations by, for example, a factor of two, then this would double all of the numbers on the vertical scale of Figure 1, but all of the points would remain in the same position relative to each other. The analysis of Figure 1 would change only if the appraisals distort volatility by different amounts in the different regions. However, that seems unlikely (not to mention unknowable.)

[9] This is probably a good place to dispel another notion that sometimes surfaces in discussions of risk and return. Often a manager will say that "Risk is important, but over the long run, the risk will wash out and all that will matter is the expected return." This is a misunderstanding of risk and its relation to return and, in fact, both the return and the risk increase over time. The exact form this takes depends on various technical features, but generally over very long periods, the greater the standard deviation of a portfolio's returns, the more likely it is that the value of the portfolio will fall below a given level.

[10] It might have occurred to the reader that we should consider breaking real estate into twenty classifications according to both property type and region. For example, hotels in the West would be one of the twenty classes. This is possible, but we have chosen not to do so because of the small number of properties in some of these classes and the resulting lack of reliability of the figures.

[11] A subtle technical point arises from our focus on constructing efficient real estate portfolios. Because of the different interactions between individual stock categories and real estate, we are not assured that an efficient portfolio of stocks and real estate will make use of an efficient real estate portfolio. In practice, though, the difference will be small and the data are not accurate enough to discern the difference.

[12] Liquidity concerns, however, generally should not be a cause to forgo the diversification of benefits of real estate, because real estate constitutes a small percentage of most portfolios. Other assets can better serve as sources of ready liquidity.

APPENDIX

Data Series and Sources

Source	Data Description
Frank Russell Company (FRC Indexes)	A quarterly time series of equity real estate returns extending from 1978 to the present. The series is broken down by income and capital gains and also by region and property type. Currently, the data base has approximately 1000 properties owned by real estate funds with an average value of about $10 million per property.
Evaluation Associates (EAFPI)	A quarterly time series extending from 1969 to the present. It is an index constructed by an equal weighting of the returns on a number of largely all-equity real estate funds. The data base currently includes about thirty-three tax-exempt funds with a total asset value of about $25 billion.
Gs & Co. Equity REIT Returns (EREIT)	A monthly time series extending from 1974 to the present. It is an equally-weighted index constructed from thirty-three REITs holding more than 80% equity assets. In comparison with the FRC index, EREIT is more heavily concentrated in shopping centers and apartments and less in office properties.
Stock, Bond, and Inflation Data	Ibbotson and Associates provide a comprehensive monthly data base that begins in 1926.

Real Estate Portfolio Analysis: An Emerging Focus on Economic Location

Charles H. Wurtzebach*

Real estate practitioners are increasingly using "economic location," rather than "geographic location," as their primary analytic tool. That trend has gained substantial support among academics and practitioners who believe "economic location" is a more effective basis on which to build the analysis of risk in real estate portfolios.

Traditionally, real estate practitioners have viewed geographic diversification as an important portfolio characteristic. "Geographic diversification" usually referred to breaking the United States into the four broad regions of the East, Midwest, South and West. However, traditional methods used to analyze the locational diversification of real estate portfolios have proved to be less effective than previously thought.

The practical result of such a move is the management of real estate assets as portfolios, rather than as "accidental" collections of individual holdings, a new phenomenon in the investment industry.

The Traditional Approach

Managers of real estate portfolios traditionally have relied upon two approaches in analyzing diversification and in planning portfolio composition, including:

1. Allocation of assets among property types.
2. Allocation among geographic regions.

Diversification among the traditional property types, which include office, retail, industrial, residential and hotel, has been effective. Several studies have demonstrated the risk-reducing power of combining a variety of property types rather than concentrating holdings in one asset category.

However, the traditional approach to geographic diversification has not been supported as

*Charles H. Wurtzebach, not a member of the Society, is Vice President and Director of Investment Research, The Prudential Realty Group.

well, either by researchers or in practice.

Three forces culminated to place significant pressure on the traditional approach:

1. Researchers began to apply Modern Portfolio Theory to the analysis of real estate portfolios.
2. The effects of wildly variable regional real estate returns made practitioners look closely at the location risk in their portfolios.
3. Increasingly knowledgeable institutional investors began to press for greater sophistication in the management of their assets.

The effectiveness of any approach to diversification depends on the availability of types of investments whose returns are not highly correlated. In order to analyze the correlation of returns among alternative investments, return data of sufficient duration and breadth are required to ensure statistical reliability. Studies of diversification within the real estate asset class have been severely hampered by lack of such reliable data.

During the mid-1980s, however, researchers acquired access to acceptable data, and studies of the asset class at the portfolio level began. A 1986 study by Hartzell, Heckman and Miles concluded that diversification across the four traditional regions had limited effectiveness. The authors' work built on a 1982 study by Miles and McCue and led them to report "these results suggest that current industry practice represents little more than naive diversification." A 1987 study by Firstenberg, Ross and Zisler found the regional approach less effective than the property-type approach. These studies generally supported work done by other researchers in 1983 and 1984 based on other, less extensive data.

At the same time, empirical evidence was beginning to cast doubt on the traditional approach. In addition, the experience of practitioners added pressure for change. Nationally, investment managers experienced regionally based roller coaster performance over the 1975-87 period. The decline of the "Rust Belt" and the emergence of the "Sun Belt," in response to the combined effects of the oil crises of the 1970s and the high value of the dollar, were followed in the 1980s by depression in the "Oil Belt" and dramatic declines in property values in cities like Denver and Houston. While New Orleans is classified geographically as a southern city and Denver is in the western region, both cities responded to the same single economic variable - oil price. Supporters of real estate portfolio analysis took this analogy a step further. They say if oil-based economies cross regional boundaries, so do those heavily dependent on the hi-tech industries, defense spending, and manufacturing.

Clearly, the real estate industry needed to find a new way to describe location for the purpose of managing portfolios.

Refining the Traditional Approach

A study published in February 1988 by Hartzell, Shulman and Wurtzebach provides a bridge from the approaches based strictly on geography to those moving toward economic characteristics. In that analysis, the country was divided into the following eight regions based on a combination of geography and economic orientation (Exhibit 1):

1. New England
2. Mid-Atlantic Corridor
3. Old South
4. Industrial Midwest
5. Farm Belt
6. Mineral Extraction Area
7. Southern California
8. Northern California

The authors describe these as "cohesive economic activity regions." State boundaries are ignored in many cases where the state's economic activity is significantly varied within its borders. The return patterns of properties in those eight regions were analyzed using updated and expanded data similar to that used by Hartzell, Heckman and Miles. The analysis showed the "eight-region categorization produces lower correlation coefficients than the traditional classification into four regions" and further "suggests that the traditional four-region analysis does not capture the impact of regional diversification."

While this approach apparently provided significant advantages, the level at which the economic characteristics of a region were analyzed was not very refined. The approach is hybrid, not truly geographic but not purely economic either.

Approaches to Defining Economic Location

A great deal of discussion in the industry today focuses on the concept of economic location. How-

---

EXHIBIT 1. Economic Geography of the United States Eight Region Approach

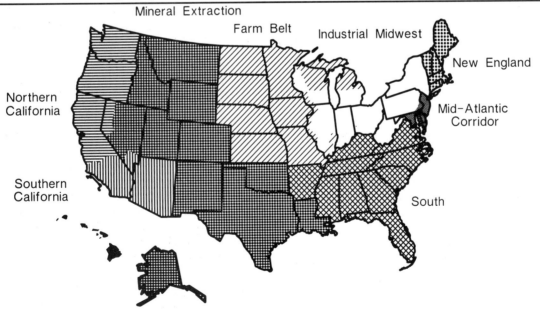

Source: **Salomon Brothers Inc, February 1988.**

ever, actual published data on either its definition or its use in managing portfolios are still scarce. To date, researchers and managers have taken two basic approaches to defining categories of locations:

1. Relative employment growth patterns.
2. Analysis of employment composition, or economic base analysis.

The Employment Growth Approach

Unpublished research on 118 individual real estate markets done by Wurtzebach and DeLisle between 1986 and 1988 identifies five common patterns of employment growth among those markets and analyzes the effectiveness of using those patterns to establish portfolio diversification categories.

The employment growth data for each of the 118 markets for 1974 through 1987 were plotted against the employment growth of the United States as a whole. Deviations from the national patterns were tested for statistical significance. The definition of patterns was made in terms of relative growth rates, not absolute growth levels, so very large markets do not skew the groupings. The five categories identified are:

Growth Category	Example Markets
Consistently Higher Growth	Atlanta, San Francisco
Recently Higher Growth	Oakland, Jacksonville
Recently Lower Growth	Houston, Miami
Consistently Lower Growth	Kansas City, Cleveland
Cyclical Growth	New York, Indianapolis

This system of analysis was tested working with essentially the same data base used by Hartzell, Shulman and Wurtzebach in their 1988 study and provides superior diversification potential. Correlations among these categories were lower.

The Economic Base Approach

Wurtzebach and DeLisle also have proposed a system of grouping the 118 markets analyzed into five broad categories describing employment characteristics in those markets:

Classification	Examples
Diversified	St. Louis, Wilmington
Energy	Houston, Tulsa
Government	Washington, San Antonio
Manufacturing	Chicago, Anaheim
Services	New York, San Francisco

Note: The authors report that these categories were intentionally designed to be broad enough to allow reliable testing against a data base of historical and forecasted returns. More narrow categories would have prevented reliable calculation of correlation and volatility figures.

Like the author's employment growth approach, analysis of the economic base approach showed it to have diversification characteristics superior to those of the traditional geographic approach. Correlation of returns among the economic base categories was lower than correlations among the four geographic areas.

The economic base approach has the advantage of facilitating the translation of sectoral forecasting to analysis of investment strategy.

Using Economic Location

The amount of work done to date on the concept of economic location will undoubtedly be multiplied many times over during the next few years. The idea is intuitively more appealing than its predecessor. In addition, initial research has suggested the concept is more effective, and the community of managers, investors and consultants has demonstrated enthusiasm for the approach. The ways in which the ideas, as they develop over time, are actually used in managing portfolios will vary widely.

For managers of large portfolios, one differentiation will likely be between those who have sufficient data to "optimize" on the category adopted and those who do not. If an investor has sufficient data to associate reliable correlation coefficients and standard deviation figures with the location categories being considered, he can use those to drive an "optimal asset allocation analysis." An efficient frontier can be developed and decision-making can be done in an explicit risk/return environment. If the manager does not have that sort of data base, portfolio composition decisions will be more subjective and probably more reflective of specific economic sector forecasts.

Another difference will occur between those using these ideas for portfolio analysis and management and those using them primarily for analysis of a specific investment decision. The emphasis of the user likely will be different if the question is one of overall portfolio allocation or one of deciding between two specific acquisition alternatives. But the question does seem to be, "How will we use this approach?" rather than, "Will it be used?"

In conclusion, managers and investors alike must address the challenge of strategy implementation and execution. Real estate is not like stocks and bonds. Should a stock manager decide to change investment strategy, he only needs to call the trading [sic] desk. With real estate, however, no central clearing-house for properties exists. The manager must have the capability to execute the strategy.

References

Firstenberg, Paul B., Stephen A. Ross and Randall C. Zisler. "Managing Real Estate Portfolios." Goldman Sachs & Co., November 16, 1987.

Firstenberg, Paul B., and Charles H. Wurtzebach. "The Portfolio Construction Process - The Competitive Edge in Managing Real Estate Portfolios." Prudential Realty Group. December 7, 1987.

Hartzell, David J., John Heckman and Mike Miles. "Diversification Categories in Investment Real Estate." Salomon Brothers, Inc. December 1986.

Hartzell, David J., David G. Shulman and Charles H. Wurtzebach. "Refining the Analysis of Regional Diversification for Income Producing Real Estate." *The Journal of Real Estate Research* (Vol. 2, No. 2), p. 85.

Wurtzebach, Charles H., and James R. DeLisle. "1989 Economic Location Diversification Analysis." Prudential Realty Group. October 19, 1988.

THE DIMENSIONS OF

DIVERSIFICATION

IN REAL ESTATE

by:

Susan Hudson-Wilson
Vice President
John Hancock Properties, Inc.

Real Estate risk is related to various factors.[1] Among them are geography, property type, lease term, financial structure, tenant industry, and property operating cycle. It is not known which of these risks are the most important from a portfolio point of view. In addition little is known about the interactions among the sources of risk to real estate returns.

Clearly one of the key objectives of any portfolio management exercise is to diversify away as much unsystematic risk as possible. Investors do not get paid for assuming risk that can be diversified away. Thus an important goal is to accurately measure and manage the risks associated with real estate investing. In this paper, we investigate two dimensions of real estate risk: the dimensions of geographic location and property type. Our metric will be the volatility of real estate returns by metropolitan area and property type within each metro area. It is conceivable that these two sources of risk dominate all of the others; decisions about financial structure, development cycle, tenant mix and lease term may all be less important than those about property type and location. At the very least, it is probable that the risks associated with property type and location can be managed, either before or after, the management of the other types of real estate risk.

One of the primary missions of this study is to explore the dimensions of property and location diversification undertaken in an effort to reduce the riskiness of a portfolio. By dimension we mean the concept over which diversification, or risk management, will be achieved. For example, the NCREIF-Russell real estate return data[2] is reported by six property categories and eight regions.[3] Thus one could, using this data, design a portfolio diversified by the dimensions of the six property types or the eight regions. Hartzell, Shulman and Wurtzebach conducted a diversification exercise using eight regions defined along homogeneous economic lines.[4]

Many pension funds and other investors approach the diversification problem in two steps; diversify by property type and then by region (or vice versa). Implicit in this step-wise technique is the assumption that the property type allocation is the same for each region and, conversely, that the regional allocation is appropriate for each property type. This must be considered an improbable assumption.

In all of these cases, the regional data may be too highly aggregated. The richness of the differences associated with the individual cities within each region and among the property types within each city is completely lost. It is likely that geographically oriented diversification opportunities exist within regions and across property types within regions. Diversification over insufficiently detailed dimensions would be as subject to question as the qualitative, or naive, diversification that has heretofore dominated the real estate industry.

We have sought to ask three questions about diversification in this study. The first is whether the property type dimension is appropriate, the second is whether the regional or metropolitan area dimension is appropriate and the third is whether property and geographic diversification are simultaneous or sequential events.

Two hypotheses will be explored in an effort to answer these questions. The first is that the definition of the real estate asset is the key to the successful identification of the correct dimensions of diversification and so the key to the successful management of unsystematic risk. The inappropriate specification of the asset will generate the appearance of, but not the reality of, diversification. A poorly diversified portfolio is a portfolio exposed to risk in unknown ways.

The second hypothesis is that geographic and property type diversification must be done simultaneously, not sequentially. That is, it is not accurate to apply a uniform geographic allocation to all property types or to apply a uniform property allocation over all geographic units. Property types in particular locations constitute the most basic dimension over which diversification efforts should be focussed.

We will proceed by examining data on historic and forecast real estate returns. These returns are calculated at a highly disaggregated level so that the answers to the regional, metropolitan and property type questions will be self-evident. The return data used is available by city, by property type.[5] Thus an asset is defined as, for example, Baltimore-Office, Baltimore-Apartment, Baltimore-Retail, Baltimore-Industrial, San Francisco-Office, San Francisco-Apartment, etc. Figure 1 presents this return data for the four assets in the Washington, D.C. urban area. It is clear that it would not be accurate to describe Washington D.C. as one real estate investment opportunity or asset. The four property types have unique cycles and amplitudes.

The next task is to distinguish between similar and different assets from among a universe of investment opportunities. In other words, we are seeking to discover the proper dimensions of diversification. In this case we analyzed thirty cities and four property types within each city. Thus we began with one hundred twenty assets.

Cluster analysis was used to discover assets with common behavior over history and into the forecast period. The clustering procedure produces groups of assets with shared attributes with respect to the level, volatility and timing of returns. From a portfolio, or risk management, perspective, such clustered assets can be considered to be substitutes for one another. The correlations of the returns within such clusters are high while the correlations between such clusters are low and sometimes negative, rendering them the appropriate dimensions over which diversification, using mean-variance analysis, can be productively undertaken.

Figures 2 through 7 present some of the clusters that emerged from the model.

Figure 2 shows a very tight cluster of three industrial markets in three south Florida cities. This cluster confirms the conventional wisdom that property types constitute an appropriate dimension of diversification and that the regional concept may sustain as well. Figure 3, however, presents the office returns for the same three cities but does not constitute a cluster. The behavior of these three markets is not sufficiently similar. This example suggests that it is not valid to assume that metropolitan areas constitute a consistent dimension of diversification.

Figure 4 presents a cluster that is consistent across the industrial property type, but is located on opposite coasts of the country, thus violating the credibility of traditional regional diversification. This cluster is consistent with the concept of economically rather than geographically contiguous regions[6] since both cities share a high-tech focus.

Figures 5 and 6 are similarly consistent over property type, but present a major challenge to the concept of regional homogeneity and a non-intuitive adherence to the concept of economic region. Finally, in figure 7 we see that the conventional wisdom on property type homogeneity is sometimes violated as well.

This analysis leads to the conclusion that regional groupings, defined either by physical contiguity or by definitions of economic structure, and the property type concept of a dimension of diversification do not sustain. It is clear that the industry's current definitions of the dimensions of diversification are inadequate. It is also clear that portfolios of real estate diversified along gross dimensions and diversified in a two-step process (property type separately from location) are exposed to unsystematic risk in some unpredictable ways. The relationships among real estate assets are surely complex. The dimensions over which diversification is to be conducted warrants significant research attention.

FIGURE 1
WASHINGTON, D.C. MSA MARKETS

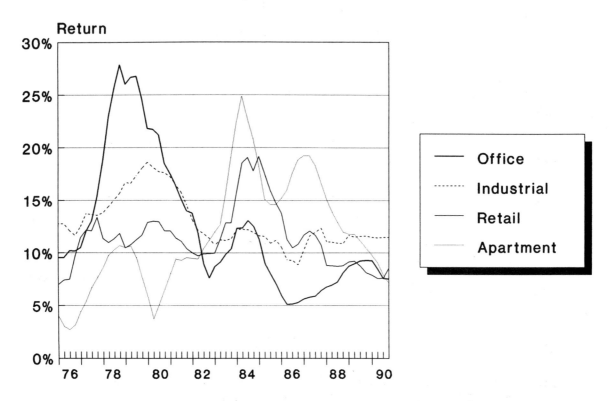

Source: John Hancock Properties, Real Estate Research

FIGURE 2
INDUSTRIAL MARKET

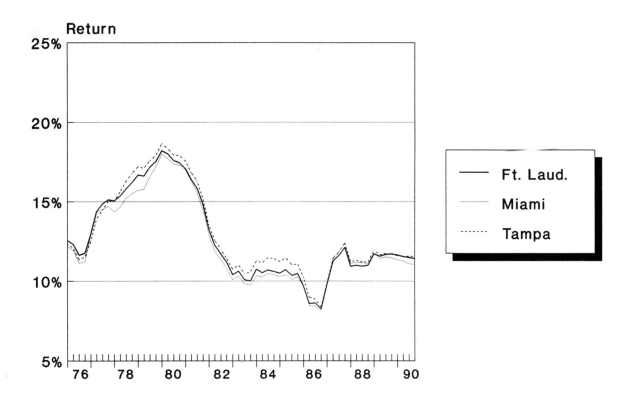

Source: John Hancock Properties, Real Estate Research

FIGURE 3
OFFICE MARKET

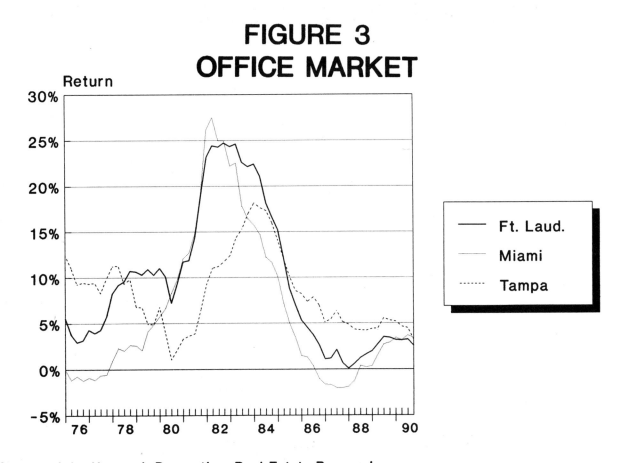

Source: John Hancock Properties, Real Estate Research

FIGURE 4
INDUSTRIAL MARKET

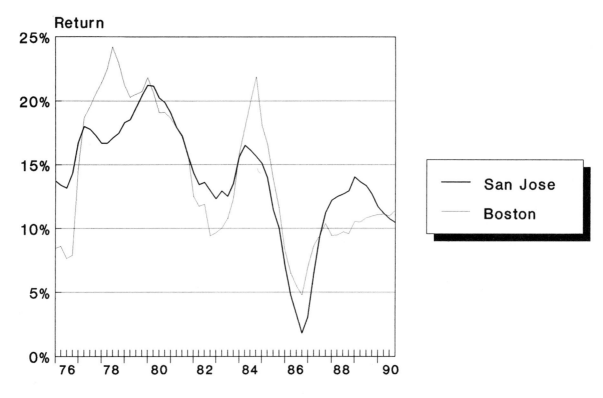

Source: John Hancock Properties, Real Estate Research

FIGURE 5
RETAIL MARKET

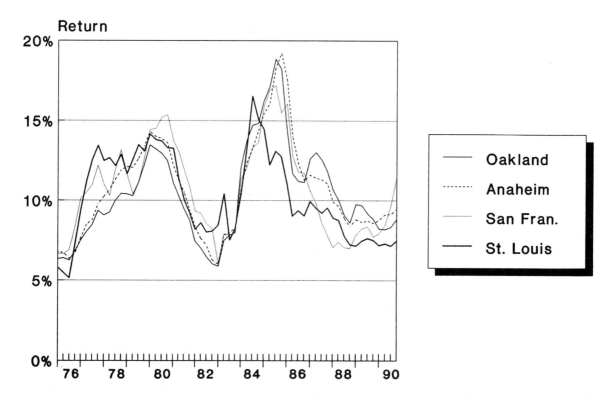

Source: John Hancock Properties, Real Estate Research

FIGURE 6
OFFICE MARKET

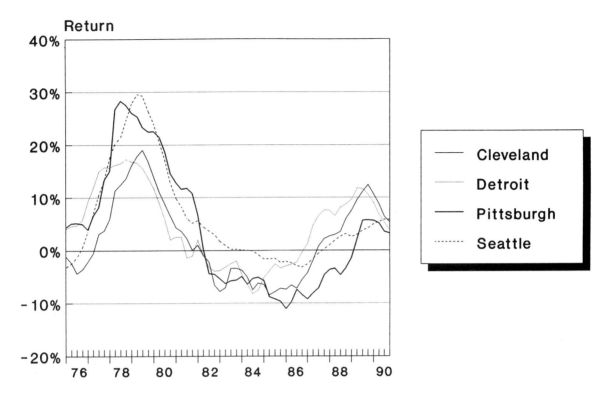

Source: John Hancock Properties, Real Estate Research

FIGURE 7
APARTMENT & OFFICE MARKETS

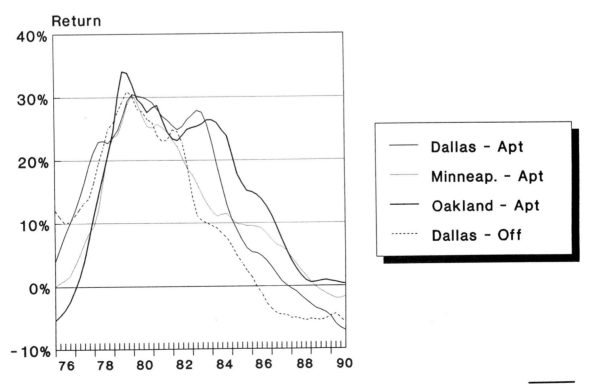

Source: John Hancock Properties, Real Estate Research

[1]Michael Giliberto, *Thinking About Real Estate Risk* (Salomon Brothers: Bond Market Research, May 26, 1989).

[2]*NCREIF-Russell Index* (New York: National Council of Real Estate Investment Fiduciaries).

[3]NCREIF-Russell index was formerly partitioned into four regions. Recently it became available partitioned into eight regions. These eight consist of the original four, each further disaggregated into two. However, the data are only available by property type within the original four regions.

[4]David J. Hartzell, David G. Shulman, and Charles H. Wurtzebach, *Refining the Analysis of Regional Diversification for Income-Producing Real Estate* (Salomon Brothers, February 1988).

[5]The data are calculated by John Hancock Properties, Inc. at the city and county level by property type within each city or county. The data are calculated quarterly from 1976 through 1995.

[6]David G. Shulman and Robert E. Hopkins, *Economic Diversification in Real Estate Portfolios* (Salomon Brothers, November 1988).

Robert E. Hopkins

David Shulman

Toward an Indexed Portfolio of Real Estate
Part II: Recent Construction

Introduction

Real estate portfolio diversification decisions are hampered by the lack of accepted measures of the dollar value of the various product types that comprise the real estate market. Without such measures, portfolio managers cannot easily compare their asset allocations with the market portfolio. And this, in turn, makes it inherently difficult to create a portfolio that matches the market. In contrast, stock portfolio managers can gauge the overall market using the capitalization-weighted Standard & Poor's 500 Stock Index (S&P 500) or other broad indexes. They can then create an indexed portfolio of stocks whose performance would replicate that of the S&P 500, for example. Bond investors, similarly, can make use of the numerous bond indexes, such as the Salomon Brothers Broad Investment Grade Index. Managers can duplicate the performance of these indexes, or they can deviate from them in a planned way according to their expectations about the different sectors of the market.

In an earlier paper, we presented estimates of the size of the U.S. speculative office market by coherent geographic region to assist real estate portfolio managers in their diversification efforts.[1] Here we present estimates of the distribution of investable real estate by product category: offices, warehouses, hotels, retail, and apartments.

Methodology

We have developed property category portfolio weights based on a straightforward method for totaling past construction by property type, accounting for inflation, depreciation and the value of the land. By measuring all new construction in the past 20 years, we have included a significant proportion (though surely not all) of the entire commercial real estate market and, by definition, the entire market for loans on new construction. The value of construction is measured by the value of contract awards estimated by Dodge/DRI.[2]

A simple summation of construction over the past 20 years would be relatively meaningless, because it would not account for inflation of values, the value of the land or the physical depreciation of the assets. Hence, we have estimated each of these components using the following procedures:

● The value of the land was assumed at a constant percentage of the value of construction at the time of construction. The percentage varies by property type from 10% for hotels to 30% for warehouses. Warehouses

---

[1] See *Toward an Indexed Portfolio of Real Estate Part I: Office Buildings*, David Shulman, Sandon J. Goldberg, David J. Hartzell, Robert E. Hopkins, and David J. Kostin, Salomon Brothers Inc, June 2, 1988.

[2] Dodge/DRI Construction and Real Estate Information Service.

have a high land component, because they tend to be relatively simple buildings on large parcels. Hotels, conversely, are generally expensive construction on small plots of land in suburban markets. Offices have high land components because of their prime locations. And in the retail segment, land costs are increased by location and the extensive land needs for parking. The exact percentages used in our estimates are displayed in Figure 1.

● Inflation in property values was measured by the Commerce Department's construction cost index for all property types.[3] We have assumed that all properties rise in value in line with replacement construction costs. Obviously, this is not the case for each property, but competition from new buildings will force it to be true on average. Land values were assumed to grow annually at two percentage points above the construction cost inflation rate.[4]

● Depreciation occurs when a building's value is reduced because the building has become outmoded or has physically deteriorated. We assumed straight-line depreciation of the improvements over a given lifetime, which varies by property type. The lifetimes used in our estimates are also presented in Figure 1.

Figure 1. 20-Year Construction Index — Land Value and Depreciation Assumptions by Property Type

Property Type	Land Value as a Pct. of Construction	Asset Life (Years)	Implied Annual Depreciation Rate
Offices	20%	67	1.5%
Warehouses	30	50	2.0
Retail	25	50	2.0
Hotels	10	50	2.0
Apartments	15	40	2.5

Source: Salomon Brothers Inc.

Any measure of the stock of real estate that is based solely on new construction misses the enhancements to value that result from rehabilitation and conversion to commercial property from other uses. This rehabilitation and conversion offsets, to some degree, the results of physical depreciation, abandonment and conversion to noncommercial uses. Thus, our physical depreciation assumptions may overestimate the net result. For example, in the single-family housing market, in which annual estimates exist for both housing stock and housing construction, the impact of rehabilitation and conversion implies an effective depreciation rate that is negative in some periods. Because of this possibility, we have calculated our index estimates both with and without the depreciation rates described above.

The methodology involves a number of simplifying assumptions: (1) We only measure construction that has occurred during the past 20 years. (2) We assume equal inflation across all property types and all regions. The estimates could be made regionally, since the Dodge contracts data are available on a county-by-county basis, but that would have been beyond the scope of this paper. (3) Our land value percentages, while reasonable, do not vary over time.

Although these assumptions may limit the precision of our estimates, we believe that the inaccuracies tend to even out and, hence, that our results are reasonable and plausible. In fact, the assumptions may make our estimates more useful for specific types of portfolios. For example,

---

[3] See "Value of New Construction Put in Place, May 1988," U.S. Department of Commerce, *Current Construction Reports C30-88-5*, for an explanation of the construction cost index.

[4] The final index values are relatively insensitive to the exact rate of increase in the value of land over improvements.

because we do not include older buildings, the index may be especially useful for gauging portfolios limited to relatively new buildings or properties in newer regions of the country or for lenders who concentrate on new construction.

Investment Implications

We estimate the current property value of recently constructed buildings at $1.3 trillion. Almost $300 billion of this is the value of the land, and the rest reflects improvements. Our $1.3-trillion estimate of current value comprises the following: $388 million of office properties,[5] $458 million of apartments,[6] $231 million of retail space, $142 million of warehouse space, and $76 million of hotels.

An indexed real estate portfolio based on our estimates would be dominated by apartments and offices. With more than 30 million of 92 million households living in rental units, the demand for new apartments over the past 20 years has been considerable. Office space construction is a derived demand from the more than nine million office jobs created since 1972. Together, these two property types account for 65% of the total index. Retail is the third-largest component of the index, with a total value equal to the sum of warehouses and hotels. Figure 2 lists the index shares of each property type.

Figure 2. 20-Year Construction Index — Index Shares by Property Type
(Percentage of Current Property Value of Buildings Constructed Over the Past 20 Years)

Property Type	With Depreciation	Without Depreciation
Apartments	35.4%	37.7%
Offices	30.0	28.2
Retail	17.9	17.6
Warehouses	11.0	10.6
Hotels	5.8	5.8

Source: Salomon Brothers Inc.

These index values appear to differ significantly from the percentage representation of the various property types in actual real estate portfolios. **In particular, apartments are significantly underweighted in most institutional portfolios, and hotels are somewhat underweighted.** For example, the $13.5-billion institutional real estate portfolio used in calculating the Frank Russell Company (FRC) Property Index includes only 4.3% apartments and 2.2% hotels, both significantly below the percentages in our index. Conversely, the office and research and development sectors combined account for 56.7% of the FRC portfolio compared with 30% for offices in our index. Figure 3 compares our index with the FRC portfolio.

Apartments and hotels may not fit the requirements of certain investors. Both property types require significant on-site management, and properties often are relatively small. The other three property types could still be balanced against a subindex of market value, however. Figure 3 also shows our estimate of an indexed portfolio that does not include apartments and one that excludes both apartments and hotels. Even if we view the FRC portfolio as one that excludes hotels and apartments, that index appears to be somewhat overweighted in offices and underweighted in warehouses and retail.

---

[5] Our $388-million estimate of recently constructed office properties compares with our earlier estimate of $300 million of speculative office space in 50 major markets. See *Toward an Indexed Portfolio of Real Estate Part I: Office Buildings.*

[6] Because the Dodge/DRI multifamily contracts include newly built condominiums, this figure overstates the "investable" apartment market.

Figure 3. Portfolio Allocation — 20-Year Construction Index versus the Frank Russell Property Index Portfolio (Percentage Allocated to Each Property Type)

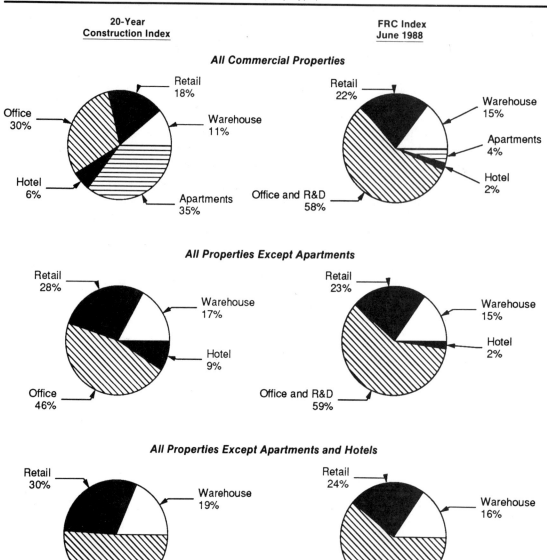

20-Year
Construction Index

FRC Index
June 1988

All Commercial Properties

All Properties Except Apartments

All Properties Except Apartments and Hotels

Source: Salomon Brothers Inc.

Variations in the Index Over Time

The index weights vary over time, as different sectors of the market come into or fade from prominence (see Figure 4). Apartment construction, for example, is extremely volatile, and as a result of past overbuilding and the negative impact of tax reform, it currently is well below previous peaks. This may limit the ability of portfolio managers, especially lenders, to invest a percentage equal to the market if they are limited to lending for new construction.

New construction lenders, in particular, may find that our index values do not match their perceptions of the market, because they do not include the current value of properties older than the normal term of their mortgage loans. We therefore reestimated the index based on rolling five-year periods of construction. This approximates the value of a portfolio of ten-year loans, some of which have been amortized or prepaid.

As is evident in Figure 4, the index shares of each property type vary significantly over our 1973-88 time frame. In particular, the apartment share dropped dramatically from 46% of the market in 1973 to 35% in 1978, reflecting the multifamily boom in 1972 (led by the real estate investment trust explosion) and the resulting bust after the 1974-75 recession. The low levels of multifamily construction that have followed tax reform may once again reduce the allocation to apartments.

Between 1975 and 1978, reduced construction of apartments and hotels and modest investment in offices pushed up the share of warehouses and retail properties in our index. According to our five-year rolling stock measure, warehouse properties' share rose from 9% in 1973 to almost 14% in 1978, while the retail share climbed from 17% to almost 23% during the same period. In 1978, a loan portfolio might have had almost equal holdings of office and retail properties, compared with our current index values of 30% and 18%, respectively. The shift reflects the considerable increase in office construction in 1980-85.

Figure 4. 20-Year Construction Index — Index Shares Using Five-Year Rolling Total Value

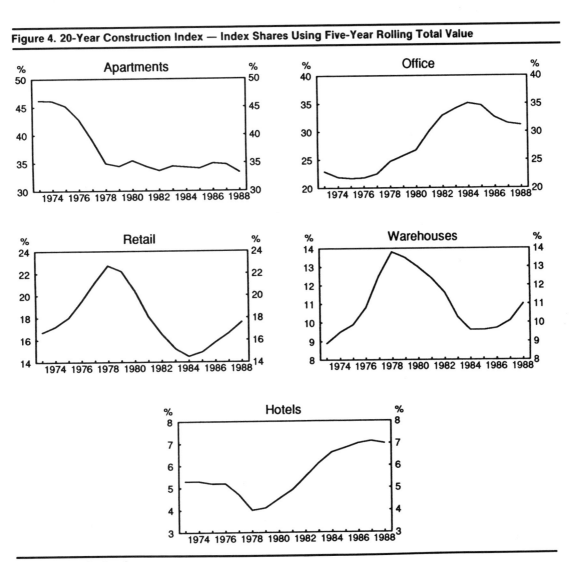

Source: Salomon Brothers Inc.

Summary and Conclusions

The 20-Year Construction Index can be a useful starting point for real estate portfolio managers on both the debt and equity sides. Because the index is a reasonable estimate of the total real estate market by property type, a portfolio manager can assess how closely his or her portfolio matches the market. Strategic or practical decisions can then be made to allocate more or fewer resources to the different property types. Alternatively, managers of relatively passive portfolios can use the index to bring their portfolios more closely in line with the market.

* * * * *

The authors wish to thank Sharon A. Meyers for her invaluable research assistance.

Bibliography

Akerson, C. 1986. "Appraising for Pension Portfolios—A Two Day Seminar." American Institute of Real Estate Appraisers.

Brachman, W.O. 1981. "Rating Commingled Funds." *Pension World* (September): 25-38.

Brown, S. J., and M. P. Kritzman, eds. 1989. *Quantitative Methods for Financial Analysts*. Homewood: Dow Jones-Irwin.

Brueggeman, W. B. and T. S. Chang. 1989. "The Real Estate Report." Goldman Sachs Real Estate Research (July).

Brueggeman, W. B., A.H. Chen, and T.G. Thibodeau. 1984. "Real Estate Investment Funds: Performance and Portfolio Considerations." *AREUEA Journal* (Fall): 333-54.

Brueggeman, W. B. and S. M. Giliberto. 1987a. "Measuring Real Estate Investment Performance: A Revised Approach." Unpublished paper, Edwin L. Cox School of Business, Southern Methodist University.

————. 1987b. "Reading in Pension Fund Real Estate Equity Investment." Unpublished paper (December).

Burns, W. and D. Epley. 1982. "Performance of Portfolios of REITs and Stocks." *The Journal of Portfolio Management* (Spring): 37-42.

Cirz, R. T. and M. S. Sorich. 1987. "Developing a Better Cash Flow Projection." *The Appraisal Journal* (January): 19-24.

Cole, R., D. Guilkey, and M. E. Miles. 1986. "Toward An Assessment of the Reliability of Commercial Appraisals." *The Appraisal Journal* (July): 422-32.

Cole, R., D. Guilkey, M. E. Miles, and B. Webb. 1989. "More Scientific Diversification Strategies for Commerical Real Estate." *Real Estate Review* (Spring): 59-66.

Conroy, B., M. E. Miles, and C. H. Wurtzebach. 1986a. "A Practical View of Real Estate and Modern Portfolio Theory." *Industrial Development* (May/June): 11-20.

————. 1986b. "Institutional Real Estate Investment." *Industrial Development* (July/August): 5-10.

Corcoran, P. 1987. "Explaining the Commerical Real Estate Market." *The Journal of Portfolio Management* (Spring): 15-21.

Corgel, J. and G. Gay. 1987. "Local Economic Base, Geographic Diversification and Risk Management of Mortgage Portfolios." *AREUEA Journal* (Fall): 256-67.

Darrat, A. F. and J. L. Glascock. 1989. "Real Estate Returns, Money and Fiscal Deficits: Is the Real Estate Market Efficient?" *Journal of Real Estate Finance and Economics* (September): 197-208.

Davidson, H.A. and J.E. Palmer. 1978. "A Comparison of the Investment Performance of Common Stocks, Homebuilding Firms, and Equity REITs." *The Real Estate Appraiser* (July/August): 35-39.

Downs, A. 1988a. "America's Educational Failures: How Will They Affect Real Estate?" Salomon Brothers Inc (May).

————. 1988b. "The Tokyo Real Estate Markets and Some of Its Impacts on U.S. Real Estate." Salomon Brothers Inc (November).

————. 1983. "The Triple Revolution in Real Estate Finance." *Real Estate Review* (Spring): 18-27.

Edwards, C. E. and P. L. Cooley. 1984. "Leverage Financing Choices for Real Estate." *The Real Estate Appraiser and Analyst* (Summer): 73-78.

Edwards, D. G. 1984. "Rates of Return from S&L Investments in Service Corporations, 1979-83." Research Working Paper Series, Office of Policy and Economic Research, Federal Home Loan Bank Board (November).

Estey, A. and M. E. Miles. 1982. "How Well Do Commingled Real Estate Funds Perform?" *The Journal of Portfolio Management* (Winter): 62-68.

Fama, E.F. and G.W. Schwert. 1977. "Asset Returns and Inflation." *Journal of Financial Economics* (November): 115-46.

Firstenberg, P. B., S. A. Ross, and R. C. Zisler. 1988. "Real Estate: The Whole Story." *The Journal of Portfolio Management* (Spring): 22-34.

————. 1987. *Managing Real Estate Portfolios*. Real Estate Research.

Firstenberg, P. B. and C. H. Wurtzebach. 1989. "Managing Portfolio Risk and Reward." *Real Estate Review* (Summer): 61-65.

Fisher, J. D. and W. N. Kinnard. 1989. "The Business Enterprise Value Component of Operating Properties: The Example of Shopping Malls."

Proceedings of the International Conference on Assessment Administration (September).

Fogler, H. R.. 1984. "20% in Real Estate: Can Theory Justify It?" *The Journal of Portfolio Management* (Winter): 6-13.

Fogler, H. R., M. R. Granito, and L. R. Smith. 1985. "A Theoretical Analysis of Real Estate Returns." *The Journal of Finance* (July): 711-21.

Friedman, H.C. 1971. "Real Estate Investment and Portfolio Theory." *Journal of Financial and Quantitative Analysis* (March): 861-74.

Froland, C. 1987. "What Determines Cap Rates on Real Estate?" *The Journal of Portfolio Management* (Summer): 77-82.

Froland, C., R. Gorlow, and R. Sampson. 1986. "The Market Risk of Real Estate." *The Journal of Portfolio Management* (Spring): 12-19.

Gau, G. W. 1987. "Efficient Real Estate Markets: Paradox or Paradigm?" *AREUEA Journal* (Summer): 1-12.

———. 1985. "Public Information and Abnormal Returns in Real Estate Investment." *AREUEA Journal* (Spring): 15-31.

Giliberto, M. S. 1989a. "Managing Real Estate Duration: A New Perspective on the Use of Leverage." Salomon Brothers Inc (October).

———. 1989b. "Real Estate versus Financial Assets—An Updated Comparison of Returns in the United States and the United Kingdom." Salomon Brothers Inc (February).

———. 1988. "A Note on the Use of Appraisal Data in Indexes of Performance Measurement." *AREUEA Journal* (Spring): 77-83.

Gold, R. 1986. "Real Estate: Can Institutional Portfolios Be Efficiently Diversified Without It?" JMB Realty, Chicago.

Goldberg, S. J. 1988. "Index of Salomon Brothers Real Estate Research Reports." Salomon Brothers Inc (November).

Graaskamp, J. A. 1988. "A Proposed Strategy for a Portfolio of Land Investments in the Path of Urban Employer Emigration." Salomon Brothers Inc (November).

———. 1987. "Appraisal Reform and Commercial Real Estate Investment for Pension Funds." Salomon Brothers Inc (January).

Grissom, T. V., J. L. Kuhle, and C. H. Walther. 1987. "Diversification Works in Real Estate, Too." *The Journal of Portfolio Management* (Winter): 66-71.

Hartman, R., M. E. Miles, K. VanMeter, and S. Lavenstein. 1984. "An Introduction to Pension Fund Investment in Real Estate." Merrill Lynch Commerical Real Estate .

Hartzell, D. J. 1988. "Salomon Brothers Real Estate Roundtable." Salomon Brothers, Inc. (April).

———. 1986. "Real Estate in the Portfolio." Salomon Brothers Inc (August).

Hartzell, D. J., J. S. Hekman, and M. E. Miles. 1987. "Real Estate Returns and Inflation." *AREUEA Journal* (Spring): 617-37.

———. 1986. "Diversification Categories in Investment Real Estate." *AREUEA Journal* (Summer): 230-54.

Hartzell, D. J. and D. G. Shulman. 1988. Real Estate Returns and Risks: A Survey. Salomon Brothers Inc (February).

Hartzell, D. J., D. G. Shulman, T. C. Langetieg, and M. L. Leibowitz. 1988. "A Look at Real Estate Duration." *The Journal of Portfolio Management* (Fall): 16-24.

Hartzell, D. J., D. G. Shulman, and C. H. Wurtzebach. 1989. "Refining the Analysis of Regional Diversification for Income-Producing Real Estate." *The Journal of Property Management* (July/August): 19-24.

Hartzell, D. J. and J. R. Webb. 1988. "Real Estate Risk and Return Expectations: Recent Results." *The Journal of Real Estate Research* (Fall): 31-37.

Hemmerick, S. 1985. "Study Sheds Light on Real Estate's Risk in Portfolio." *Pension and Investment Age* (January): 11-12.

Hoag, J. W. 1980. "Towards Indices of Real Estate Value and Return." *Journal of Finance* (May): 569-80.

Hopkins, R. E. 1988. "Ranking Metropolitan Areas: A Long-Term View." Salomon Brothers Inc (August).

Hopkins, R. E. and D. G. Shulman. 1989. "Toward an Indexed Portfolio of Real Estate, Part II: Recent Construction." Salomon Brothers Inc (January).

———. 1988. "The Economic Resurgence of the Midwest." Salomon Brothers Inc (July).

———. 1987. "Ranking Metropolitan Growth: A Real Estate Tool to be Used With Caution." Salomon Brothers Inc (June).

Hornick, P. 1983. "Applications of Portfolio Theory to Real Estate." *Real Estate Review* (Summer) 88-92.

Hudson-Wilson, S. 1989a. "Quantitative Methods in Real Estate Analysis." In Stephen J. Brown and Mark P. Kritzman, eds., *Quantitative Methods for Financial Analysis*. Homewood: Dow Jones-Irwin.

———. 1989b. "The Dimensions of Diversification in Real Estate." John Hancock Properties, Inc. (August).

———. 1988. *Real Estate: Valuation Techniques and Portfolio Management*. Charlottesville, VA: The Institute of Chartered Financial Analysts Continuing Education Series.

Ibbotson, R. G. and C.L. Fall. 1979. "The United States Market Wealth Portfolio." *The Journal of Portfolio Management* (Fall): 82-92.

Ibbotson, R. and L. Siegel. 1984. "Real Estate Returns: A Comparison with Other Investments." *AREUEA Journal* (Fall): 219-42.

John Hancock Properties, Inc. 1988. "A Review of the New York City Office Market." John Hancock Properties, Inc. Real Estate Research.

Jordan, S. 1989. "San Jose/Silicon Valley Research and Development and Office Markets." Salomon Brothers Inc (January).

Jordan, S. and D. J. Kostin. 1988. "Atlanta Real Estate Market." Salomon Brothers Inc (February).

Kau, J.B. and C.F. Sirmans. 1984. "Changes in Urban Land Values: 1936-1970." *Journal of Urban Economics* (January): 18-25.

Kelleher, D. 1976. "How Real Estate Stacks Up to the S&P 500." *Real Estate Review* (Summer): 60-65.

Kostin, D. J. and S. J. Goldberg. 1988. "An Update on the National Office Market." Salomon Brothers Inc (May).

Krutick, J. S., D. G. Shulman, and J. W. Giles. 1988. "The Improved Operating Outlook for the Hotel Industry." Salomon Brothers Inc (September).

Lauritano, M. and J. Peterson. 1989. "Review of the Chicago Real Estate Market." John Hancock Properties, Inc. (October).

Lepcio, A. 1988. "The Mechanics of Office Rent Escalation." Salomon Brothers Inc (January).

Lillard, J. 1988. "Overview of the Real Estate Market." In S. Hudson-Wilson, ed., *Real Estate: Valuation Techniques and Portfolio Mangement*. Charlottesville, VA: Institute of Chartered Financial Analysts Continuing Education Series.

Locke, S.M. 1986. "Real Estate Market Efficiency." *Land Development Studies*.

Marmer, H. S. 1989. "Is Equity Duration A Useful Concept?" *Canadian Investment Review* (Spring): 51-55.

McMahan, J. 1981. "Institutional Strategies for Real Estate Equity Investment." *Pension Trust Investment in Realty*. Practicing Law Institute (November/December).

Melnikoff, M. 1984. "A Note on the Dawn of Property Investment by American Pension Funds." *AREUEA Journal* (Fall): 401-7.

Miles, M. E. 1989. "Real Estate as an Asset Class: A 25-Year Perspective." Salomon Brothers Inc.

———. 1984a. "Commerical Appraisals for Institutional Clients." *Appraisal Journal* (October): 550-64.

———. 1984b. "Institutional Real Estate Investment." *AREUEA Journal* (Fall): 215-18.

Miles, M. E., D. J. Hartzell, D. Guilkey, and D. Sears. 1989. "Is a True Transactions Based Real Estate Index Possible?" Salomon Brothers Inc (July).

Miles, M. E. and T. McCue. 1982. "Historical Returns and Institutional Real Estate Portfolios." *AREUEA Journal* (Summer): 184-99.

Miles, M. E. and M. Rice. 1978. "Toward a More Complete Investigation of the Correlation of Real Estate Investment Yield with the Rate Evidence in the Money and Capital Market." *The Real Estate Appraiser and Analyst* (November/December): 8-19.

Peiser, R.B. 1984. "Risk Analysis in Land Development." *AREUEA Journal* (Spring): 12-29.

Pittenger, W. L. 1986. "Time/Value Relationships in Development Projects." *The Real Estate Appraiser and Analyst* (Winter): 33-41.

Ricks, R.B. 1969. "Imputed Equity Returns on Real Estate Financed with Life Insurance Company Loans." *Journal of Finance* (December): 921-37.

Robichek, A.A., R.A. Cohn, and J.J. Pringle. 1972. "Returns on Alternative Investment Media and Implications for Portfolio Construction." *Journal of Business* (July): 427-43.

Rosen, K. T. 1988. "The Apartment Market: A Changing Demographic and Economic Environment." Salomon Brothers Inc (March).

Rosen, K. T. and S. Jordan. 1988. "San Francisco Real Estate Market: The City, the Peninsula, the East

Bay." Salomon Brothers Inc (October).

Ross, S. A. and R. C. Zisler. 1987a. "Managing Real Estate Portfolios Part 2: Risk and Return in Real Estate." Goldman Sachs Real Estate Research (November).

————. 1987b. "Managing Real Estate Portfolis Part 3: A Close Look at Equity Real Estate Risk." Goldman Sachs Real Estate Research (November).

Roulac, S.E. 1981. "How to Structure Real Estate Investment Management." *The Journal of Portfolio Management* (Fall): 32-35.

————. 1976. "Can Real Estate Outperform Common Stock? *The Journal of Portfolio Management* (Winter): 26-43.

Sale, T. S., III, ed. 1985. *Real Estate Investing.* Charlottesville, VA: The Institute of Chartered Financial Analysts Continuing Education Series.

Salomon Brothers Inc. 1989a. "Inflation and Real Estate: Will This Time Be Different?" (March).

————. 1989b. "Real Estate Market Review." (April).

————. 1988. "Diversification in Real Estate Portfolios." (November).

————. 1986. "The Relative Risk of Equity Real Estate and Common Stock: A New View." (June).

Seibald J. D. 1988. "The Hypermarket Experiment in America." Salomon Brothers Inc (July).

Shulman, D. G. 1989. "Real Estate and Inflation: Will This Time Be Different?" Salomon Brothers Inc (March).

————. 1988. "New York Metropolitan Area Office Market." Salomon Brothers Inc (July).

————. 1987. "Appraisal-Based Returns After the RREEF Write-Offs." Salomon Brothers Inc (August).

————. 1986-88. "Real Estate Market Review." Salomon Brothers Inc (May 1986-October 1988).

————. 1986a. "Rent Projections in the Context of a Rent Cycle." Salomon Brothers Inc (October).

————. 1986b. "The Relative Risk of Equity Real Estate and Common Stock: A New View." Salomon Brothers Inc (June).

Shulman, D. G., S. J. Goldberg, D. J. Hartzell, R. E. Hopkins, and D. J. Kostin. 1988. "Toward and Indexed Portfolio of Real Estate Part I: Office Buildings." Salomon Brothers Inc (June).

Shulman, D. G. and R. E. Hopkins. 1989. "Toward an Indexed Portfolio of Real Estate, Part II: Recent Construction." Salomon Brothers Inc (January).

————. 1988. "Economic Diversification in Real Estate Portfolios." Salomon Brothers Inc (November).

Shulman, D. G. and S. Jordan. 1989. "A Graphic History of U.S. Office Space Supply and Demand, 1972-88." Salomon Brothers Inc (February).

Shulman, D. G. and D. J. Kostin. 1988. "London Office Market Report." Salomon Brothers Inc (September).

Sirmans, G. S. and C. F. Sirmans. 1987. "The Historical Perspective of Real Estate Returns." *The Journal of Portfolio Management* (Spring): 22-31.

Smith, K. V. 1980. "Historical Returns of Real Estate Equity Portfolios." *The Investment Managers Handbook.* Homewood: Dow Jones-Irwin.

Smith, K. V. and D. G. Shulman. 1976. "The Performance of Equity Real Estate Investment Trust." *Financial Analysts Journal* (September/October).

Smith, L. B. 1987. "Adjustment Mechanisms in Real Estate Markets." Salomon Brothers Inc (June).

The Handbook of Basic Economic Statistics. 1985. Bureau of Economic Statistics, Inc. Economic Statistics Bureau of Washington, D.C. (November): 97-101.

The National Council of Real Estate Investment Fiduciaries. 1988. "Current Value Reporting by Real Estate Fiduciary Managers." *Real Estate Accounting and Taxation* (Fall): 36-46.

The NCREIF Report. 1984. Washington, D.C.: National Council of Real Estate Investment Fiduciaries (Spring).

Titman, S. and A. Warga. 1986. "Risk and the Performance of Real Estate Investment Trusts: A Multiple Index Approach." *AREUEA Journal* (Fall): 414-31.

Vandell, K.D. 1978. "Default Risk Under Alternative Mortgage Instruments." *Journal of Finance* (December): 1279-69.

Webb, J. R., R. J. Curcio, and Jack H. Rubens. 1988. "Diversification Gains from Including Real Estate in Mixed-Asset Portfolios." *Decision Sciences* (Spring): 434-52.

Webb, J. R. and J. H. Rubens. 1987. "How Much in Real Estate? A Surprising Answer." *The Journal of Portfolio Management* (Spring): 10-14.

Webb, J. R. and C.F. Sirmans. 1982. "Yields for Selected Types of Real Property vs. the Money and Capital Markets." *The Appraisal Journal* (April): 228-42.

————. 1980. "Yields and Risk Measures for Real Estate, 1966-1977." *The Journal of Portfolio Management* (Fall): 14-19.

Wilson, A. R. 1989. "Probable Financial Effect of Asbestos Removal on Real Estate." *The Appraisal Journal* (July): 378-91.

Wurtzebach, C. H. 1989a. "Assembling an Equity Real Estate Portfolio." *Investing* (Fall): 87-91.

————. 1989b. "Real Estate Portfolio Analysis: An Emerging Focus on Economic Location." *The Actuary* (June): 4, 6-7.

Wurtzebach, C. H. and D. J. Hartzell. 1990. "Comparing the Performance of City Center and Suburban Office Investments." *Real Estate Review* (Winter): 39-42.

Zerbst, R. H. and B. R. Cambon. 1984. "Real Estate: Historical Returns and Risks." *The Journal of Portfolio Management* (Spring): 5-20.

Zisler, R. C. 1988. "Toward the Discipline of Real Estate Portfolio Management." *Institutional Investor* (September): 22-25.